in Publication Data

travel—1945-
via (Pass) date

74–6253

Enjoying Europe

Lawrence and Sylvia Martin have spent a large part of their not-inconsiderable married years traveling and living in areas of the world far removed from the United States. Some of the fruits have been:

ENGLAND! *An Uncommon Guide*
PARIS! *An Uncommon Guide*
SWITZERLAND! *An Uncommon Guide*
EUROPE: THE GRAND TOUR! *An Uncommon Guide*
THE STANDARD GUIDE TO MEXICO
THE STANDARD GUIDE TO THE CARIBBEAN

By Sylvia Martin:
YOU MEET THEM IN MEXICO
I. MADAME TUSSAUD (A NOVEL)

If they didn't like what they saw or heard or experienced, they moved on. If, on the other hand, *Gemütlichkeit* was pervasive, they stayed a month or a year, or went back as soon as they could arrange it.

Here you'll find the Martins' choice of European cities and villages, lakes and mountains, love nests and castles. Again and again they have gone back, refined the best of the best for discriminating travelers. Much of what you will read has appeared in their previous books, now unavailable. What's here is not "How much does it cost?" but "Where is it and how did it all come about?"

Enjoy Europe as it deserves to be enjoyed, and as you deserve to enjoy it, whether you backpack, luxuriate at the Ritz, or stay at home with a good book—this one, of course.

To David and Justine C

123456789MUBP798765

Library of Congress Cataloging [

Martin, Lawrence, date
  Enjoying Europe.

  1. Europe—Description and [
—Guide-books. I. Martin, Sy[
joint author. II. Title.
D909.M28   914'.04'55
ISBN 0-07-040625-1

Contents

INTRODUCING—

Here we are, a married couple indivisible and individual, one Mr. and one Ms., who in what seems ages ago promised to love, honor, and obey *each other* (a difficult pledge to keep) and to write articles and books together. Having produced our sixth travel book, mainly from the best parts of our others, we take it to the publishers.

They say, "Congratulations! But you haven't written an Introduction!"

"We don't want to do that."

"Oh! Why don't you?" they inquire.

"Because," we answer, "we have written introductions to various sections, and we just don't feel that we have any more Prologue-type stuff in us."

"But," they say, "you must, even though the Contract doesn't specify it. And it should emphasize the joy of travel in Europe."

After consulting each other we say, "It's silly to write about 'joy' just because it appears in the title: if the book itself doesn't reveal that Europe is enjoyable—even while troubling, thought-provoking, and misadventuresome as travel often is—then, you should excuse the expression—*Pfut!*"

"We agree in general," they nod. "But we still feel that the book needs an introductory Hello."

"Like what," we ask, "for instance?"

"Like those fifty Swiss businessmen you watched in Thun, who, when they descended from their motor coaches, tipped their hats to one another and shook hands all around."

"Hm," we mutter. We consult each other, disagree, make up, and recall that, speaking of Switzerland, our best Hello, our most enjoyable greeting, happened there.

On one of our earlier trips to Europe we entered Switzerland through a canton we had never heard of. We had come by Swiss postal bus from Merano in the South Tyrol, a long and tiring ride. After going up and over and down a couple of mountain passes, the bus rolled into a place called Müstair, and our eyes snapped open. For suddenly the buildings were different. Here and there stood a lordly white house decorated with strips of geometric designs. The signs were in a strange language. The men and women walking homeward from the fields looked a distinctive breed—dark and long-limbed, with wide round eyes. A handsome people.

"Where are we?"

"In the Land, I think, of Elsewhere."

From across the aisle a mustached, pince-nezed gentleman spoke. "You are in the Grisons," he said in careful English. "In German, the Graubünden; and in Italian, I Grigioni."

We were as excited as if we had discovered that a new country had been added to Europe—a country fresh, unhurt, other-planetary—in short, Elsewhere.

The yellow post-bus went through places with queer names: Tschierv, Zernez, Muottas Murag, Susch, Tschuggen. Now and then the language condescended to be guessable, as Il Fuorn (the Furnace), and Il Munt for Mountain, Piz for Peak. The road coiled upward and then unwound, flinging off *munts* as it rolled on.

We stopped at Davos for the night. The hotel receptionist, a willowy young woman with velvet eyes, combined the poise of a princess with a friendly warmth that would have melted the century-old crust of a wheel of hobelkäse, the cheese that outlives people. She admitted to being a Rhaetian. We confided our ignorance of her country—for the Grisons is more than a canton, if less than a nation. To its people it is Rhaetia and their speech Romansh, Switzerland's official language number four. Theirs is the largest canton, the most thinly populated, the most thickly mountained and valleyed. Our Rhaetian princess taught us a Romansh lullaby:

"Cu ais que cha la naivetta
croud' e crouda d'un cuntin?"
"Taidla, taidla, ma figlietta,
Su in tschêl ais un mulin."

Strange, but easier than the Dead Sea Scrolls. *Figlietta* must be
"little daughter." Less obviously, *naivetta* is *neige, nieve*—snow.
Mulin is mill. *Tschêl* is *ciel,* heaven. *Cu ais que cha* is our old French
friend, *qu'est-ce que c'est. D'un cuntin* is continually, and *taidla,*
listen. So—

"Why is it that the snow
Falls and falls continuously?"
"Listen, listen, little daughter,
Up in heaven is a mill."

Years passed, and we found ourselves in St. Moritz and the
Engadine in a year when winter was refusing to give way to
spring. This San Murezzan (a more interesting name than St.
Moritz) had little to remind us that we were again in the Grisons.
Along came a sunny day for a walk in the lovely valley between
Guarda and Scuol. Beyond Bos-cha a peasant woman passing us
on the path smiled and said, *"Allegra!"*

We mumbled something, and when she was out of hearing
examined her word. *"Allegra*—happiness, joy. She was saying, 'Be
happy'?"

As if to clear matters up, a small boy and a small girl came
skipping hand in hand. *"Allegra!"* they cried. Trigger-happy, we
gave them back a double *Allegra.*

We stopped to rest on a knoll. Gold-and-brown butterflies
danced around us. Spring was busting out all over in the valley
below, where the river Inn rollicked on its way to Innsbruck, to

the Danube, to the Black Sea. We breathed the air of an earth newborn. A village lay on a slope, all white and architecturally embroidered. Tarasp Castle, right for any third-son-of-the-peasant tale, stood proud on its rock in the middle of the valley. The world was strange and wonderful. *"Allegra!"* we shouted at the valley. "Be happy! Have a good time! Hope all your folks are joyful!"

ENGLAND

Our affair with England began in the nostalgic era when one could travel, if one had to—and we had to—on five dollars a day. For years we kept dropping in on the lady, drawn to her and her antique furniture, her gardens, and the way she served tea. We became enamored.

We fell in love with our eyes open. We see her faults and have small hope of reforming her.

She is charming and exasperating. But she never palls. Shakespeare saw her in Cleopatra:

> Age cannot wither her, nor custom stale
> Her infinite variety; other women cloy
> The appetites they feed, but she makes hungry
> Where most she satisfies. . . .

England, that half-an-island, is infinitely various. There is not one England; there are as many as you have time and hunger to discover. York, Winchester, Norwich, Bath have in common only their unlikeness. The many cathedrals are not the same cathedral with variations; each has a distinct personality. This truth applies to castles, parish churches, Stately Homes, inns, Tudor houses, hills and moors, dales and streams. Each half-timbered cottage has aged after its crotchety or amiable fashion, leaning and bulging in its own gafferish way.

An American, whose home is a young continent that his technology has largely standardized, is slow to realize how multiplex a nation can be, even one only the size of Minnesota, after men have lived there a sufficient number of centuries. History adds a fourth dimension to geography's three. England's two thousand years have endowed the human landscape with every tint and eccentricity that time can give. A town or village that has lived through Roman occupation and Saxon, Danish, and Norman invasions; that has suffered feudal wars, gloried in the Elizabethans, put up with the Stuarts, flourished with the House of Hanover, and is able to chronicle the defection of its American colonies in a brief line, is bound to have something we Americans cannot boast of.

George Babbitt's nephew from Zenith says, "Salisbury (or Chester, or whatever) is all right, but I wouldn't want to live there." No one asked him to live there. No one is even so unkind as to remark, "Zenith, Ohio, may be a great little town, but who crosses an ocean to see it?"

As with England, so with that concentration of it called London. New York is wonderful; it has better this and greater that, but it doesn't have the Abbey, the Tower, the Houses of Parliament, Georgian squares, Regency terraces, Wren churches, Trafalgar Square, the Inns of Court. There is more than one New York in New York, but they are not as diverse as the Londons that London contains. You can adventure at least six different ways out of Trafalgar Square and find yourself in six times six different Londons.

England, thickly populated with the English, with Eric Knight's Sam Small, Housman's Shropshire Lad, and all the people out of Dickens; with parrot-faced dowagers, buxom barmaids, wispy small-town girls, tweedy country gentry, Cockneys and bobbies, seedy peers and clerks in striped trousers—England bears looking into.

If you travel on one of those Europe-in-a-flash tours, you may come away disappointed. You ought to. Cleopatra can't be wooed and won in three days. Stay three weeks and you will find her tantalizing and infuriating. Stay three months, and you will feel a stab of guilt when you catch a sudden glimpse of the Stars and Stripes over the Embassy in Grosvenor Square. Enjoy, enjoy! A guilty love is better than none.

MOSS IS THE STUFF
If you're in London on or about October 21, go to the Law Courts (Fleet Street and the Strand) to watch the Quitrent Services. "*Oyez! Oyez! Oyez!*" cries the usher. After preliminaries, the presiding personage in a black silk gown, lace stock, velvet court suit, and full-bottomed wig commands: "Tenants and occupiers of a piece of waste ground called the Moors in the county of Salop, come forth and do your services!"

A gentleman in a cutaway and pin-striped trousers walks to a table on which lie two bundles of twigs, a billhook, and a small hatchet. Solemnly he takes up the hatchet and chops a bundle of faggots in half. With the billhook he chops the second bundle.

The personage, after a judicial pause, pronounces two words: "Good service!" The twig-chopper bows and retires, amid a relieved buzz of comment.

But hush! Order in court! Now the personage is summoning the tenants and occupiers of the Forge in the parish of St. Clement Danes.

The same man of the cutaway responds. He goes to an adjacent table, where he takes up one by one—counting aloud slowly and distinctly before laying each item down—sixty-one nails and six oversize horseshoes. When he has finished, the personage speaks: "Good number!"

Thus, for another year the tenants of the Moors and the Forge are secure. They have paid their rent. That is, the Corporation of London, represented by the City Solicitor, has paid their rent for them to the Crown, represented by the Royal Remembrancer.

But there are no tenants. The Moors and the Forge don't exist—except in a peculiarly English sort of way.

It's like this.

At some time not known, a king of England gave somebody and his heirs for eternity a piece of land called the Moors somewhere in Shropshire for the price, or nominal annual rent, of one billhook and one hatchet, each of which had to be proved of good quality by cutting clean through a faggot of wood. (In time the size of billhook and hatchet shrank; so did the faggots.)

In the same way, at some other time also unknown, but thought to be in the twelfth century, another king of England gave a farrier some property called the Forge somewhere on the Strand, in return for sixty-one nails and six horseshoes a year. (The shoes were not for a six-legged horse; two were spares. The nails represent ten per shoe, with one spare.)

The ceremonies of paying the rent on these two properties were well established by the time royal records began to be kept.

Why not forget the whole thing?

No! This is no ordinary country—this is *England*. The properties and their quitrents are on record. Therefore they exist. If they exist, they have tenants who must pay the rent. The unknown tenants of these two unknown properties are, by eternally temporary default of flesh-and-blood people, the Corporation of London.

Don't laugh. Remember, this comedy has been played for at least 750 years, which is awesome.

(Those horseshoes, by the way, are outsize because they were made to fit a knight's battle steed, the original farrier having been horseshoer and armor-repairer to the Knights Templar.)

About fifty parcels of land are held "of the Crown." They are gifts for some service rendered to a monarch by a nobleman, a borough, an organization, a favorite. A quitrent was exacted in return. The quitrent could be anything the generous or capricious monarch happened to think of.

A Scottish baron holds his property on condition that he blow three bugle blasts whenever the sovereign hunts the stag on the nearby moor.

The Marquess of Ailesbury, who holds Savernake Forest of the Crown, must be prepared to tootle on his twelfth-century ivory horn when the sovereign pays him a visit.

The lord of Archer's Court in Kent must accompany the sovereign on Channel crossings with a silver bowl in case of royal seasickness.

Kidwelly Castle in Wales must provide the monarch, when he (or she) happens by, the services of a knight in battle dress.

The laird of Dunstaffnage Castle, Scotland, can call his place his own only if he spends one night each year in the roofless castle ruins.

The Duke of Wellington and the Duke of Marlborough must each pay a flag a year for their right to own and occupy the palaces built for their illustrious ancestors in gratitude for the victories of Waterloo and Blenheim.

The Munro of Foulis (Scotland) holds whatever he holds on condition he pay the Crown annually a bucket of snow.

"The Crown" is not only the King or Queen. Every year the present heir to the throne, as Duke of Cornwall, has received from his Duchy two greyhounds, a pound of pepper, a hunting bow, a pair of spurs, a load of firewood, a pound of herbs, a gray cloak, one hundred shillings, a salmon, and a pair of gloves. The ceremonies and receptions having to do with these particular items date to 1337. British coinage has now been changed, but shillings are still available.

Many subjects hold this land or that privilege so long as they pay a rose, or a bouquet ("plucked in midsummer," reads one command), or flags, or gloves.

The official who keeps the books and collects the tokens is the Royal Remembrancer. The Remembrancer's office is so old that its origin is lost. He must have been the earliest accountant-royal.

One wonders what sort of books he keeps, what receipts he gives, where he stores the mossy stuff he collects. The Wellingtons and Marlboroughs have together paid him, by now, more than three hundred flags. What does he do with them? Or with the nine hundred years of leggings provided by the village of Ketton, Rutland?

As to those nails and horseshoes paid by the "tenants" of the Forge—sixty-one nails and six horseshoes per year are bound to create a storage problem after a few hundred years. But it turns out that the same horseshoes and nails have been in use for ages. Every year the Remembrancer takes them out of his files, dusts them off, carries them to the court, and after the ceremony wraps them up and files them away again. So that's all right. But they are a special case. We worry about all those greyhounds paid to the Duke of Cornwall; but knowing the English feeling about dogs, we hope that they too are made a special case.

What happens if someone neglects to pay, or is unable to deliver, or delays? We picture a laird in Scotland just come into his inheritance, reading a stern note:

> To the Munro of Foulis:
> Sir: I am directed by Her Majesty to bring to your attention the fact that your annual Bucket of Snow is in arrears. . . .

The Munro replies Special Delivery that he dispatched one Bucket of Snow by registered mail in plenty of time, and holds H.M. Post Office receipt No. TX-7782513-stroke 8 in proof withal and therewith.

By return courier OHMS our Remembrancer informs the Munro that investigation reveals a bucket of dirty water received, and calls attention to the terms of the holding, which require that said Bucket of Snow be not only dispatched but delivered as *snow,* and reminds His Lairdship that there is the Tower. . . .

But there are survivals less worrisome.

For some unknown reason High Wycombe, a town near London, weighs its mayor on November 9. The scales are set up in the center of town, and not only the mayor but his lady and the aldermen are—as it were—thrown in.

The Olney Pancake Race on Shrove Tuesday is more widely known, since the town of Liberal, Kansas, yearly challenges Olney for a transatlantic pancake trophy. Olney's event is first known to have been held in 1445; it brings crowds now. On signal, a score of aproned women run a course of 415 yards, each tossing a pancake in a pan. The finish is at the parish church, where the verger gives the winner a buss, called for some reason the Kiss of Peace.

A really ancient affair, about nine centuries old, is the marital-happiness contest for the flitch of bacon at Dunmow in Essex. Aspirants must appear before a judge and jury of maidens and bachelors, and prove their married lives have been unmarred by any "household brawles or contentious strife," and that they haven't, for the last year and a day, repented of marriage even in thought. The trial lends itself to the kind of cross-examination not always easy to keep within bounds. But it bowled along hilariously until the press woke up to it. Now it's a self-conscious affair.

November 11 is St. Martin's Day. More than two hundred years ago the founder of St. Martin's Church in Fenny Stratford, Buckinghamshire, left a trust ordaining that six tiny cannon be fired annually to commemorate the building of the church. The cannon, the size of quart mugs, are known as Poppers, and are on view. (Nearby is Stony Stratford, whose two inns, The Cock and The Bull, gave rise to the phrase "a cock-and-bull story.")

On Easter Monday in Hallaton, a village in Leicestershire, they celebrate "Hare-Pie Scrambling and Bottle-Kicking" Day. After church a pie, originally of hare but now of beef, is cut up and scrambled for on the rectory lawn. Then is the turn of the bottles—no longer bottles now but small casks filled with beer. And instead of being kicked they are wrestled for. How did all this originate? It seems that a village woman was once upon a time attacked by a bull as she crossed a field. A running hare diverted the bull's attention. As a thank-offering she bequeathed a field to pay for these festivities. They don't seem entirely to the point and must be hard on the rectory lawn.

If you visit Oakham, capital of England's smallest shire, Rutland, you will see—in the hall of the Norman castle—walls adorned with horseshoes. Every peer of the realm who passes through Rutland has to present a horseshoe to the castle. If he hasn't a spare he must borrow it from his horse.

Parliament in London is rife with cultural fossils. In the House of Lords they have a fine cavalierlike rule for stopping a bore. Any lord can rise and move "that the Noble Lord be no more heard." What could be more sensible? On the other hand, they open debate obliquely. Someone moves for "the papers." That starts things. The papers never appear. There are no papers.

In the Commons, note the red line that runs along the floor beside the two front benches. An M.P. who steps over his red line commits a foul. When it happens, the other side cries "Order! Order!" The culprit (he may be the Prime Minister himself) becomes rattled and humbly apologizes. The lines are two swords' lengths apart and were fixed in days when gentlemen wore swords and were likely to use them.

And although swords haven't been worn for two centuries, the pegs in the Commons' cloakroom still bear looped red tapes from which the swords, when no longer allowed in the chamber, were suspended.

The Speaker of the House is a very important person. He must be impartial, and his decisions are final. The Commons choose him from one of their number. When nominated, he rises and shakes his fist at nominator and seconder, indicating clearly he doesn't want the post. Each then takes him by an arm and conducts him to the Chair.

This sham reluctance goes back to the days of Charles I, and even earlier, when being Speaker was dangerous.

The ceremony surrounding the man and his office is something we hope you'll have a chance to witness. You're standing in the lobby when a constable on duty shouts, "Mace! Hats off, strangers!" In marches a Messenger of the House wearing tails, a chain of office, and a medallion of Mercury. After him comes the

Serjeant-at-Arms in silk court dress, carrying the 14-pound silver-gilt mace. Mr. Speaker follows, dressed in gown, full-bottomed wig, knee breeches, and buckled shoes, and attended by his train-bearer, chaplain, and secretary. When Parliament is in session this happens at the opening of each day's sitting, just before 2:30 P.M. Monday through Thursday, and 11 A.M. on Friday.

The mace is the symbol of the Commons' powers. In the House it rests on a rack. If it's not there, no business can be done. Once a member who wanted to stop debate effectively did so by running off with the mace.

About 10 P.M. the House begins to adjourn. A Government leader rises to move "that this House do now adjourn." If you think the Members will now get up and head for the door, you haven't learned about moss. This is only a signal opening a new phase of debate. After about half an hour, Mr. Speaker declares the House adjourned.

Instantly the light in the clock tower is switched off, informing London that the great talk-shop is putting up its shutters. Inside, a constable on duty shouts, "Who goes home?," a cry that has been heard here for almost three hundred years, and tells of times when streets were unsafe and citizens out late traveled in groups, often with an armed retainer.

Occasionally, customs do change. For hundreds of years the sovereign chose the sheriffs of the shires by marking a list with a pen or stylus. But one time, when the list was brought to Queen Elizabeth I, she was knitting in her garden and no quill was handy. The high-handed Queen wouldn't wait; she stabbed holes in the list with her knitting needle. Since then, every monarch uses a knitting needle for the job.

The ceremonial of the King's Champion was the most dramatic of all medieval survivals. After his coronation the newly crowned King sat at the banquet table in Westminster Hall. In came the Lord High Constable, the Earl Marshal, and the Lord High Steward, all on horseback. Hard on their heels came the King's

Champion, wearing the King's second-best suit of armor, riding a horse, carrying lance and shield. A herald blew a trumpet blast and proclaimed: "If any person, of what degree soever, shall deny or gainsay our Sovereign Lord to be the rightful heir to the Crown of England, or that he ought not to enjoy the same, here is his Champion, who saith he lieth sore and is a false traitor, being ready in person to combat him."

This was done at three advances to the King, the Champion each time throwing down his iron gauntlet (clang!). As no challenger ever spoke up, the hardest part of the Champion's task was to back his horse out of the great hall.

The drama was last played at the coronation of George IV in 1820. The Champion has to be a man of the Dymoke family; properly, its head. But in 1820 the eldest Dymoke was a clergyman, rector of Scrivelsby in Lincolnshire. His twenty-year-old son was permitted to do the honors, on a white horse borrowed from Astley's Circus. He performed so well that the King drank his health out of a gold cup.

In every generation the Dymokes still produce, as did the Marmions before them, the King's Champion. Now he carries the royal standard in the coronation procession, dressed in a tabard like the jack in a deck of playing cards, and has no gauntlet to throw.

LONDON

Both London and Paris preserve the heart of their matter —London, the City; Paris, La Cité.

But Paris is reasonable and London is not. Its confusion is partly the fault of the Thames. After following a fairly east-west course, it suddenly swerves at Waterloo Bridge and becomes a north-south river at the Houses of Parliament. The streets follow it, tumbling south and west.

In the beginning was the City, a port and trading center surrounded by a Roman wall. The wall is still there—invisibly, like the British Constitution. And there are invisible walls that never did exist, around squares, hamlets, villages, and towns. They formed London in unconformity by growing into one another while refusing to give up their identities.

And now a skyscraper metropolis is taking shape around, between, and on top of perfectly happy incoherence.

We first tackled London with the aid of a large detailed map and can confidently give you this counsel:

Study the map—that's essential. How else will you learn, if not London, humility?

I

Like the button on a loose robe, like Humpty Dumpty's nose in the immensity of his face—is Trafalgar Square. It is the patch of London which most nearly expresses England, Britain, the Empire that is gone, and the Commonwealth that remains. It is a major traffic hub, and the downtown of the English spirit. If it weren't there, you'd be looking for it, knowing in your stranger's heart that something was missing.

Trafalgar Square wheels around a 168-foot column atop which Lord Horatio Nelson submits to pigeons. At the base, Landseer's bronze lions, looking imperial but benign, in the British way, afford footholds for orators, dissenters, and scrambling children. Fountains play. Modest flower beds defy the fumes of swirling traffic.

Ranged round the square are offices of various Commonwealth nations; Admiralty Arch, framing the Mall which leads to Buckingham Palace; Charles I on a horse, facing Whitehall, where he lost his head; the National Gallery, a famous art museum with Corinthian portico; and St. Martin-in-the-Fields, the eighteenth-century church often copied from memory by homesick English colonials in America. —And who is this, overlooking "the full tide of human existence" from in front of the National Gallery? The rebel patriot George Washington, father of another country—in a rather poor copy.

Sitting on the parapet beside George Washington, you find no

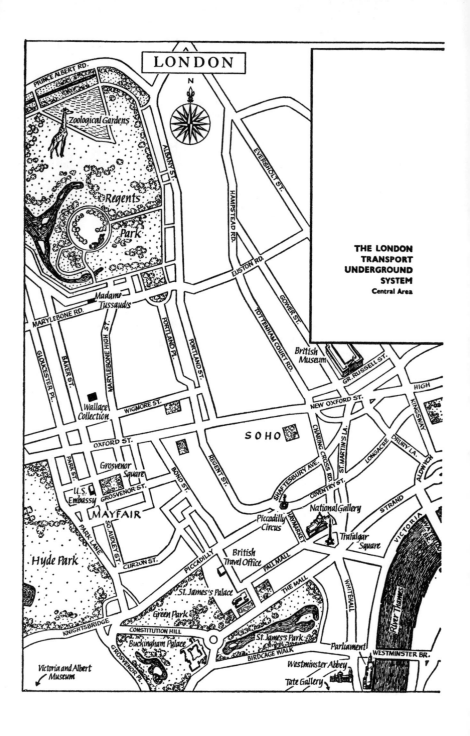

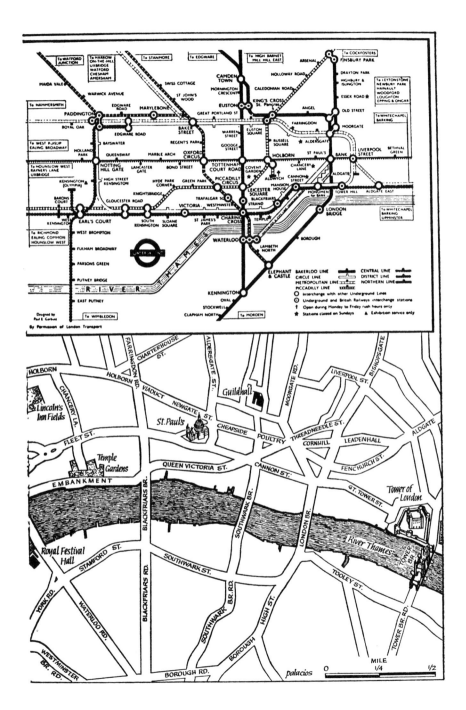

problem in deciding where to go first. The compelling prospect is straight across the square down Whitehall to Big Ben on the Parliamentary clock tower.

II

Whitehall, neither white nor a hall, is a broad half-mile of government offices leading to the climax of the Houses of Parliament and Westminster Abbey. Its name comes from a long-gone palace which Henry VIII took from Cardinal Wolsey. In Whitehall he married Anne Boleyn. In Whitehall, he died. Trafalgar Square covers the site of its stables. Reminiscent are the two mounted sentries of the gorgeously uniformed Horse Guards. Stoically they endure exclamations and cameras. A booklet begs tourists not to drop money down their boots: "the coins cause nasty bruises."

About halfway along the historic government avenue is narrow Downing Street, where the Prime Minister lives and works at No. 10, a quiet Georgian brick house. A constable or two are the only guards.

When Henry VIII descended upon Whitehall he abandoned a palace that began in the eleventh century, when Edward the Confessor needed someplace to live while presiding over the building of his Westminster Abbey. Parliament was then permitted to use the old palace. The present complex of buildings —officially, the Palace of Westminster but better known as the Houses of Parliament—is a rare triumph of Victorian pseudo-Gothic. It replaces the real thing which, incredibly, was still standing until 1834, when a workman burning old tax receipts let the job get out of hand.

One building that survived the fire is Westminster Hall. The awesome structure of stern Norman strength displays beautiful windows and a superb hammerbeam roof. In its use as the royal great hall it had a courtly gallery and painted walls. Charles I heard his death sentence here. We shiver in it not only because it is cold but for its sensation of ruthless power.

Westminster means "West monastery." It was a Benedictine abbey outside the west wall of the City. About 1050 Edward the Confessor, a Saxon king brought up in exile in Normandy, had the old abbey church pulled down and began a new one in the cruciform Norman style. It was finished just in time for him to be buried in it. A year later William the Conqueror had himself crowned there. It has been a church of tombs and coronations ever since.

Edward's church lasted two hundred years and was rebuilt in "Early English" to give him a grander resting place; he had been sainted.

Magnificent! is your instant impression on stepping inside and looking down the length of the nave, then up at the roof's height and vaulting. But attention wobbles, drawn to the clutter of funerary furniture and fixtures at eye level—tombs, memorials, chapels, shrines, the Poet's Corner with Chaucer and Shakespeare tributes. . . . "Look out, you're standing on Dickens!" "Watch it yourself, you're on Thomas Hardy!"

The finest item in this intramural cemetery is Henry VII's Chapel with its exquisite fan vaulting. The most endearing is the fierce little red-and-gold lion at the feet of Mary, Queen of Scots. Mary is in the south aisle, and in the north lies Elizabeth I, her sharp-nosed face in effigy as familiar as someone known in life. Edward, who began all this, is enshrined behind the high altar. Near him is the Coronation Chair of 1300, still in use, with Scotland's Stone of Scone under it.

There's something left of the old abbey itself—the beautiful octagonal Chapter House, the Chapel of the Pyx, and the Undercroft with a small museum of royal effigies. "Pyx?" you ask. It was the place where the standard coins and their dies were kept and where money was yearly assayed in the good old days when its worth was solid.

Architectural Note. "Norman" in England is Romanesque on the

Continent. "Early English" is early Gothic; "Decorated" comes next, and "Perpendicular" (Perp. for short) is the final, extra-decorated stage. This kind of knowledge, though scant, gives one a fine feeling of confidence. When you look at Henry VII's Chapel, think "Perp."

Westminster was the first part of London to develop outside the wall. It was a royal settlement. The City was a town of prickly merchants jealously guarding their rights. A road—the Strand—connected the two, entering the City through a gate with portcullis. The gate is symbolized now by a column, Temple Bar, where the sovereign still has to stop and ask His Worship the Lord Mayor for permission to enter.

"Bar" is an old word for gate. As for "Temple," it refers here to the medieval domain of the Knights Templar. They were expelled and the precincts leased to lawyers. This position between Westminster and the City, says historian Trevelyan, "helped the English lawyer to discover his true political function as mediator between Crown and people."

Two Temples they are—Middle and Inner—divided by Middle Temple Lane. These are the greatest of the four Inns of Court. Their gardens and chambers have known famous men, from Raleigh to Dickens and Blackstone of the *Commentaries.* The twelfth-century Round Church of the Knights Templar still stands. In Middle Temple Hall, Shakespeare's *Twelfth Night,* written on order for Elizabeth I, had its first performance.

The other two Inns of Court are Gray's and Lincoln's, the last with lovely lawns and trees. On High Holborn, the spectacular black-and-white Tudor frontage of Staple Inn (once still another Inn of Court) lingers on.

III

As residential London spread beyond the old wall, it left the City high and dry. Thousands work in it, few live there. It's the financial center of London. Among the blocks and cubes of office buildings are the small lovely churches of Christopher Wren. Here too is his greatest work, St. Paul's Cathedral. It was begun in 1675 on the site of older cathedrals dating back to 604.

One glance and you see that St. Paul's belongs to a style of mind entirely different from Westminster Abbey's. It is a secular style, cool, composed, speaking of no great fear of the Cosmos. The interior is like an ecclesiastical palace. The dome is considered in size and beauty second only to St. Peter's in Rome.

Lord Byron managed to express his views on both St. Paul's and London in two bitter lines:

> A huge dun cupola, like a foolscap crown
> On a fool's head—and there is London town!

IV

The Tower of London occupies a hill on the City's eastern boundary.

Having won the Battle of Hastings (1066) against the Saxon Harold, William the Bastard, now earning the sobriquet of Conqueror, came to the City gates and parleyed. There were many Normans in the town because good jobs had been available under Edward the Confessor, a Normaniac whose only concession to Saxon customs had been to grow his hair and beard. In due time a deputation went out to William and invited him to be king.

No king made London—London made a king.

The Tower was built to keep the Londoners from changing their minds.

It began with the big square keep, or White Tower. It grew and grew, extending with walls, bastions, baileys, barracks, other towers, and a variety of structures covering eighteen picturesque acres.

We did our homework before Tower-going; and then found that it's all very well to know that Walter Raleigh suffered long

imprisonment in the Tower, that Lady Jane Grey passed her brief
queenship in the Tower, that the little princes were smothered in
the Tower, but . . . At first we kept asking, "Which tower of the
Tower?" There are nineteen. After a while we didn't care. It was enough to sit on a bench in
the watery sunlight, watching the ravens hop about on Tower
Green, thinking shudderingly of the block and the ax (the site is
marked)—remembering that on Anne Boleyn, by special cour-
tesy, the two-handed sword was used; the ax was clumsier.

By Tudor times peaceful coexistence had been established
between City and Crown. Like the knights of old in purification
vigil, the new monarch spent at least one night in the Tower, and
then rode from it through the City to Westminster Abbey for the
coronation.

That is how seventeen-year-old Jane Grey happened to be
there. She came to make ready for her coronation. She went
instead to the block. Before that, she was hurriedly moved out of
the White Tower to the Yeoman Gaoler's house, while Mary
Tudor, soon to be abominated as Bloody Mary, was escorted to
the White Tower. Among Mary's attendants was her half-sister
Elizabeth. It was by the oddest historic chance that three women,
queens, were all together in the Tower preparing for separate
destinies.

Soon after, Princess Elizabeth was back, brought by barge,
entering with furious protest by the water gate—her sister's
prisoner. She was so certain of execution that she debated send-
ing word to Queen Mary begging for the sword, as with her
mother, instead of an ax.

And then you see her returning in triumph, visiting her cell
before going to the White Tower. And at last she comes, in gold,
crimson, and ermine, through a cheering, adoring City, to be
crowned in Westminster. There never was a woman like her, and
the best place to think of her is in St. John's Chapel of the White
Tower—a gem of the purest and strongest Norman architecture
you'll ever see. She will have prayed there, to the English God
created by her father when he separated the Church from Rome

to marry Anne Boleyn, who died because she bore Elizabeth instead of a son.

V

Pass under Admiralty Arch, at Trafalgar Square's southwest corner, and you find yourself on the Mall, running straight to Buckingham Palace.

The palace began as a cozy mansion George III bought as a dower house for his wife, the queen of whom a wit remarked on her fiftieth birthday, "I do believe the bloom of her ugliness is wearing off." George IV had his architect Nash build something grander around it, at vast expense. The result, though not a success, became the permanent royal abode when Queen Victoria moved in. An uninspired pseudo-classic frontage is all you see when pressed against the iron fence, trying to watch the Changing of the Guard—a ritual much better enjoyed at Windsor Castle.

On the left as you walk up the Mall is beautiful St. James's Park; on your right, the Duke of York's Steps and monument, Carlton House, Marlborough House, and the back of St. James's Palace.

For this palace, go through Stable Yard and Cleveland Row to see its red-brick Tudor gatehouse and puppetlike sentries. Henry VIII had St. James's built as a country lodge. Charles II found it convenient. Ambassadors are still accredited to "the Court of St. James's."

You are now in the West End, developed during Charles II's reign as an aristocratic suburb. Charles gave Nell Gwyn a house in Pall Mall which is still there, home of an insurance company. He was sometimes seen in unkingly attitudes chatting with her over her garden wall.

Since the eighteenth century this part of town has been pre-eminently Club-land. On Pall Mall and St. James's Street are the famous Regency clubs. White's, at No. 37 St. James's, is the oldest. It began as a coffee house.

St. James's Square was laid out by Henry Jermyn, Earl of St. Albans and a favorite of Charles II, who gave him much of the land hereabouts. His self-named Jermyn Street, with its quality men's shops, runs parallel to Piccadilly, where Fortnum & Mason's reigns as Europe's prettiest department store and Burlington Arcade's handsome shops attract the tourist trade.

VI

To carry on with palaces and the residential problems of royalty, go next to the suburban village of Kensington.

William of Orange, invited to take over when James II had tried the British too far, liked open spaces, clean air (he had asthma) and Dutch comfort. Kensington was his choice—it was far more open then, late in the seventeenth century—and his palace was built around a country house he bought from an earl. His successors, the Georges I and II, liked it too. George III, for country life, preferred Kew Gardens.

One day the Duke of Kent (fourth son of the third George) came home from a Continental junket with a pregnant wife and empty pockets. The couple arrived breathless—hurry, hurry; the child must be born in England for possible succession to the throne. They were hastily installed in Kensington Palace.

That is how a baby girl named Alexandrina Victoria came to be born here in 1819. In her bedroom, eighteen years later, she wrote in her diary: "20th June. —I was awoke at 6 o'clock by Mama. . . ." She was hustled downstairs in her dressing gown to be informed by the Archbishop of Canterbury and the Marquess of Conyngham "that my poor uncle, the King, was no more, and had expired at 12 minutes p. 2 this morning, and consequently that I am *Queen*."

Victoria's nursery, bedroom, and staircase are in the part of the palace given over to the pleasing London Museum, which is one day to be moved to a home of its own. The State Apartments of William and Mary, also on view, were designed by Wren. Princess

Margaret and family (not on view) have been living in a third part of the palace.

Another man who liked open space, comfort, and clean air was Cardinal Wolsey, and whether you're a palace-lover or not, you must see Hampton Court, some thirteen miles out of London. This is the palace built by Henry VIII's Cardinal in the enchanted days when he could do nothing wrong. He himself supervised every detail. The red brick is warmer, somehow, than other red brick. The towers, gateways, and courtyards are just the right size for affection. The decorative stonework and ornamental chimney clusters are happy. An almost childlike delight must have gone into the making of Hampton Court.

Of course, Henry VIII took it. Wolsey died of an illness in time to save his neck.

There have been changes since Tudor times. The State Apartments (forty rooms) and the part near the gardens were built by Wren for William and Mary. The gardens were famous in Wolsey's time. They still are.

Finally, go on to Windsor, where Windsor Castle, begun by the Conqueror, remains the oldest and largest royal residence still slept in. This mightiest of English castles, seen from afar, looms many-towered and tremendous on its mound. Nor does it disappoint on close acquaintance. You can spend a full day sightseeing in it—a half-day if the sovereign is in residence. And every morning at 10:30 the Changing of the Guard begins with a band marching the New Guard up the street and into the castle grounds for the ritual maneuvers which end with the band marching the Old Guard out. You can watch freely; there's no imposed barrier, as at Buckingham Palace. It's a wonderfully colorful spectacle with the scarlet uniforms against the gray stone, and almost archaic in this world of nuclear warheads. English tradition is a stubborn thing, bless it.

The most beautiful part of Windsor Castle is St. George's, the heraldic chapel of the Knights of the Garter. The Knights still meet there; the choir displays their heraldic fittings and banners. The lacy stone vaulting of this regal church is something to weave into dreams.

Henry VIII is buried beneath the floor with Jane Seymour, a wife who kept her head. Queen Victoria's memorial chapel to her Albert was created with the taste that helped give "Victorian" a bad name; luckily it is in an annex.

Windsor is a pleasant town, and a good place to stay if you tire of hectic London and would like to make friends with the Thames. At Windsor the pleasure Thames begins—seventy miles of boating, pretty villages, and attractive towns (interrupted only by Reading) to Oxford. Just across the river from Windsor is one-street Eton with its famous public (private) school, founded by Henry VI in the fifteenth century.

VII

Here and there in London are things one doesn't want to miss, or will see next time, or will come upon as a personal discovery. Mme. Tussaud's, the waxworks, is not one of these—everyone goes there. But among the others are the British Museum (requiring strength of character and feet); Dr. Johnson's House and the Guildhall in the City; Carlyle's House at 24 Cheyne Row in Chelsea; and the Wallace Collection in Manchester Square. The Wallace is not too big, and every item—furniture, miniatures, paintings, small objects—is special. The house was built for an eighteenth-century duke of Manchester.

Finally, if you're an American, be sure to walk around Grosvenor Square, which has become "Little America." The point is made in a fine way by the statue of Franklin Roosevelt on the greensward, the gift of the British nation. It is made in a different way by the American Embassy, a brutal structure by E. Saarinen adorned by an aggressive eagle. In 1785, four years before Washington took the oath as first President, John Adams bobbed up at No. 9 as first American Minister to the Court of St. James's.

It was a modest beginning to the Americanization of a Georgian square, cordially welcomed by a city that has ingested centuries of styling and remained as distinctively English as the Mad Hatter.

SHAKESPEARE-ON-AVON

Think on thy Proteus, when thou haply seest
Some rare noteworthy object in thy travel. . . .

When Shakespeare penned this version of "Don't forget to write," he didn't dream that he himself would be a "rare noteworthy object"; that because of him Stratford-on-Avon would become the world's literary shrine. He was no egoist, merely a hard-working genius breaking out into a new field.

Everyone in England for the first time visits Shakespeare's home town. The statistics say so: Stratford comes next after London. More than a million visitors a year make their entrances and exits, paying homage to the fact that there's no business like show business.

It was not always so. In Shakespeare's own day the theater wasn't even allowed within London. You had to go across the river to unsavory Southwark to see a performance, and if you were respectable, you didn't go. Even if you were Queen Elizabeth I and had ordered a Shakespeare play, in a special performance, you arranged to see it outside the City wall.

Stratford was then a sober market town. The return of the local boy who had made good, with a coat of arms and money enough to buy the biggest house in town, was a slap in Virtue's face. After his death, when a troupe of his old colleagues came to put on a play of his, the town fathers paid them—*to go away*.

Not until 250 years after the Bard's death did Stratford wake up to its mission. In 1769 the landlord of an inn rallied his reluctant townsmen to celebrate the poet's birthday. The great Garrick organized the affair. There were fireworks, cannon salvoes, processions, a public banquet—everything but a Shakespeare performance.

For the next hundred years this type of commemoration prevailed. "The Birthday" became a bore. But Stratford was saved by Charles Edward Flower, a whiskered giant of a brewer. (Flower's Ales are still drunk wherever in Warwickshire men say "Cheers!") In 1870, when the burning local question was a Shakespeare monument, Flower spoke up, and his voice was loud: "The monument we want is a theater."

A theater in a market town? Preposterous! Only London had theaters. The London press ridiculed the project as an "elaborate burlesque of national respect for a great memory." It made the mistake of calling Stratfordians "nobodies." The brewer roared, "We've waited three centuries for the Somebodies. Now we'll show them what the Nobodies can do."

He gave two acres of ground on the river, raised $5,000 to put a theater on it, and willed a good part of his fortune to the playhouse.

In April 1879 the first-night curtain rose on *Much Ado About Nothing* and many empty seats. Two weeks later a small audience generously applauded the end of the first Shakespeare season. There seemed no reason why there should be another. But Flower was a stubborn man, and year after year saw a Shakespeare season.

When Charles died, his brother Edgar carried on, and then Edgar's ten sons. Outstanding in this bouquet was Archibald Dennis Flower. When in 1926 the theater burned down he said, "Just as well. It was too small." He kept performances going in a local movie house while he went with his wife to the United States and talked 2,000 Americans out of nearly $3 million. If you manage to see a performance in the excellent new theater (which is again too small), be proud that America helped.

Do what you can short of committing mayhem to see a Shakespeare play in the Shakespeare theater. Here a great company performs in the most comfortable of auditoriums and in an air of excitement that fills the whole town. Stratfordians may live off the tourist business, but to a man they are Shakespeare fans. The first time we were there fierce debate raged in street and shop. It was charged that the producer had slandered Romeo and Juliet by reducing their grand passion to puppy love. In the pubs indignation waxed over the bitter and rebuttal was hurled from behind the stout. A little old lady of Back Lane shook her fist under the nose of an actor we were drinking with and cried, "Don't meddle with our Shakespeare!"

On our last visit it was a controversial Hamlet, and the head waiter of the Shakespeare Hotel stood by our table roundly denouncing the brilliant actor's interpretation. Between acts the theater lobby had seethed with argument. We had that rare, choking, first-night feeling.

When the first Flower woke them up, Stratfordians began rediscovering their town. They stripped from their homes, shops, and inns the ugly fronts of later centuries and revealed the fine half-timbering which had lined the streets in Shakespeare's day. Hidden fireplaces, cupboards, paneling, beams, all the handsome Elizabethan details have been restored. Every building connected with the Poet and his time is lovingly preserved. The town is a monument shared by Stratford with the world.

It's a handsome town, but the trouble is that the world has too many people determined to see it—to queue up for Shakespeare's birthplace, the New Place Estate, Anne Hathaway's Cottage, Mary Arden's House, the Elizabeth Knott garden, Harvard House, the view from Sir Hugh Clopton's bridge, the Avon's swans, the footpath Will used to take when courting Anne. . . . The hotels fill up from April through October, and so do the sweet meadows Shakespeare knew—with campers.

The best time to come is early or late in the season, and even so pray for bad weather.

It was in early season and bad weather that we found the parish church empty. Here the Shakespeare family worshiped. Here the infant Will was baptized; here he is buried. In a row lie others of the family, all in line in front of the altar.

Trinity Church is interesting in itself. Raise the hinged seats of the choir stalls and examine the misericords, especially the one in the second stall from the altar, on the south. It portrays a fight between a man and wife. He is pulling her hair and biting her thumb while she pulls his beard, tries to gouge his eye, and kicks him in the groin. On the right is one even livelier. A man is birching a naked woman's buttocks. He's sitting on her neck, she is upside down, and a dog is biting her leg. Young Will probably tipped up these seats many a time before or after the service. He wrote, one remembers, *The Taming of the Shrew.*

OXFORD

Oxford is a university inside an industrial city of 106,000 population. The university consists of thirty colleges, each self-contained within its own walls. Each college consists of a series of buildings surrounding quads (quadrangles). Behind the quads are gardens. Figure an average of two quads per college, add gardens, add thirty chapels, dining halls, and libraries (the parts usually but not always open to visitors), and you see that as a sightseer you are up against something formidable. Then there are other notable buildings, the famous High Street, the Broad Walk, the meadows. . . .

What's the best way to master this complexity? One expert worked out an ingenious walk taking in everything of interest. It begins with a 145-foot climb to the top of Magdalen Tower, followed by a one-mile perambulation of the Water Walks and of Magdalen's groves and gardens. Just for a start!

A non-system advanced by some veterans is to follow your nose, saunter where you will. But this is for the tourist with plenty of time.

Our own system, designed for a minimum of physical labor and a maximum of reward, is of course the best. It concentrates on the four most interesting colleges. It involves basic knowledge of the layout from advance mapwork.

Let your first act be to buy the local guidebook—at the hotel, the nearest bookstore, or the information office in the tower at Carfax, which is the center of town. The best is *Alden's Oxford*

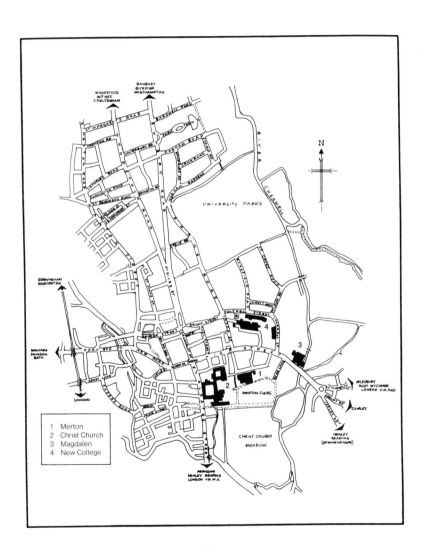

1 Merton
2 Christ Church
3 Magdalen
4 New College

Guide (it has sold at this writing more than 368,000 copies). Less detailed, but sufficient for the hurried, is *A Day in Oxford.*

Having done your homework, you will know that the part of Oxford that interests you is a half-mile square, bounded:

> on the west by Cornmarket and Magdalen streets,
>> plus the nearer parts of St. Giles's and St. Aldate's;
> on the north by Broad and Holywell streets;
> on the east by Magdalen College;
> on the south by Christ Church College and the Broad Walk.

In this crowded area, the colleges most worth visiting are Magdalen (pronounced *Maudlin*), New College, Merton, and Christ Church.

Begin by walking on the Broad (you never say "street"; it's un-Oxonian) to that curious round-front building, the Sheldonian Theater. On the way, note on your left Balliol and Trinity, but do not let them divert you. That would be fatal.

The Sheldonian was built in 1668 by Christopher Wren for university commemoration ceremonies. He was inspired by the Theater of Marcellus in Rome, but a very English cupola has got stuck up on top. Spend no time on the Sheldonian's interior, but take the stairs (an easy climb) to the cupola for the eight-sided view of roofs, spires, pinnacles, towers, domes, and, on the east, gas tanks. By recourse to your map, see if you can identify the buildings in view.

SPECIAL NOTE. We've brought you to the cupola not merely for the view but also to appreciate the fact that you needn't be concerned with architectural dates and periods. It's a relief to see that everything is hopelessly jumbled, and that a comparatively simple structure may combine Gothic, "classical," and an individuality that can only be called fantastic.

Coming down now, advance south with firm tread into the maze. It begins with Old Schools Quadrangle, on which rise the Divinity School, the Tower of the Five Orders, and the Bodleian, one of the world's richest libraries. There is also the statue of the Earl of Pembroke, and over the ground-floor rooms ahead and on your left the names of the "faculties" of the Old Schools that moved out eighty years ago to give the Bodleian more space. There are things worth exploring inside, such as the fine hall of Divinity, and those parts of the Bodleian the authorities will admit you to. If you are off-season or off-hours for the Bodleian, and if you have a good-looking young woman in your party, remember that even librarians are human. Let her run interference. But not now—later. We are bound for Magdalen.

If our tread has been firm enough, you and we suddenly erupt into an open space. Before us in the center grass plot is a freakish building: Radcliffe Camera, now a Bodleian reading room. Colleges cluster: on the east, Hertford and All Souls; on the west, Exeter and Brasenose, and over the roofs of Brasenose, Lincoln. Resist the impulse to call on them. (All about here is the locus of David Frome's *Mr. Pinkerton Finds a Body*, a whodunit that makes good Oxford bedside reading.)

On the south side of the square is venerable St. Mary's, the university church, with a long history we can't stop for. It fronts on the High, on which we walk eastward toward Magdalen's imposing tower. At the corner of Queen's Lane we stop for a backward look at the High. This is the best vantage point from which to see that fine street. But charge tourist propaganda with exaggeration when it speaks of the High's "streamlike meanderings." One slight curve doesn't make a meandering.

So we pass into Magdalen, conceded to be the wealthiest and loveliest of the colleges. It's the only one making use of Oxford's waterways. Magdalen has six quadrangles and some fifty acres of grounds. Wander through the quads, find the cloisters (by way of that passage through the Muniment Tower), then amble about the gardens and meadows. Watch the young men playing bowls on the greens with their girl friends. Look at the college deer in the enclosed park called the Grove; we hope that for you they'll be leaping and hurdling and not merely nibbling.

Magdalen's campus (a word never used at Oxford) is idyllic. In fact, its out-of-doors is more rewarding than the indoors. So when you have looked and walked your fill in the meadows where Joseph *(Spectator)* Addison, Edward *(Decline and Fall)* Gibbon, Prince Rupert, and Charles *(Cloister and Hearth)* Reade walked before you, let us decamp by the exit on Long Wall Street and head for New College.

We go north, turn into Holywell, and after a hundred yards pass through a gate on our left and through the old city wall.

We are in a college six hundred years New, and here both outdoors and in are fascinating. Invade the Hall, a splendid room with oak ceiling and linenfold paneling. (Compare with your own college commons room if it had one, or your fraternity or sorority dining room.) Pass on to the lofty chapel, with its ornate reredos, the Joshua Reynolds window, the fourteenth-century window, and misericords (look under choir-stall seats). It has, besides, the great statue of Lazarus by Epstein, and an El Greco. The Greco, easier for an enthusiast to walk off with than the Lazarus or the windows, has put an end to casual sightseeing. No wandering about alone any more. When the attendant leaves, you go. On the way out, promenade the wood-vaulted cloisters and the generous expanse of garden bordered by the old wall.

But don't leave New College by the way you came in. To save footwork, leave by the gate on New College Lane. As you follow this narrow alley into Queen's Lane, watch out for the traffic, which can't make the turns without mounting the sidewalk.

Why not pop into Queen's—very briefly? After all, we've got half our chore done—two colleges down, two to go.

Queen's has eighteenth-century pseudo-classic façades and a colorful hall by Christopher Wren. But the inner essence of Queen's isn't something you can see. Possibly you can feel it. It is eccentric, and therefore typical of academic England. Members are summoned to dinner by trumpet instead of by bell. For Christmas dinner the main dish is boar's head, ushered in by carols, all to celebrate the escape of a scholar who, attacked by a wild boar in a nearby forest, had the presence of mind to thrust his copy of Aristotle down the beast's throat. Naturally the animal fell back and died. After the boar's head, a normal week is allowed to pass. Then, on New Year's Day, the Bursar hands around needles and thread, saying, "Take this and be thrifty." Buried in this admonition is an atrocious pun in French on the name of the founder, de Eglesfield—*aiguille* plus *fil*. Got it?

One wonders if they're able to go through all this without feeling a little silly. But a titterer can always sober himself with the fact that Queen's has the largest collection of Slavonic books this side of the Soviet Union, and that anyone who wants to know what a certain medieval boyar said to a hostile hetman has to come here.

So on to Merton, but—

What is that sign across Queen's Lane? "The condition of this tower is dangerous. Please do not park or linger."

That's the church of St. Peter's-in-the-East. The tower is tired, having stood up for almost eight hundred years. Why not have a look around? But quickly—this time we *must* get to Merton.

Your local guidebook will tell you that the crypt is the oldest part and the most celebrated, but will fail to add that it is nearly always barred. You can look through the bars, however, and glimpse the old pillars and arches built about 1150. All the centuries from William the Conqueror's eleventh have left behind some reminder in stone in this small church. When last we were here we missed Merton because we peered at every stone in the churchyard looking for the grave of James Sadler, the first English spaceman. We never found it, but we did find the tablet in the west wall of the nave.

James was a dependable baker in the High until he read in the papers of the Montgolfiers' balloon ascents in France. He deserted his ovens and devoted his life to getting into orbit. Filling with hot air a homemade balloon sixty yards in circumference, he ascended, in 1784, to 3,500 feet—the first Englishman to get so far off the ground. The next month he did it again. Twenty-seven years later he achieved his greatest triumph, getting blown from Birmingham to Boston (*their* Boston, not ours) in under four hours—for those days practically breaking the sound barrier.

Saddler was the first human being to travel as fast as twenty-five miles an hour and live to be congratulated. Somewhere in the churchyard a space six feet by two and a half waited for him to crack up, but he never had an accident and died in bed at seventy-five.

Dropping in on St. Peter's makes a good change of scene. The peace and quiet here is like that at Gray's Stoke Poges.

But duty calls, and picking up our firm tread we advance upon Merton. There is a peril on the way—how to cross the High. The traffic is continuous and remorseless, and the only stop light is at Carfax, too far away. But we as guides have our limits; we have no formula for circumventing Oxford's traffic. We will assume that you have crossed, have found Logic Lane, have turned from it into Merton Street, and have discovered on your left the college gate.

Approach Merton with deepest respect. It is the oldest Oxford foundation, dating from the thirteenth century. The buildings which house it compose the most interesting lot, architecturally, in the university.

See as much of it as you can, but certainly these: the thirteenth-century chapel, famous for its 650-year-old painted glass; the medieval library, with some old books still chained; the hall, rebuilt in Victorian times but retaining the antique atmosphere; the seventeenth-century Fellows' Quadrangle; and the Treasury or Muniment Room, the oldest college building in Oxford. Although talk about the weather—the oldest, most universal English preoccupation—did not originate here, it was here developed; the first consistent weather-recorder was a Merton sage.

In the Middle Ages, when to be controversial was dangerous, Merton was a hotbed of speculation. This college advanced the cause of free circulation of ideas—hats off to it. And an extra cheer for being the alma mater of Max Beerbohm—essayist, parodist, caricaturist, and author of the fantasy on Oxford university life, *Zuleika Dobson*. Admirers of the Incomparable Max should visit the new Beerbohm Room, where his original drawings, books, manuscripts, and only dab at oil painting are on exhibit. Before leaving Merton, do the gardens, Dead Man's Walk, and the terrace on the city wall (views).

Back on Merton Street, a walk west of some two hundred yards brings you into the Canterbury gate of Christ Church. Largest of the colleges, its 500 undergraduates are several thousand fewer than those of even a modest midwestern "cow college." (All the colleges together have about 7,200 undergraduates, of whom about 1,200 are women.) Nevertheless "the House," as Christ Church is called, has been educating youths into men for more than four hundred years—among them Philip Sydney, John Locke, Ruskin, Hakluyt, Wesley, William Penn ("sent down"— which means kicked out—for nonconformity), "Lewis Carroll," Gladstone—and so on down a long roster.

One of its several peculiarities is that the college chapel is also the cathedral of Oxford. Another is that Great Tom the 6¼-ton bell in Tom Tower, bongs 101 times at 9:05 P.M. On the last stroke all the porters shut the college gates.

From Canterbury quad bear right into Peckwater quad. It has the library; you can skip this if your time is short or your feet hurt. Skirting the Canons' Garden, go into Tom quad, the largest in Oxford. It fails to be as impressive as the Great Court of Cambridge's Trinity or King's College, possibly because it is too large for the height (or lowth) of its buildings. The gateway-with-tower on the northeast corner is called Kill-Canon because of its draftiness.

Under the Tom Tower you find the grand staircase (elaborate ceiling) leading to the hall, one of the glories of the house. It has portraits by such masters as Reynolds, Gainsborough, Lawrence, Millais, Kneller, and Lely. Your eye will be drawn to the famous Henry VIII, ascribed to Holbein, which has typed that monarch as conclusively as Gilbert Stuart's Washington has done for the immortal George.

This noble medieval room has seen noble doings. Henry VIII, Elizabeth I, James, and Charles I were here. Charles, doomed, his head good for only five more years, assembled here those Members of Parliament who were loyal. On leaving, take the right-hand stairway down to the kitchens, where an ox could still be roasted whole.

After all this, don't feel depressed by not getting excited over the chapel-cathedral. It is not one of England's great churches.

Now that we, with your help and our system, have at last managed to see Merton, we are going to leave you. As you went along you may have seen, here and there, new structures being built to add to the lively architectural confusion; for example, some dormitories that look like Florida hotels. Amid the ancient stonework the effect is startling—as if Granny had gone giddy. One of these is at Queen's College; another is at St. John's. Three new colleges are abuilding: Nuffield, endowed by the automobile tycoon, in a gabled style that attractively straddles Gothic and modern; St. Catherine's and St. Anthony's. The last, designed by a modernist Danish architect, should be, with its land- and water-scaping, a beauty.

If Magdalen's Water Walks did not give it away, you would hardly know that Oxford was on the Thames and the Cherwell. They call the Thames the Isis here, and you find it at Folly Bridge, south of Christ Church. From here to Iffley is the famous stretch of river where the college races are rowed. That other river, the Cherwell (*Charwell*), is for leisurely punting and canoeing. Boats can be hired at Folly Bridge and Magdalen Bridge. From Folly you can board a steamer for a river trip to Henley or Windsor. Given good weather—and when we did it, the weather was glorious—the two-day float to Windsor through locks and along idyllic shores is unforgettable.

We went out one evening to meet the undergraduates in their favorite pubs: the Turf, the King's Arms, the White Horse (a few hoof-steps away in the Broad), the Bear Inn near Christ Church, and the bar of the Randolph. We found these solidly packed, with an overflow into corridors and out of doors. The Turf, up an extremely narrow alley off narrow New College Lane, was the oddest, having a "garden" populated by empty bottles, rejected lettuce, and primitive chairs and tables, some occupied by youths who were being alone with the universe. The expedition was a failure, for there wasn't room for even the skinniest tourist. And if there had been? The collegians form a club, a group of clubs. Nowhere do you feel so much the complete outsider as right in the thick of them.

During the Long Vacation, mid-June to mid-October, the colleges are easier to see. The undergraduates are gone, taking some atmosphere with them; tourist hordes are there instead. The last ten days of May are wonderful, with the cricket matches, boat races, ceremonies, and balls—but all the hotels are packed with parents, relatives, and sweethearts.

OF CANTERBURY AND YORK

When William of Normandy was a boy his father, about to go off on a pilgrimage to Jerusalem, presented the child to his worried nobles as his heir. "By my faith," he said, "it is not my will to leave you without a lord. I have a little bastard here who will grow, if God please, to be a gallant man."

The gallant man had an obsession about legitimacy. In putting himself right with God, William built more than thirty abbeys in Normandy. When he decided to invade England, a blameless Christian country, he wangled the Pope's support. But that wasn't enough to quiet his conscience. He had the equivalent of a state White Paper written in Norman chronicles and woven into the Bayeux Tapestry. He had himself crowned not only in London but in Winchester, the old Saxon capital, King Alfred's city. He began to build churches in England even before he had conquered it all.

Once begun, the church-building boom continued, as on the Continent, for 400 years. It studded little England with more than twenty cathedrals and a thousand handsome lesser churches. Architectural marvels were accomplished, not by architects—there weren't any—but by master masons, craftsmen who had worked their way up from the stone quarries to leadership in skill, daring, and invention.

Who were they?

When the books say "Edward the Umpth built" they're short-cutting. What they (and we) really mean is that Edward gave an order and appointed someone to see it through. The someone then hired a master mason, who in turn hired journeymen masons, carpenters, quarrymen, glaziers.

A monk named Gervase described what happened when the choir of Canterbury Cathedral burned down in 1170. He was there. People, he said, went mad with grief, "cursing God and His saints for the destruction of their church."

When they recovered sufficiently, the monks sent for both French and English craftsmen. Among them was "a certain man of Sens, William by name, one who was of great energy. . . . So they sent the rest away and engaged him, on account of his sparkling genius and his great reputation for work."

Nothing is known about this William except that he had already built a cathedral in the French town of Sens. "—Therefore he set himself to the work of bringing stone from over the sea. He designed, with great ingenuity, machines for loading and unloading ships, for moving cement and stone. He produced moulds for the use of the sculptors he had collected."

William of Sens fell from a scaffold and was too badly injured to carry on. The monks then engaged "William the Englishman." Of this second William even less is known. Yet these two Williams introduced Gothic architecture into England, and the main fabric of Canterbury—that most inspired and historic of English cathedrals—is their work.

It was begun, however, by an earlier William—the Conqueror—under his appointed archbishop, Lanfranc, in 1070, only four years after the Battle of Hastings.

I

Chaucer's pilgrims, you may remember, were bound for Canterbury, "the holy, blissful martyr for to seek."

The martyr had been, in life, Thomas à Becket, the able chancellor and dearest friend of Henry II, a king with a large sense of statecraft. Henry, plunging into a power struggle with the Church, made Thomas à Becket the new archbishop of Canterbury, primate of England.

As chancellor, Becket had glittered, showing a fine taste for gold, jewels, and ermine. Becket as archbishop suddenly transformed himself into an ascetic and flagellant, a churchman more papist than the Pope. All Europe followed the moves and countermoves in the struggle of these two iron-willed men for supremacy. There came a day when Henry cried out for deliverance from Becket, calling his own men cowards. Four knights quietly slipped out of his court, traveled to Canterbury, and hacked the archbishop to death in his cathedral.

It was a sensational murder, as cool and principled as Julius Caesar's. The results were far-reaching. Becket became at once a martyred saint of universal appeal. To win pardon, the King, barefoot and stripped down to his shirt, walked through Canterbury town and submitted to a flogging before his dear enemy's shrine.

The cathedral was a charred wreck when Henry II came to be purged. He went down into the crypt. In his day, and since early Christian times, the pilgrimage churches enshrined their saints and relics below ground. The crypt was an architectural survival from the era of persecution.

Canterbury's crypt is mostly Norman. It's a great church in itself, vaulted, pillared, and as rugged as the soaring pile above is graceful. St. Dunstan had been drawing the pilgrims. With miracle-working St. Thomas, the crowds became so great and the monks so officious in hurrying them along those underground pillared avenues that riots erupted.

Something had to be done.

By 1220 the cathedral of the two Williams was ready. St. Thomas' remains were moved from the crypt up into the church behind the high altar, in a gold and jeweled shrine. The "Translation" was attended by people from all over Europe, high and lowly. It was performed with such splendor that four successive archbishops took fifty years to pay the bill.

Chaucer was writing more than 150 years after the Translation, just about the time when the cathedral was building a new nave and transepts. Another century-and-a-half saw the culmination of labor and love—Bell Harry, the exquisite "lantern"; that is, the windowed central tower.

Henry II lost his battle with the Church. A later Henry, the Eighth, won it. He began his reign only four years after Bell Harry was proudly completed. One of his first acts after dissolving the monasteries was to seize St. Thomas' golden shrine and scatter the bones.

Opposition rose against his radical religious measures. He suppressed it with executions and by creating—if destruction can be called creative—the abbey ruins which dream so sweetly in the green and pleasant land.

II

Churches can be tiresome unless they pass a miracle.

An easy way to make the miracle happen is to visit the abbey ruins of Tintern, Rievaulx and, above all, Fountains. They are beautiful stone forms with minimal distractions. Their floors are of the greenest turf. Their pillars and arches frame wooded hills. Architecturally and romantically, their effect is still as described by John Aubrey in the seventeenth century:

"They breed in generous Minds a Kind of Pittie; and sett the Thoughts a-worke to make out their Magnifice as they were when in Perfection."

If you plan to see Fountains, loveliest and most extensive of the ruins, you'll go to York and drive (25 miles) or take an excursion bus from there. We found a difficulty intruding itself—once in York, we could hardly bear to leave it, even for an excursion.

A walled city on the river Ouse, seat of an archbishop, York is one of England's most colorful provincial capitals. It is vigorous, dynamic, and has much to show: the wall and its gates, the medieval street called the Shambles, fine old houses, the entrancing Castle Museum, and a church in full "Magnifice."

York Minster is no place for an attack of yawns. If you're statistics-minded, be impressed by the fact that this is the largest of all English churches. Be impressed, further, by its wealth of stained glass. One window alone—that at the east end—displays, says an expert,"the greatest single area of 15th-century glass in Europe." There's a glorious fifteenth-century stone screen with wrought-iron gates, a wonderful chapter house, a Norman crypt with weird, hellish sculpture, and much else.

We caught the tremendous church in the mid-tide of thorough restoration. A railroad with hand-propelled rail trucks snaked all around inside. An iron elevator, rising at the transept-crossing like a misbegotten pillar, lifted hard-hats to dim nests of roof work. Here and there, in deep holes, squatted archaeologists examining, drawing, and writing the story of Norman and Saxon leavings. The clangor and hammering, contagious excitement, and stumbling tour parties halted for services while the dust settled briefly.

"This sort of thing," we told each other, "should go on always."

For a couple of hundred years, while the central cathedral of the north slowly rose, pilgrims and Yorkshiremen knew it as work in progress. They skipped around masons, carpenters, stonecutters, glaziers, tilers, and the workmen who dug and carted, mixed mortar, and hoisted stones into place.

The drama of kinship with the past is over now. But York is wonderful, and where else in the world can you move so gratifyingly from Magnifice to the Kind of Pittie that sets the Thoughts a-worke?

RYE AND WINCHELSEA

There exists in the United States an organization called the Society for the Restoration of the Dukedom of Normandy.

"What in the world have Americans got to do with Normandy?" you ask sharply. "And restoration to whom?"

"Restoration to England," we reply glibly. "When William the Conqueror took England he retained his Normandy dukedom. His successors finally lost it to the French and spent the lives of thousands of ordinary medieval Joes to get it back, and never did."

"So what concern is it of ours?" you ask, and rightly. "That would play hell with NATO, giving Normandy back to England. How do the Normans and the French feel about it?"

"The Society has never asked them. Actually, its main concern is genealogical. Each member traces his lineage back to some Norman knight who helped William beat Harold and the English in 1066."

This fictitious dialogue breaks open a fact not known to many who visit England—that for the greater part of English history the main enemy was France. You know the names of Poictiers and Agincourt, of Joan of Arc, of Napoleon and the Black Prince. They're to the point. The French kept making quick strikes at the English Channel ports. The English did the same to the French side. This went on even between wars. Raiding and counterpiracy were endemic.

That is why, in Winchelsea, you may see a man go up to the top of the old fortification known as the Strand Gate to gaze out at sea in the direction of France. What looks he for? A French invasion fleet. He and his predecessors have been staring out to sea from the Strand Gate for some seven hundred years. They have been keeping watch and ward for an enemy fleet such as the one of 1357 which all but did for Winchelsea, and the other, twenty years later, which burned everything combustible in neighboring Rye.

Rye and Winchelsea are sister towns, but each has its own vivid personality. If you see one, you're bound to see the other as well, for the distance between them is almost exactly the length of New York's Central Park from 59th to 110th—less than three miles.

Both are officially towns, but Rye has eight times Winchelsea's population. Rye is hilly and black-and-white (half-timbered). Winchelsea is level and of stone. Both used to be ports. They were added to the Cinque (pronounced *Sink*) Ports by, it is thought, William the Conqueror. Channel waves and currents have removed them from the sea.

I

Rye has a people inured to trudging up and down steep cobbled streets, keeping house in ancient dwellings, amusing tourists, and getting scraped by lorries (trucks) in its narrow main street. At the top of its hill are the parish church and town hall, and on the cliffside the Ypres (pronounced *Wipers*) Tower and museum, from which there is a glorious ("Oh, I say!") view of Winchelsea and the Channel. The church clock is one of England's oldest still in working condition. It has two eighteenth-century quarter-boys who strike the quarter hours, but not the hour itself. We gathered with a multitude to watch them do it. Alas, all we got for our pains was a slight movement, and the cherubs went dead for another fifteen minutes.

Inside, you see the 18-foot-long pendulum swinging back and forth. The climb to the clock works and belfry chamber for another view is worth making if you're fit.

Rye is a busy place, tourist-packed, and with more traffic than is good for it. High Street is lined with souvenir shops, but there are better shops above, near the church. Rye pottery is the buy.

Mermaid Street is a steep line of some of the most picturesque houses in any English street. Just off it, on West Street, is the house where Henry James lived and wrote.

The Rye golf links, about a mile and a half out on Rye Harbor (buses), are famous and draw golfing tourists too timid or lazy to journey all the way to St. Andrews in Scotland.

The inns are old and among the sights. On one visit, when we walked in to have a look at the Mermaid, a surly landlord shooed us out—he wasn't having anyone darken his door who might not spend money. He isn't there any more. On our last trip we lunched at the Flushing, a fifteenth-century house with a sixteenth-century mural in its dining room. We were invited to poke about in the medieval cellar, which once had a private door on the sea side for smugglers. Smuggling was an important business in the Cinque Ports.

II

Winchelsea, with a population of about six hundred and an area of about a dozen city blocks, prides itself on being England's smallest "town." It's a delightful, open, sunlit place. Sunlit? Yes, even in the rain it has a smiling aspect. The few streets are wide and grass-verged, the lovely houses well kept. Nothing cramped here, and no hurry. Why ever did Henry James choose to live in Rye with this serene and gracious little town next door?

French raiders ruined the beautiful abbey church, but what remains is still in use and there is enough to please mightily. Within are the tombs of the Alards, fine work beautifully lighted. You lift your eyes to the delicate windows and the contrasting heavy crossbeams of the roof, and your heart lifts too. The tombs in the graveyard grow flowers.

The museum, in the medieval Court Hall, is a treat. Look for the primitive painting on wood of St. Leonard, puzzlingly dated 1300–1400. The sweet gentlewoman in charge demonstrated for us the horrible man-trap. "Now stand well away," she warned. She kicked an iron gadget and the great teeth came together with a crash. "Snappo!" she cried merrily. "It has probably torn many a poacher's leg off, that!" See the Armoury, a handsome stone mansion, one of many fine old houses.

We kept our eye on the Strand Gate, wanting to see the keeper perform the ancient rite of scanning the horizon for the French invasion fleet. Not seeing him, we pursued him through the town. But it would have taken a man-trap to catch him. He's the local odd-job man, and we were always one job behind him. Keeping the Gate is one of his odd jobs. His pay for it was five dollars a year. Winchelsea has had a continuous line of mayors and Keepers of the Gate. The inductions, on Easter Monday, take place in the Court Hall and faithfully follow the medieval ceremonies. When Winchelsea was thriving, Edward I came to confirm Magna Carta, and Edward II set out from here for the Battle of Crécy. The French paid sudden and bloody visits. Then the sea took a hand, first drowning it, then silting up the harbor; and it was reborn where it now stands, two miles inland. That is why you find it with broad streets in a grid pattern—a medieval planned town.

III

From either Winchelsea or Rye:
Down the coast about twelve miles is Hythe. If you have children in tow, or are yourself a railway enthusiast, go there and buy a round-trip ticket on the miniature railroad. The Romney, Hythe & Dymchurch is an honest-to-goodness commercial line. It runs fourteen miles to Dungeness (which is no place) on a track of 15-inch gauge, with real if pint-size locomotives and cars. Every trip is a festival. Crowds come to ride. As avid as the children are the locomotive engineers who visit on their day off their own main-line jobs to polish the engines and beg for a chance in the cab. During World War II the tiny railway did a man-size job hauling pipe for Operation Pluto, armed with ack-ack guns, in this corner of the Blitz.

Remember the Battle of Hastings—1066 and all that? This being England, it wasn't fought at Hastings. But you're very close here to where England's most important historical events began, so why not look at the places?
In September 1066 William the Bastard, leaving Normandy in

the capable hands of his wife Matilda (he'd wooed her by pulling her around by the hair and kicking her some), set sail for England with all the men he could muster in a thousand ships of the long, slim, curved-prow Viking type. They beached at Pevensey. Earl Harold had been expecting them, but had had to dash up north because Harold of Norway had chosen this inconvenient time to attack. William was incredibly lucky—Earl Harold was a great warrior.

At Pevensey, William flung up a makeshift castle within the walls of a Roman fort, and then sailed down the coast a little way to Hastings, which provided a better haven. Harold, having beaten his Scandinavian foe in a terrible battle, had no time to rest. He came south as fast as he could.

Pevensey has the remains of William's castle, the one that replaced the hasty wooden structure he put up on landing. The Roman wall surrounds it.

Hastings, once an important Cinque Port, is now a seaside resort. Very little of the old survives—some narrow streets, fishermen's houses, a fishing museum, a smuggler's cave, and the scanty ruins of another of William's castles.

The "Battle of Hastings" was fought seven miles to the northwest of the port, at a place in the open which the Conqueror called Battle and where he had an abbey built to make good a vow to the Almighty.

An attractive small town, with a broad, country-like main street, has grown outside the abbey. Its chief point of interest is, of course, the abbey, even though it now houses a school. A fee is charged to see the ruins and grounds. The grand battlemented gatehouse frowns down on High Street. Its colorful companion is the Pilgrim's Rest, a fine half-timbered house, once a maison-dieu (pilgrim's hostel). It's a good port for tea and worth examining within and without. There are many fine old buildings in and just off High Street.

The nearby village of Sedlescombe has an odd church. All along the roads and lanes hereabouts you see venerable thatched cottages sporting TV aerials. The rolling countryside of the Downs and the Weald has few spectacular moments, but is deep green pastoral country, very satisfying any way you wander.

SHERBORNE WITH MRS. CHUBB

Back in the days when we were a-courtin', a project that drew us together was collecting American town songs. One that sticks in the mind went like this:

> I wandered the whole world o'er
> And then I found Desplaines. . . .

Chorus: Happy town, happy town, never can be beat.
           The streets are paved, conditions best—
           You will like Desplaines.

Years later, wandering the whole world o'er, we came to Sherborne, a town in Dorset we had never heard of. Its soft-colored stone and the grace of the curving, ascending High Street caused us to break into "Happy town, happy town!"

We were on a walking tour. Hotels were beyond our budget, so we stayed in bed-and-breakfast homes—which turned out to afford closer contact with England and the English than the hotel route. We found in a side street a house named The Brambles, with a hand-lettered card in the window: "Bed and Breakfast. Mrs. Chubb."

Mrs. Chubb's parlor was like a set in a Victorian play. Plush-framed photographs, "God Bless Our Home" in needlepoint, and a penmanship diploma decorated the floral wallpaper. Wax flowers bloomed on tables under glass bells. Whatnots were thickly populated with knickknacks, among them Mrs. Chubb's two most prized possessions—a rose of Jericho and a stuffed owl.

Mrs. Chubb was a skipsy woman with big blue eyes, a country-girl's complexion, and a way of mounting the stairs to the bedrooms in effortless, airy flight, talking all the while. She was both genteel and larky. There was a teenage daughter, speechless and shy, floating ribbons from hair and dress. Our praise of her breakfast of ham and eggs with butter-fried potatoes brought a flush of deep Dorset red. At the upright piano we tried to teach Chubb, Jr., the real Dixie beat, but it was Mrs. Chubb who caught the rhythm. For three days we were part of a sprightly family.

Before leaving we contributed our laudatory inscription to the Guest Book, and read the comments of preceding guests. "Short visit but sweet." "Comfortable digs." "*Joli ménage.*" The week before, a multitude had descended upon Brambles: "Noble & Harris, Furniture Removers. 4 men, one lady, 2 children, one dog, Plymouth to London." After them came "Three maids from Lady Rugge-Price. Miss Hinks, Miss Bolan, Miss Wall." They had put their heads together and composed this:

> If from home you have to wander,
>   Never fear.
> There's a welcome and good cheer
> At The Brambles in Sherborne dear
>   With Mrs. Chubb.

It is perilous to return after long absence to a place where one was vividly happy. But we had to see Sherborne again to check dutifully on whether it was worth urging on other travelers. And perhaps we could pay our respects to Mrs. Chubb, who was so alive then that we did not doubt she was still so.

At the railway station we inquired after her and The Brambles. Neither was known.

This time we put up in style at the Digby, former mansion of the great family of these parts. We admired the slow curve of Low Cheap and High Cheap, the inviting shops, the ageless houses of russet stone, the timbered inns, and the long green hill smiling down on all of it. Our relief was enormous. Sherborne is blessed with that indefinable quality called presence.

This small (pop. 7,000) ancient town has a fine abbey, a complex of buildings mostly fifteenth century but dating back to 705. Most of what is not church is one of England's oldest public schools, founded in 1550. The boys dine in a paneled Great Hall, watched from a niche by a childlike statue, blue, white, red, and gold, of Edward VI, their Founder. At one end of the complex are medieval almshouses of antique stateliness.

In the church, we liked the slab erected, as it said in carved script, "in Remembrance of a Great Hailfstorme," May 16, 1709, "which ftopping the courfe of a fmall river weft of this Church caufed" a flood in the abbey garden "running with fo rapid a stream" that it forced open the north door and was "2 foot 10 inches high as it paff'd out at this South Door."

A couple of Sherborne's inns are so old they seem to have grown like oak trees out of the ground.

Sherborne has wealth and breeding and a famous hunt center known as the Melton Mowbray of the South. Its golf course is panoramic, its visitors are gentry. The town is full of old gossip. In the seventeenth century, for instance, Sir Kenelm Digby, the handsomest man of his day, married Venetia Stanley, the most beautiful woman. When Sir Kenelm's mother objected to Venetia as a notorious courtesan, he replied that "a wise man, and a lusty, could make an honest woman out of a Brothell-house." And so he did, to the extent that a portrait of Venetia hangs in the State Apartments of Windsor Castle.

We quested after Mrs. Chubb. Taking tea at the Spindleberry, we sounded out Mrs. Spicer over her homemade cakes. New to Sherborne, she guessed that the provision merchants across the Cheap might know. From them we learned that a Miss Chubb sold dresses in a shop down the street.

We popped in, and there was our Miss Chubb, no longer beribboned, still shy, but less speechless. She took us home to her Mum, warning us that Mum was getting on, her memory not what it used to be.

The Chubbs, no longer taking "paying guests," now lived on Hound Street. Mrs. Chubb's snowy-white hair made her eyes look larger and bluer, like those of an unwinking doll. Her skin was as fair, and flawless. She was still light on her feet and larky.

"Eighty-three!" she said of herself. "And not a spot on me!

Doctor says he's never seen anything like it!" She chattered away, going back and forth in time with skipping ease. "I used to bathe Mr. Churchill. 'Twas back in 1898. I'd run away from home to London and found work in a bath-massage house."

"The stuffed owl, Mrs. Chubb?"

She took us into the parlor—and there everything was, just as we remembered: the whatnots, the flowers under glass, the penmanship diploma. The piano was gone; Chubb junior had grown up and married, taken the piano, and given his Mum grandchildren.

"And there," said Mrs. Chubb, "is Owl, sitting in the window. The night constable likes Owl. When he passes he blinks his light at him. 'I like to see him blink back at me,'" he says. She laughed like a girl.

"And the rose of Jericho?"

She was delighted that we remembered it, and pointed out its bowl in the Victorian clutter. "It's still blooming."

Lawrence said, "Just like you, Mrs. Chubb." She blushed and dropped a curtsy.

She brought out a pile of yellowed guest books, blew the dust from each. She stopped at one she said was the right year—our year.

We opened it, lightly arguing with her. But she was right. Here was the page, here the faded inscriptions: "Noble & Harris. . . . Three maids from Lady Rugge-Price. . . .," and the verse:

> If from home you have to wander,
> Never fear. . . .

And under that, our own contribution: "When Hitler's gone, we'll be back."

We marveled over her memory. We cried triumphantly, "We said we'd be back, and here we are!"

But Mrs. Chubb was looking at the message with a frown. "Yes," she said, "they all come back." Still she stared. "But who," she asked, "is this Hitler? A queer name. I don't remember *him* staying here."

ELY AND CAMBRIDGE

I

A backwater drenched with history, most of it dramatic and some of it unintentionally comic, Ely is inhabited by 10,000 undramatic souls and dominated by its strangely lovely cathedral. This church is usually likened to a great ship under full sail. To us it looks no more like a ship than a windjammer ever looked like a cathedral. The notion stems from the way you see it, on approaching from miles away, apparently rising all alone from the flats.

Close at hand it is, at first, not impressive because hard to encompass. Walk toward it slowly, and its greatness begins to speak to you. Every style of Gothic, from Norman to Perpendicular, asserts itself in this glorious stone pile.

The most remarkable feature of the long interior is the octagonal central tower and lantern. The church was finished in 1187 in Norman style. One February morning in 1322, just after Matins, the central tower crashed down, ruining the choir and leaving a great hole. The shape of that hole gave the sacristan, Alan of Walsingham, the idea of something new—an octagon. It was, and is, an engineering victory on a grand scale. It is held up by careful balancing of weight and by corner posts of oak 65 feet long. But the technical feats, though they wring a salute, don't prolong wonder. Does it matter how the posts were searched for all over England, how they were jockeyed into position, and what weight they've supported for 600 years? What does matter is the combined effect of bold strength and airy beauty.

There's a profusion of extraordinary things: the richly decorated Monks' and Priors' doors, the undercroft, the roof bosses, the carved misericords, the imaginative and capricious stone carving on the capitals and above the choir stalls (those Imps of Ely), and the fifteenth-century carved and painted transepts. And the superb Lady Chapel. And the choir's vaulting. A gloomy day doesn't bring out the extravagant details. But on a sunlit day, what you see brings to mind that line from Shakespeare's *Henry V*: "The singing masons building roofs of gold."

As you come out of the cathedral, whether the sky be bright or dark, the military jets you can't see make themselves heard. They too are part of Christendom as we Christendumkopfs have made it.

There's little more for you in this lowly, stony town except St. Mary's, dating from 1215, and King's School, part of the cathedral precincts.

We stood in grounds muddy from much rain and watched rubber-booted schoolboys slosh to what looked like a reconditioned Elizabethan tithe-barn. We talked with a bright youngster who asked to look through our "Pictorial History of Ely Cathedral." He read about his school: "What better setting could one hope to find for a school? And who would exchange the lovely old buildings in which the boys live and work and play for any of our modern erections? Most of them date from the Middle Ages."

Our boy said he'd been visiting a friend during the holidays. "He goes to that big new technological school near Hatfield House—you know it?" We did. "Well—" Yearning and envy were in that one word. Then the thin shoulders straightened and the clear young eyes accepted fate. "It's not the same thing at all, is it?" "No, not at all," we said gently. With gloomy pride he sloshed on to the Middle Ages.

Ely's history is weird; its boys of King's School grow up with it. Ely was an island in the Fens and on a muddy river populated by eels—an unlikely site for human habitation. Yet it was already hoary by the time William the Conqueror came up against Hereward the Wake. It had a double monastery of monks and nuns when the Venerable Bede was young. (He must have been a boy once.)

Long long ago, in Saxon times, the daughter of an East Anglian king was married to Tonbert, a lord of Mercia. She was Etheldreda, but her name was either *pronounced* Awdrey or *was* Awdrey. It is hard to get Angle-and-Saxon affairs straight.

This lady refused to accord her husband the expected privileges. The story omits any ensuing painful scenes and does not give Tonbert's reactions. All we next know is that he died. Etheldreda-Awdrey then did an unaccountable thing. She took another husband, this time King Egfrid of Northumberland. She gave him the same "Don't touch me" treatment. Egfrid, either short-tempered or healthier than Tonbert was, insisted. Etheldreda fled. Egfrid pursued. His hairy Northumbrian hands were stretched out to seize his bride, when suddenly some waters rose to foil him. Etheldreda was saved. Egfrid went back to Northumbria and was heard from no more.

One assumes the chase took place over the marshes, and that the waters of rescue were the eely river Ouse, because in honor of the miracle a nunnery rose on the Isle of Ely. Etheldreda was its founder and first abbess. She died there in 679 of a quinsy, or inflammation of the throat, contracted from kneeling from midnight to daybreak on cold, damp stone floors. But she laid her fatal illness to divine punishment for having fondly worn a necklace.

Ten years passed, and her sister Sexburga (a name fraught with possibilities) discovered Etheldreda's body to be perfectly preserved; looked around; and by another miracle found a beautiful white shrine all ready for it. Sexburga became the second abbess. From the beginning, whoever touched the coffin was immediately healed of whatever ailed him. Pilgrims came in great numbers.

When Sexburga died, her niece Ermenilda succeeded her, and she too died a devout virgin. These two were buried near

Etheldreda—who by now was definitely called St. Awdrey—and Ely had a peculiarly holy triple shrine of female saints. But in 870 marauding Danes sacked the place and slaughtered the nuns. Many decades later the sainted Dunstan gave Ely a new start as a Benedictine monastery. He built a church around the remains of the three saints. A fourth was soon added—Wihtburga, another sister of Etheldreda.

Wihtburga was an acquisition of Ely's abbot Brihtnoth, a vigorous, Teddy-Roosevelt type. Seeking to increase Ely's sanctity potential, he took encoffined Wihtburga "not very reputably from its resting place at Dereham," said our "Pictorial History."

"Not very reputably" shyly conceals an epic of tenth-century body-snatching, the kind of enterprise that helped make the pilgrimage era lively.

Brihtnoth saw no reason why the minor-league monastery of Dereham should own the remains of Ely's great saint's sainted sister. He hatched an elaborate plot. He and his monks made a festive trip by boat to Dereham, inviting its monks and townsmen to a "feast of brotherly love."

Brihtnoth and his stalwarts wined and dined the Derehamites into a stupor, and in the stilly night made off with Wihtburga's coffin. Twenty miles overland they had carried it, to the banks of the Ouse, when they heard the Derehamites panting in pursuit. They tumbled the saint and themselves into the waiting boat and began to row and pray frantically.

The men of Dereham intercepted the boat at a bend. Running along both banks, they pelted the monks with clods of earth and stones. Some of the heroes suffered bruises, but they won the great race and Wihtburga. She was safe with them because Ely was well fortified.

A century later William the Conqueror, triumphant through most of England, stood among his men on land dry and firm enough to hold them and stared over the quaking, wetter land to the fortified, holy Isle of Ely. He faced no small problem. Ely would not surrender and could not be taken. Its resistance leader—Hereward the Wake—from a camp in the miasmic marshes had long been waging successful guerrilla warfare against the Normans. He had won the reputation of sorcerer. The whole look and feel of the place, the Isle's ancient sanctity, and Hereward's uncanny appearances and disappearances, filled the Normans with superstitious terror. But William was experienced in taking impregnable strong-points. He settled his men to starve Ely out, and meanwhile busied them with building a three-mile road over the marshlands.

In due time an emaciated delegation from Ely came out ready to give up and to betray Hereward by showing the Normans the way to his camp. To prove their good will they brought along a sorceress who offered to work her powers against those of Hereward. William built a wooden tower in which he imprisoned the enchantress and had her pushed well ahead of his advance. Hereward couldn't resist setting fire to the tower. The Normans charged, and fought in the light of flames that revealed Hereward's position. The sorceress, forgotten, was left to burn. So ended the last organized resistance to the Conqueror.

William caused the present great church to be built around the hallowed Awdrey-Etheldreda, Sexburga, Ermenilda, and the stolen Wihtburga. Early in the twelfth century it was ready for the sainted four. Hordes of pilgrims were attracted, especially by the great fairs in June and October. As at Canterbury, there wasn't enough shrine-room for them. The apse had to be pulled down and the cathedral extended eastward with a six-bay presbytery in which a new shrine was erected. In 1252 Awdrey-E. was "translated," Henry III coming to the dedication of the new shrine. If you ask, a verger will point out where it stood.

Around the octagon eight sculptured corbels (projections for supporting timbers and arches) portray scenes from the life of this Etheldreda the Unready. The illustrators did not choose the most interesting episodes.

Awdrey-Etheldreda has her reward on high. But on low, the English language has immortalized her in its own way. It has appropriated her name for the word "*tawdry*."

Ely's great markets were called St. Awdrey's Fairs. In time this was elided to S'tawdry. Like all fairs, they were crowded with stalls selling gimcrackery, fripperies, trinkets. *"Tawdry"* crept into the language as a designation for the kind of trash you get stuck with at a fair. So at long last the story comes full circle with the strange irony that a religiously virtuous woman who believed her death was punishment for wearing a necklace should have her name thus enshrined in the language.

You might call it an inverse miracle.

II

In traveling, a change of scene and pace is just as welcome as it is in the routine of home and office. Such a change is yours if you go from Ely to Cambridge, a distance of seventeen miles.

Ely is heavy with old, unhappy, or hard-to-believe things, with impossible Brihtnoths and Wihtburgas, with faceless Angles and Saxons. The land is so flat as to be almost concave, more sky than landscape. Everything is so quiet you can hear the past tick.

And suddenly, Cambridge. Suddenly, because you don't merely arrive, you erupt into it. Cambridge is dynamic. It is movement, activity, youth, a living drama played against a marvelous back-drop that began building in the thirteenth century and faces not yesterday but tomorrow. "Many shall run about, and knowledge be increased," saith the Bible somewhere. And here are the many running about, mostly on bicycles—some breasting the wind with streaming beards—and knowledge is being increased like everything.

Milton and Pepys went to school here. So did Tennyson, Byron, Newton and Bacon, Wordsworth and Macaulay. In the Cavendish Laboratories behind Corpus Christi College, Thomson and Rutherford did their revolutionary work in physics, and the Russian Peter Kapitza nursed along the idea that became the first sputnik. As the many run about, you can almost hear the final countdown, beginning with Erasmus and marking off the centuries to C. P. Snow of Christ's College.

Of course, if you come in the "long vac," the summer vacation, the effect is not the same. Then you erupt into fellow tourists, who are running about on their own feet. Then Cambridge is merely beautiful.

"Oxford and Cambridge," people say—seldom, "Cambridge and Oxford." For not a few, however, Cambridge comes first as a tourist experience. The colleges are not as chaotically jumbled as at Oxford. Each displays itself more fully, and you feel less intrusive and more welcome among them. The town is pleasanter, Oxford having become industrialized. The river in summer is both a public way and an integral part of the university; you can go boating among the colleges. But—

Caparisons are odorous, as Mrs. Malaprop, without benefit of college education, said. If you ask us: "Which one should I visit, Oxford or Cambridge?" we must answer, "It would be a pity to miss either." If you then say: "But I haven't time for both. So which should it be?" we can only tell you that in our family the vote is a one-to-one tie.

We had a time taking you and ourselves around Oxford, if you remember. Oxford, in growing, had to compress itself within medieval walls. Cambridge, never walled, spread out gracefully and naturally. It is therefore easier to see. You can walk over much of it in a day, if your metatarsals are as sturdy as Gothic arches. Your program could run like this:

1. For orientation and preliminary survey, go up one side and down the other of the seven-eighths of a mile of main street—a continuous thoroughfare changing name from south to north: Trumpington, King's Parade, Trinity Street, and St. John's Street.

The parade of colleges on this stretch, from Trumpington north, reads: Peterhouse, St. Catharine's (with Queen's behind it), King's (with Clare behind it), Caius, Trinity, St. John's. Across from St. Catharine's are Pembroke and Corpus Christi.

The oldest, structurally, is the part of Old Schools called Regent House. Old Schools (lecture halls) is between King's and Caius and behind the classical Senate House which serves for end-term ceremonies. (The oldest structure in Cambridge, actually, is the tower of St. Benet's Church in the street of that name, parts of which are absolutely Saxon.)

2. Go to King's College and, letting nothing else distract you, visit its chapel, which is on the north side of the Great Court, the one with the fountain in the middle. (By the way, where Oxford has quads, Cambridge has courts.)

King's College Chapel is a late stone-and-glass flowering of Gothic. It is one of the most ornately beautiful structures of the Western world. The walls are mostly stained-glass windows reaching from the floor almost to the intricately fan-vaulted roof eighty feet above. The sixteenth-century screen is a glorious wall of woodcarving. In every detail this chapel is a marvel. A church without aisles or pillars, it is daringly original.

King's College was founded by Henry VI in 1440 as the link of higher education to his Eton. As a young man he directed the planning of King's College Chapel and laid the first stone in 1446. Sixty years later Henry VII, the first Tudor king, visited Cambridge and was so excited by the half-built church that he not only took it in hand but left money for the work to go on after his death. Henry VIII finished it—on the screen are carved the arms and monogram of Anne Boleyn.

It gives one pause to think about that sixth Henry. Was an architect lost to the world because he had to be a king?

It gives one to think about the seventh Henry too. His reputation for miserliness had made him look small-souled.

Buy at a table the pamphlet "King's College Chapel: Comments and Opinions"—pro and con from noted appraisers since 1564, Queen Elizabeth I being the first. It's hard to believe anyone could ever say a word against it. Yet here is one William Gilpin in 1769: "Its disproportion disgusts." And Sir Anthony Carlisle, 1804: "Its ornaments are in bad taste." Theirs was an age that misprized both Gothic and Shakespeare. At the other extreme is Wordsworth with three sonnets.

This superb church should be experienced in action as well as in repose. Don't miss the candlelit evensong at five-thirty. (Check on the time with the college porter.)

3. Concentrating on the west side of the main street, walk in the courts and go through to the Backs. Since you are at King's College, begin there. When you pass through the archway of the building at the west end of the Great Court, you find yourself on a dream of a lawn going down to the river Cam. This is King's piece of the Backs.

"*The Backs*" is the name given to the river frontage—the lawns, gardens, and meadows behind this row of college buildings. Here, where weeping willows bow down to the water and birches stand tall and little bridges curve above the shining river, may well be the loveliest man-made landscape in all England.

You can't walk along the full length of the Backs because there is no connection between one college and another. You keep going in and out. The colleges are beautiful and various enough to make this a pleasing exercise. You can float along the Backs on the river. If foolhardy, rent a punt—a clumsy boat which must be poled along. The unskilled finds his pole stuck in the mud, himself frantically hanging on it, the punt floating away. To be safer, rent a canoe. (Boat hire at Magdalene Bridge and at Mill Lane; summer.)

4. The main street runs into Bridge Street at St. John's. At this point you'll be tempted by the Round Church. Succumb. Go in and rest your weary feet. This is the Church of the Holy Sepulchre (one of four round churches in England), dating from 1130 and looking much older. While resting, buy and read the leaflet about the church.

But don't pass by St. John's College, the one with the heraldic gateway. It has a Bridge of Sighs over the Cam, and its courts are wonderful.

5. Walking west on Bridge Street, visit Magdalene (*Maudlin*) College. If you can be there during term between 2:30 and 3:30 P.M. you can see the Biblioteca Pepysiana, the library left to his alma mater by that excellent public servant, avid diarist, and

confirmed flirt, Samuel Pepys. The original *Diary* in his original shorthand is there. The two courts of this college and the broad gardens beyond are delightful.

6. Visit Emmanuel College if you want to pay your respects to the memory of John Harvard, founder of the first American college. It's off St. Andrews Street. Christ's College is nearby.

FROM GUZZLE DOWN TO THE TAH

A village we have marked down for our next stay in England is Barton-in-the-Beans. It's in Leicester, surrounded by history if not, as the name promises, by beans. Two miles away is Market Bosworth and that Bosworth Field where, in the second period of the Wars of the Roses, Richard III was so anxious to trade his kingdom for a horse and died of failure to find a buyer.

Young Sam Johnson taught school in Market Bosworth. His home was a few miles away, in Lichfield, where the "Lady of English cathedrals" asks to be seen. On another side is Nuneaton and the George Eliot country—but who reads her any more? Nearby too is Birmingham, a kind of Detroit, and Arnold Bennett's Five Towns. More appealing is Ashby de la Zouch, a name railway conductors aspire to shout.

Ashby de la Zouch! It reminds us of the curious pronunciations with which "every shires end of Engelonde" (to borrow a line from the fourteenth century) is embellished. The English Language, U and non-U, and the place names, are not the least fun of gadding about the sceptered isle.

In the United States, to counter the boredom of the ruler-straight road and the prairie on both sides, the motorist and his back-seat drivers invent license-plate games. England has fewer such roads and landscapes than a three-toed sloth has toes. If your ambition is to see England you meander with the road lanes. You round the shoulder of a hill, and there is a finger sign pointing to—what's it say?—Careless End. A few miles farther on, or the next day, you encounter Butter Tubs or Pity Me. And you begin the English game: collecting odd names.

Our vivid recollections of the Lake District are not of

Wordsworth and the morals he discovered under stones, but of such signs and the places they enticed us to. "This is the Wettest Spot in all England!" one outside Keswick proclaimed with pride; and another, "Dollywagon Pike." That one we pursued. No Dollywagon is there, but a pike with a panorama fit to make baby sit up and gurgle.

Names like Guzzle Down are a delight and a provocation. In Exeter we and an English couple saw a sign in the window of Watty's Delicatessen: "Box Lunches Put Up." We went in and ordered. Mr. Watty cried: "Stop! Put up lunches? Such things I don't do!" We propelled him outside. "Dear me," he said, "I meant to take that down years ago." "Must we call in the constabulary?" we asked.

So now as we motored toward Torquay along the South Devon coast with four Watty lunches, we debated where to picnic. Reggie looked up from the road map. "There's a Guzzle Down ahead! The fated spot!" But we never found it. We went through it, backed up, circled it, perhaps parked on it, but were unable to identify it.

This will happen, and should not dishearten. It lends zest to the sport. These tiny hamlets—and they are the ones with the fantastic monickers—are shy, well tucked away. But they *must* be there. The guidebooks may know them not, but Her Majesty's Ordnance maps do not lie. It is worth a little effort to run down villages dubbed Totterdown, Land of Nod, Wendens Ambo, Christmas Pie, Tom's-by-the-Woods, Helion Bumstead, and Lurking Hope.

Among our triumphs are Great Snoring in East Anglia, and in the Cotswolds the lovely hamlets of Slaughter—Upper and Lower—and the three Swells, Upper, Lower, and Nether. (Upper is the beauty.) Weary-All Hill was another achievement, but being in touristed Glastonbury it hardly counts as a triumph.

The curious appellation is only half, and the lesser half, of the pleasure of serendipity. The more delicious part is the way the English pronounce their home-sweet-homes.

In the Cotswolds we asked a shepherd if we were on the right road for Snowshill. He had "nur 'earn o't." But we found it. Its people call it Snozzle. The map shows that the nearby hill is Snowshill Hill. Pursuing this clue, we learned that the natives call it Snozzle-l. You see what must have happened in early unlettered days, and lives on? Snows Hill got eroded to Snozzle. A later generation asked itself why it wasn't called Snozzle Hill, the mound being the outstanding feature. In time it got worn down again to Snozzle-l Hill. A newer generation will crumble it to Snozzle-l-l. One hesitates to peer further into the future.

Shakespeare probably knew the place as Snozzle. In *King Henry IV, Part 2,* he mentions Wonscot village in Gloucestershire. You won't find it on the map, but you will find Woodmancote.

If you think our Snozzle-l conjecture farfetched, consider the finding of the sober, noted semanticist Mario Pei examining Torpenhow Hill near Plymouth. He discovered that *Tor, Pen,* and *How* all meant "hill" in, respectively, Saxon, Celtic, and Scandinavian. Along came a generation who didn't know this but did know a hill when they saw one. "Their final contribution," Mario Pei records, "makes the name Hillhillhill Hill."

Cornwall is far from the Cotswolds, and different, and even refuses to admit itself English. There they have a cute place with a cute name—Mousehole. You'd think not even a Cornishman would tamper with that. But half the population calls it Moozle and the other half Mewzle. In Sussex, Bosham is Boz'm. Olney, the famous pancake-race town, is called Ooney.

In London the taxicab drivers subject names to the same wear and tear. Your man, pointing out places of tourist interest, will show you Mobblotch, Spaws, the Ahzes of Pahment, and the Tah. It is as if New Yorkers had reduced Brooklyn Heights to Blintz —and after all, why not?

On the Welsh border we crossed the breadloaf hill called The Longmynd, and passing the Stiperstones found ourselves in a village proclaiming itself to be Ratlinghope. We climbed out for a stretch, a breath of Shropshire (Salops) air, and bumpers of Welsh ale. To break the awkward silence the advent of strangers produces in remote country parts, Lawrence said to the tavern keeper, "Pleasant village, this. How are things in Ratlinghope?"

"Ratling what?"

"Hope. Ratlinghope," and he indicated the road sign.

"Nur 'ear o't place. Any o' you lads?"

Chorus of negative grunts from two elderly lads and a kibitzer bent over shove ha'penny.

"What be name o't village then?" asked Sylvia, who is quick on catching dialects.

"Rattrup, ur be."

Later, on that run to Dollywagon Pike, we found ourselves in a lush green valley by a tumbling stream under Pendragon Castle. Legend, that engaging liar, says it was built by King Arthur's father, Uther Pendragon. Here nestles the village of Mallerstang. A name with a fine ring to it, steel clashing on steel! Wary by now, we asked the Oldest Inhabitant—there's usually one lurkhoping about—what the place was called.

"Iz be Mors'n."

"Be Mors'n? Mallerstang be Mors'n?"

"Aye, be Mors'n."

"Where be they bury rest o' name?"

"Bury? Churchyard be— "

Churchyard be blowed.

In Norfolk, where in the lavender country Snettisham village lies not far from Sandringham Hall, country home of the royal family, there is a rumor that the girl who became Queen Elizabeth II giggled every time she heard the village name uttered— Sneez'm. And what of Sevenoaks, which when we first visited it years ago was a royal-oaky village? It has since grown and developed into a suburban dormitory town for well-padded lumpen-bourgeois, London stockbroker yeomen who call it Sennocks. The next step is Snooks.

The denizens of Slaithwaite, Yoiks—poddon, Yorks—in the Coln valley on the edge of the moors and the Brontë country, call their huddle of cottages Slowitt. Hard by is the den of the Dragon of Wharncliffe. The dragon is no more, he died when it came to be pronounced Wantley. In the same riding the Duke of Rutland's Belvoir Castle, a visitable Stately Home known as the "lordliest place in England after Windsor Castle," is downgraded to "Beaver."

As for Windsor Castle, it hasn't yet become "Winkle." And to be fair, it must be admitted that the people of Wiltshire who call Hardenhuish "Harnish" or "Harnsh" have a case.

But to return to Barton-in-the-Beans. Research suggests that thirty or so years ago it was called Barton-le-Beans. The *le* points toward the Norman Conquest. What happened to provoke this late reform? Did the villeins revolt against the bad grammar of singular article tied to plural noun? The 160 villagers must have split into factions. "Why not Barton-*les*-Beans?" cried the liberals. The radicals staged a sitdown on the village green, waving signs: "Go the whole hog. Call it Barton-les-Haricots-Verts!"

A compromise was reached.

Can you imagine living without strain in a place called Barton-in-the-Beans? A brash American tourist is bound to come by, and leaning out of his car, bawl at a commorant in the ingratiating way some of us have: "Hey, doc, what's-a-name-a-this-place?"

"Barton-in-the-Beans."

"In-the-what?"

Defiantly: "In-the-Beans!"

"Beans? You sure? Hear that, Molly? Boy, is that one for the book!"

"Looks like Barton-in-the-Soup to me," says Molly in a deep contralto.

From the yokel—no, local—point of view, an uncomfortable situation. Here's a people, eternally on the defensive against the expected guffaw, the ribald comment, the curled lip, the overt sneer, brought to despise their ancestors for fastening such a label on their Barton. The children pleading with Dad and Mum to tell them *Why?* The villagers unable to shuck the moss-grown 900-year-old name—equally unable to move to a locality with a comelier cognomen, such as Furtherfits, Jollyboys, Pratt's Bot-tom, Elmer's End, Bachelor's Bump. . . .

The man who knows the why and wherefore must surely be the parish vicar. He is a mild, abstracted, silver-haired old gentleman with the washed-out blue eyes of one who has spent them on the fine print of antiquarian studies more than on the message of the heavens. He has written a monograph: "The Brasses of St. Cuthbert's and St. Jude's Parish Church, Barton-in-the-Beans, Leics. Privately Printed."

We must get to him. For when we find out the why of Barton-in-the-Beans, then at last we will know England.

FRANCE

PLEASURES AND PAINS

I

The only trouble with your French will be the Parisian; he will not understand it.

The French have an Academy to guard their language, keep it weeded, clip its hedges, and warn trespassers off the grass. In addition, every Parisian seems prepared at the first sound of a Berlitzed tourist to constitute himself deputy sheriff of the tongue of tongues. The stilly face, the utter lack of response, informs you that your passed-with-honors is a barbaric yawp.

"The French," said Professor Higgins in *My Fair Lady*, "don't mind what you say, really, so long as you pronounce it correctly."

When, in New York, a visiting sage from the Sorbonne speaks of "Brode-vay," Americans are quick to make a shrewd guess. And when in our kitchen he remarks brightly, "Zees eez zee Vestangooze?" it doesn't take us longer than a chuckle to know that our refrigerator interests him.

But if in Paris you ask your way to the Place de l'Opéra, you're likely to be stymied unless you handle *l'opéra* with three short, incisive strokes of the vocal oar, ending with the throaty "rah" high over the water. Only then does your Parisian dip his own blade to carry you safely to shore.

In the thirteenth century St. Louis, a decent king, remarked, "It is a bad thing to take another man's goods because *rendre* is so difficult that to pronounce it makes the tongue sore by reason of the r's in it."

To return another man's goods is still painful to a Frenchman, but only the stranger shares St. Louis' feeling about that "r." The trouble is compounded when he has to say *rue*—and it can't be dodged. Such a tiny word, but that trick "r" is followed by the even trickier "u." Together they lay demands on the tongue and require throat-work deep as the tonsils.

When you ask for butter you're up against a double "r" smeared by a preceding "eu." *Beurre* should be banished. It wouldn't hurt Parisians to adopt "butter." Look what they've already taken: *le box, pique-nique, les girls, sandwichs, un dancing.*

If you talk your native English (or German, or Spanish) at the Parisian, he is churlish, so you might as well learn and use fearless French. The rewards are great. For French is grand, sonorous, and delightful.

Writing this in our hotel room, we become aware of a notice under the desk's glass top: "MM. les Voyageurs are prayed to announce their departure before midday."

"MM. les Voyageurs!" That's us—we! One has suddenly become a compeer of M. Marco Polo.

You're waiting on the railway platform and the long international express rolls in (Istanbul - Beograd - Innsbruck - Zurich - Basle - Paris - Bruxelles), with silver letters centered on the dark blue coaches: COMPAGNIE INTERNATIONALE DES WAGON-LITS ET DES GRANDS EXPRESSES EUROPEENS. Declaim the line and it sings like something out of Homer.

Even the Paris Métro provides poetry. Where English reads: "Warning: Emergency cord. $25 fine for wrong use," French has—but let's put it into free verse:

Il est défendu de se servir
Sans motif plausible
Du signal d'alarme
Et du frein de secours.

II

"Restaurant" is French. It is the place where you "restore" yourself. English can't handle food and dining services without borrowing from French. Think, for example, of *chef, maître, café, menu, à la carte, table d'hôte, entrée, dessert.* Add the names of dishes and sauces, and you have a *feast,* which comes from *fête,* a celebration.

Eating, for the French, is not merely "devouring with the mouth," as Dr. Johnson (an Englishman) inelegantly defined it. It is an intensification of life. Mark Twain, the Innocent Abroad, caught the spirit in his first dinner in Paris: "It was a pleasure to eat where everything was so tidy, the food so well cooked, the waiters so polite, and the coming and departing company so moustached, so frisky, so affable, so fearfully and wonderfully Frenchy!"

France is the imperial power of cookery, Paris the capital of the culinary empire. The Parisian must keep up with restaurant news and gossip.

"Chez Raoul? It lacks, alas, of being as it should."

"What is it you say? Where can one ingest better *quenelles de brochet Nantua?*"

"I grant you the *quenelles.* But the *oeufs à la croustade,* they are not as of old."

"And what of the *rognons aux trois moutardes?*"

"They taste now as if lowered to two mustards."

Soon after, Raoul misses the Durands on Thursdays. Then, catching himself wondering why the Duponts no longer come on his *rognons* day, he feels a warning chill in the region of that sixth sense which kept his father and grandfather in business. He does not seek out a Madison Avenue firm or a gimmick. He looks into his soul and his kitchen.

Was there a time when the restaurant did not exist? In 1801 an English traveler discovered one in Paris. Great was his excitement and admiration. He wrote of the "empress" at the *caisse* "whose concern is to collect from the gentlemen-in-waiting the cash which they receive at the different tables."

He exclaimed: "By heaven! The bill of fare is a printed sheet of double folio, the size of an English newspaper. It will require half an hour to con over this important catalogue!"

In short, he described the establishment you find today.

We communicated our researches to Marthe, a lady-in-waiting at our favorite restaurant. "Ooh la-la!" she said. "The first restaurant? It was when the serpent served the apple."

"*Mais oui!*" said Michel, the *maître*. "And men have been paying the bill ever since."

"Chauvinist!" cried Marthe.

Even that word, so popular with Women's Lib, is French, derived from a soldier of Napoleon named Chauvin, a super-patriot. His American counterpart was the naval officer of the War of 1812 famous for a tipsy toast at a banquet: "My country, right or wrong!" But "Decaturist" has not entered the language.

III

Hôtel is a French word which originally meant a large house. The cap over the "o" signifies that a letter has been dropped. In Old French the word was *hostel*. From "large house" hotel reached out to stand for "hostelry" and to embrace "hospitality."

Still today the busy word is applied to other buildings than those lodging strangers. *Hôtel de ville* is the town hall, *hôtel de poste* the main post office. In Paris the Hôtel de Soubise and the Hôtel Carnavalet are aristocratic homes turned into museums. The Hôtel des Monnaies is the mint, the Hôtel Dieu a hospital: God's house. And no, the Hôtel des Invalides is *not* for sick travelers.

These etymological remarks are designed not only to clear up a puzzling ambiguity. They point to another fact—that a French hostelry may be any kind of large house. At least eight out of ten Paris hotels are carry-over buildings from some older purpose, or architectural shells of no specific purpose. This is as true of the lordly Crillon and Ritz as of the lowly Quai Voltaire and Saints Pères. The Crillon occupies half an eighteenth-century palace; the other half shelters the Automobile Club. The twin of this palace houses the Ministry of Marine. All three tenants seem happy inside the same pseudo-classic skin designed by Gabriel as street furniture for entrance to the Rue Royale.

Through the decades and centuries the old buildings have suffered convulsions. Many were erected in the candlelight era. When gas arrived, so did pipes; with electricity, wiring; with running water, more pipes. In hotels unable to afford upheavals, pipes and wiring were simply run up and through the walls in plain view. Your room may display a multiplicity of these, like tracks and sidings on the approach to a major railway station.

Your hotel may be shabby and yet retain an air, like a dowager duchess of faded beauty and presence. The grand staircase by which the beau monde once mounted to the ballroom now leads to rooms 101-130. The exquisite boudoir from which the Duchess of Frou Frou scandalously eloped with her hairdresser, two hundred years ago, is now *W. C. Dames.* In the *cour d'honneur,* where the Marquis de Bon Secours was pinked in a duel with the Chevalier de Mauvais Sang, cars are parked. Marble fireplaces yawn emptily at radiators, and a chandelier twinkles dimly in the reception hall.

Here you have a hoary structure, in its way as comfortable as an old shoe, harboring virtues and frustrations not to be found in the ultramodern hotel, which is as flatly fresh as a coat of varnish. It has had to submit to the further indignity of the installation of baths and toilets. And this addition demands, like Virginia Woolf's modern woman, a room of its own.

As a mere segment of a vast and splendid chamber, your room may be higher than it is wide, making you as cozy as a tadpole in a well. The clothes closet being nonexistent, much space is taken up by that clumsy piece of furniture, the wardrobe. Its warped doors groan open to betray a few twisted or splintered hangers. Washbasin and bidet taps read C for *chaud* (hot) and F for *froid* (cold). Take not their word for it.

For quiet, you have asked for an inside room and are pleased with the charming courtyard it faces, until in the middle of the night you are wrenched out of sleep by a metallic clangor. The *hôtelier* has converted the old coach house into a garage with an iron shutter for a door.

Many phenomena reveal themselves only after lights-out—mysteriously creaking boards, a whispering pipe, a dripping tap, a chuckling water closet.

When Lafayette inhabited what is now the St. James and Albany, we suspect he was acquainted with the night-gurgling water box in 314. In the morning after the first night, we called for help. A *mécanicien* arrived. His tampering was interrupted by our *valet de chambre*, who reached out, gave the brass lever a flip—*et voilà!* The *mécanicien* shrugged and went off, and we gave the vally-de-sham a birthday necktie we hated. But when we returned at night the water box was chuckling as happily as ever. For three weeks we lived with that gleeful lunatic of a box, flipping its lever.

Because these buildings were erected in spacious days, they have ceilings fifteen feet tall and windows to match. These open inwards, all ten feet or so at once, in two longitudinal halves.

Here you are, in bed costume, ready for the final chore —arranging a window for the night. Examining, you discover a bronze, lozenge-shaped knob which moves an iron rod ten feet long. Strength of wrist is required. Nothing about the knob tells you whether you are locking the window or releasing it from the rod's grip. You turn and tug—nothing gives; you reverse and tug, and it's still *ancien régime*. Rage seizes you. You pound the woodwork; you twist; you jerk—and suddenly the window comes apart with a screech as of a hotel being ripped down the middle. All round the court the veterans among the guests are probably muttering, "There's 314 going beddy-bye."

Well, you have learned this—the window has a mind of its own, but it *does* open.

It won't do to wax confident, for this is only the first step. You are standing with part of one wall open to the chill night. Step 2 is to make the window stay open at the gap you guess suffices for introducing the required oxygen. It is a problem because left to itself the window bangs shut. You think: a rope or cord. But even if you had one, there's only the bed to tie it to. Which means that if the occupier of the farther bed has to go in the night, he may break his sleepy neck.

"Try Straps, dear," suggests your wife, distracted from the *roman policier* (detective story) she's reading propped on the pillows. Good; but how the devil are you going to reach your suitcase, dubbed Straps, when, if you let go the window, it will shut and you'll have all the tugging to do over again? Ask her to lend a hand? You're not that desperate yet! So stretch the torso, hook a foot around that chair leg, draw the chair to you, and arrange it to keep the window temporarily at bay. You get down on your knees and drag Straps from under the bed. Ah . . .

But Straps won't do. It stands too low. The window sweeps over it.

"If I were you, I'd try Big Red," says the back-bed driver.

Big Red is *her* suitcase, practically a trunk. It contains most of the suits, dresses, and shoes, whose grand total amounts to her having nothing to wear. Big Red is in the little anteroom on the far side of everything. To drag it to the window, you have to move the desk (which doubles as breakfast table). While you are doing this the window nudges the chair aside and slams shut, causing you to leap and your wife to cry, "My God!"

Eventually, Big Red does the trick. Rejoicing is modified as you realize that, comes the dawn, you will have all this to do in reverse.

However, the only remaining task is to arrange the ceiling-to-floor drapes so artfully that they will shut out the morning light without excluding the air. Your keen intelligence makes child's play of this.

You tumble into bed with a sigh, when—*sacré bleu* and name-of-a-dog—you have to tumble out again to get rid of the damned bolster. This comes wound up in the bottom sheet. If your attack on it is too vigorous, you'll have to remake your bed. You extract it. You heave it into the farthest corner. You douse the lights. You lie panting. You have earned a night's repose.

At this moment you hear a remembered voice. It is the W.C. box beginning to gurgle happily to itself.

PARIS

I

Through the middle of Paris runs the river Seine. In mid-river is an island, the Ile de la Cité. Paris began there with a Celtic tribe called the Parisii.

A footbridge, the Pont des Arts, crosses the river from the Louvre to Cardinal Mazarin's domed Institute. It's the right place to begin an acquaintance with the City of Light. The island lies before you, ship-shaped, dipping into the water a pointed prow, raising a clean-lined hull, and towing at its stern the small Ile St. Louis.

The prow is the Square du Vert Galant, named for the best if raunchiest of French kings, Henri IV. His is the Pont Neuf behind it, the oldest and handsomest bridge. The conical towers on the left belong to the Conciergerie. Two spires shoot up: Notre Dame and the Sainte Chapelle.

Notre Dame, at the island's east end, has a happy story.
When Bishop Maurice de Sully, newly consecrated, began to

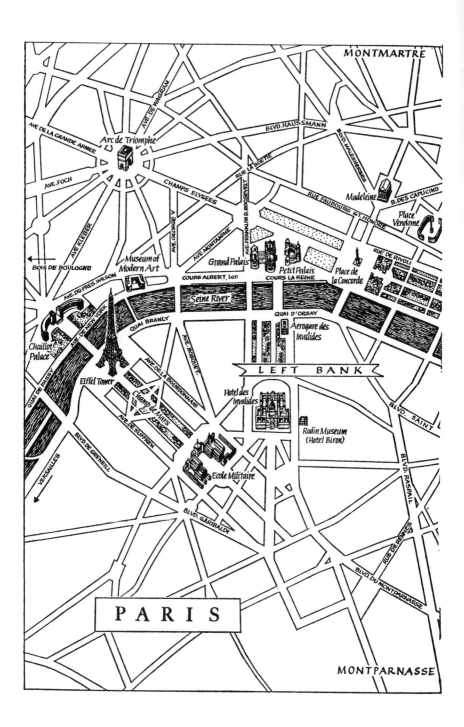

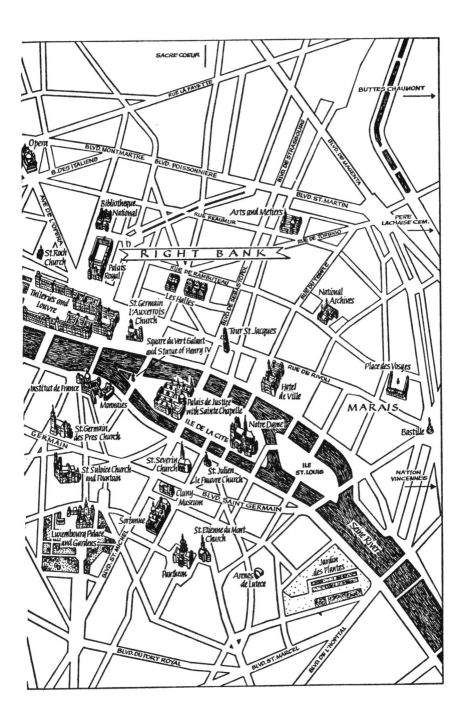

demand a new cathedral (the one in use was merely three hundred years old), Paris was a small island town. Louis VII lived in an old palace at the western end, a sad and unlikeable Capet without an heir. In casting off Eleanor of Aquitaine, he had managed to lose a good part of his kingdom.

The time seemed wrong for a tremendous project. But all over France cathedrals were rising, trying out the innovations introduced thirty years earlier by Abbot Suger of St. Denis. Pointed arch and ribbed vaulting were raising the roof in more senses than one. Rivalry was so intense that there were loud protests against "the disease of construction."

Maurice de Sully had caught the disease. He infected the King.

Work began in 1163. Two years later the King's third wife gave birth to a son—a child so unexpected that he was called the God-given. A great groundswell of joy raised the cathedral. By the time the façade was finished Philip Augustus—the God-given—had reconquered what his father had lost. He was a founder of the capital of France, as against the capital of the Franks.

The best place to enjoy the gift of Paris to Gothic architecture is from a bench on little Viviani Square (Left Bank). A hop, skip, and jump across the river, the cathedral extends its full length, from towers to long, rounded apse. Here you can see that the famous façade is actually a huge decorative screen. In medieval times it was brightly painted and gilded. The Ile de la Cité was a warren of narrow streets crammed with houses and shops that marched right into the river on stilts. From the maze Notre Dame shot up like a sunburst.

It was the first building to make people proud to be Parisian.

Under the second spire is Paris' most beautiful church, the Sainte Chapelle. But you have to search for it. You'll find it in an interior courtyard of the Palace of Justice.

In the dingy yard stands a small, regal, thirteenth-century structure containing two chapels, one above the other. The lower, richly painted, was meant for royal underlings. Find and climb the narrow winding stairway, and you pop above the floor like a jack-in-the-box into a vaulted chamber that may make you expel an "Oof!"

It's sublime.

The thirteenth-century windows are walls of glowing glass. Arrange to visit when the sun is shining through those windows. Every inch of wall that isn't window is ornamented with painted designs and colored-glass mosaics. The stonework flows upward with easy strength and grace. Gothic had found itself.

Here is the best of Louis IX, canonized as St. Louis.

When young, before he became repellently saintly, this grandson of Philip Augustus was a thoroughly good king. At twenty-four, religion and life were joyous to him. It was then he learned that the Crown of Thorns was for sale, Emperor Baudouin of Constantinople having pawned it for a loan from Venice. The Middle Ages saw a brisk trade in holy relics, and this one was among the holiest. Louis bought it and built the Sainte Chapelle to house it. When consecrated in 1248, this royal chapel was so resplendent that descriptions of it stun the mind.

The Conciergerie, attached to a nineteenth-century Palace of Justice covering the site of an older palace, is all that remains of the island's medieval royal residence.

It became the Revolution's central prison. The dread Revolutionary Tribunal sat in the old palace; and Fouquier-Tinville, public prosecutor, lived in the quay-side towers. At the Terror's height he was condemning to death fifty prisoners a day.

The most famous prisoner was the Widow Capet, better known as Marie Antoinette. On October 16, 1793, she walked up the nine steps (they now lead from the lawyer's restaurant) to the Cour de Mai and into the cart that carried her to the guillotine.

As you are conducted through the prison chambers and corridors, it's hard to realize that these were originally the royal apartments of Philip Augustus. When built, in the new Gothic style, they were considered the most beautiful in Europe.

Before it became a prison the Conciergerie was the residence of a royal deputy, the Concierge, who looked after things when the king was away. His title became the European term for caretaker, which is why your hotel porter is a "concierge."

Near the island's prow Henri IV, the Vert Galant, rides a horse on his bridge, the Pont Neuf, facing his Place Dauphine. Behind him, low on the water, extends a little park which is a pleasant place to be if you can endure the lovemaking couples or are yourself half of one. The first Bourbon was a lusty lover. Historians have soberly compiled a list of fifty-six mistresses. But there were two women he could not love: his wives.

II

The Right Bank is the Paris of elegance and imposing effects. No other capital can equal the magnificence of its downtown —that broad central corridor of two miles stretching from Louvre to Étoile and including the Tuileries, the Place de la Concorde, and the Champs Elysées. Its famed vistas are being marred now by skyscrapers; *mais* (as they say), *que voulez-vous?*

The Louvre began as a fortress protecting a new city wall, and kept growing. François I, patron of Leonardo da Vinci and Cellini, ordered its transformation into a Renaissance palace in 1546. It lengthened slowly, through many reigns, and may well be the longest palace ever built.

As a museum the Louvre has no peer. Among its sensational items are the *Winged Victory*, the *Mona Lisa*, and the *Venus de Milo*.

For local interest you will want to see: Titian's portrait of François I, looking very pleased with himself; Boucher's adorably naughty *Odalisque*, who may have been Mme de Pompadour; Gabrielle d'Estrées and her sister in the bath (Gabrielle, the blonde, was the Vert Galant's best-loved mistress); and the Medici Gallery, where Marie de Médicis is shamelessly flattered by Rubens in nineteen huge panels. Henri married her when Gabrielle mysteriously died just as he was about to make her an honest woman. An annex, the Jeu de Paume, houses the Impressionists. It is, after the Louvre, the most visited of museums.

Oddly, the Vert Galant began and ended his life at court with an unlovely Médici. The first was the Queen Mother, Catherine, who arranged his marriage to her daughter and then, while the festivities were still going on, coolly organized the massacre of the Protestants, including the bridegroom's party—her wedding guests. There's nothing good to be said about that woman, but she left her mark.

At the Louvre's west end, Catherine de Médicis built the Tuileries Chateau for herself. It has disappeared, leaving its garden.

The "French garden" is Italianate. It was born here in the Tuileries when Catherine decided she must have a Renaissance garden for her new chateau. The design was based on terraces ornamented by fountains and statues.

Too late Victor Hugo cried out, "There is nothing more brutal than a straight line!"

The Tuileries covers more than sixty acres. It's a flat oblong sliced down the middle by the Grande Allée, a wide dirt-and-gravel walk. The two halves are divided symmetrically into plots (*parterres*) with lesser *allées* between them. The plots are neatly patterned with grass, low hedges, and lower flower beds. Along the *allées* stands a regularly spaced company of statues—132 in all. The western part is a make-believe woods where the court could picnic. It is formed by *quinconces*—trees arranged in fives.

A garden is a compromise between art and nature. The French prefer a minimum of nature and a maximum of art.

You get used to the patterned landscape with its untouchable green stuff. You may even grow to love it. Now and then you hear the watchman's shrill whistle—a child has tripped over the low border and fallen *on the grass!* You shudder.

The most intimate of French gardens is in the Palais Royal, one-time palace of the dukes of Orléans. It is surrounded by eighteenth-century buildings of honey-colored stone. Under them runs an inviting but run-down shopping arcade. Above are some of the city's desirable apartments. Colette lived in one, Jean Cocteau in another. We lived there too—in a modest hotel, now converted into some more of those desirable apartments.

This interior square was made in 1781 by Philippe, Duke of Orléans, to climb out of debt. It became immediately popular. You went to the Palais Royal for its shops, cafés, restaurants, theaters, gambling salons, pawnshops, prostitutes. You went to promenade and gossip, hear a concert or attend a ball, buy a pink ice or order a banquet. The Revolution began here. Camille Desmoulins, mounting a café table, persuaded a lighthearted crowd to march with him in a political demonstration. They were fired upon. Two days later they stormed the Bastille.

The Place de la Concorde is something that happened to a rubbish dump outside the city wall as Paris moved westward. Louis XV had his architect Gabriel design this grandest of eighteenth-century squares. How could they know they were preparing a stage on which the next Louis, the sixteenth, would die?

Rue Royale—short, wide, gracious—was also created when the wall was torn down (1732). At the first intersection stood a medieval gate. The Rue St. Honoré is on the east, the Rue du Faubourg St. Honoré on the west. This is the junction of the pre- and post-Revolution fashion streets.

From a millinery shop on St. Honoré came Louis XV's last mistress, Mme. du Barry. From another came Marie Antoinette's dressmaker, Rose Bertin. The Lafayettes lived in what is now the Hotel St. James and Albany. Robespierre roomed at 398. From the steps of St. Roch, then the fashionable church, Napoleon Bonaparte put down a royalist uprising with the "whiff of grapeshot" that opened his path to greatness.

The Champs Elysées comes in two parts. From Concorde to the Rond Point it's a park; from there to the Arc de Triomphe, a tree-lined commercial avenue and celebrated promenade. *Hélas!* office buildings are crowding out the mansions, even threatening the cafés.

Its climax is the Arc de Triomphe on the Étoile. Napoleon, having divorced Josephine, wanted his arch finished in time for his entry with his new bride. When the day came, in 1810, the arch looked complete but wasn't. Architect Chalgrin, in desperation, had built it up in wood covered with canvas and painted to look like stone.

Years later when the arch was completed and Napoleon again rode under it, he was in no position to enjoy it, being dead and on his way to his tomb. Under the arch lies the Unknown Soldier of World War I.

Napoleon's tomb—the largest and most pompous this side of the pyramids—is in the Hôtel des Invalides, an ornate palace ordered by Louis XIV as a home for old soldiers.

You lean on a marble balustrade and look down into a marble well at a huge block of red porphyry on a green granite base. Napoleon lies not only well in the well but well in his tomb, in the innermost of six coffins. Around are twelve colossal figures of Victory. Everything is oversize, to the scale of Napoleon's coronation-robed statue, which is eight-and-a-half feet tall. What a shame he can't lean beside you. The little man would have loved it all.

Three squares, each of a different period, would be Essence of Paris if they could be bottled.

The Place des Vosges in the Marais was Henri IV's contribution to the good life—perhaps a protest against palaces; he planned to live there. The first architectured square (1605), it is still intact, with its fifty-six red-brick houses, the blue slate roofs, the arcades. Whenever about to be overcome by shabbiness and age, it manages to get itself restored. Mansions more in palace style rose round about. Among them is the Carnavalet, where Mme. de Sévigné lived and wrote those soppy and gossipy letters. It is now the wonderful City of Paris museum.

The Place Vendôme, another planned square, was designed by Mansart for Louis XIV, who once had his equestrian statue in the middle. Very lordly, and still a luxury enclave, it now centers on an imitation of Trajan's column with Napoleon on top, Roman-robed.

The Place de l'Opéra belongs to the *Belle Epoque*. The famous opera house is like a grande dame under whose lorgnette swirls the city's most nervous traffic, dodged by whole tourist families on nimble-toe between the Café de la Paix and the American Express. It was designed by Charles Garnier as the showpiece of Louis Napoleon's uneasy empire. The interior, as Henry James reported, is "gold upon gold." (Ceiling frescoes by Marc Chagall.)

III

For views high and wide: the Eiffel Tower, Sacré Coeur, and the Chaillot Palace.

The first two—freaks—are the most familiar landmarks of Paris.

Parisians called the Eiffel Tower "the tallest lamppost in the world." Ironmaster Gustave Eiffel built it as an exclamation point for the World's Fair of 1889. It was to be temporary. Its removal would leave a 1,043-foot slit in the sky, and something comparable in the minds of tourists and Parisians.

Sacré Coeur, on Montmartre, looks as if it arrived by way of Constantinople and Oz. Built in repentance for the Franco-Prussian War, it was finished just in time for World War I. The huge white pseudo-Byzantine basilica with breast-like domes is continually painted by artistic-looking artists who try to sell to embarrassed tourists on the Place du Tertre. It rose coinciden-tally with the thirty-year creative frenzy that produced Renoir,

Van Gogh, Gauguin, Toulouse-Lautrec, Utrillo, Seurat, Picasso—and had no relation whatever to it or them.

Across the river in Passy is the double "palace" of Chaillot, with a superb view from its terraces through the Eiffel Tower and along the Champ de Mars to the École Militaire. The Chaillot's two buildings are filled with museums. The most rewarding are the Museum of French Monuments (architecture) and the Marine Museum.

IV

The Left Bank is the home of the mind, cradle of art, literature, and intellect. Its self-conscious role is to kick conformity in the seat of its pants. This it does in cafés and hole-in-wall rooms around the Establishment's noggin—the university—and the Establishment's guardian of culture—the Institute of France.

In appearance the Left Bank is very different from the Right. Short on vistas and palaces, it's a crowded, lively area of old streets, intense vigor, and oddities both human and material.

Tradition and the Boulevard St. Michel divided it into two parts: the Latin Quarter and St. Germain des Prés.

"Latin Quarter" refers to the university, was a term bestowed by Rabelais, and speaks of the time when the learned and the learning everywhere had a language in common. Which is why Thomas Aquinas, Dante, Erasmus, and Calvin were equally at home here.

The university itself is called the Sorbonne, after its major college. It began on St. Geneviève Hill in 1112 with Peter Abélard (anti-hero of the strange love story of Abélard and Héloïse), a brilliant rebel against the Establishment of his day. The colleges are widely scattered. There is no resemblance to Oxford or Cambridge.

To begin at the river—behind Viviani Square squats St. Julien le Pauvre, gnomelike remnant of a twelfth-century church. For three hundred years it was the university's meeting hall. When parts began to fall down they were lopped off. The hoary oddment is still a church, Greek Orthodox.

Around this church and big St. Séverin is a small maze of medieval streets. Napoleon was squalidly lodging in the Rue de la Huchette when opportunity knocked. Beside No. 14 you find the windowless slit named Street of the Fishing Cat *(Chat qui Pêche).*

Boulevard St. Michel, student Main Street, specializes in cheap quick-service cafés. A little way up from the river you come upon the railed garden of Cluny, guarding the scanty remains of Roman baths. Entrance is around the corner.

Its beautiful little mansion in "flamboyant Gothic" was built in 1480 by the abbots of Cluny as their *pied-à-terre* in Paris. Now a museum of medieval art, its glory is the set of tapestries called *The Lady and the Unicorn (La Dame à la Licorne).* They are the loveliest ever woven.

"Boul' Mich" climbs Montagne St. Geneviève, a hill named for Paris' patron saint. She was a woman with a gift of speech, who performed her best miracle by talking the conquering Franks out of killing their prisoners. She talked so powerfully that their chief, Childeric, not only capitulated but ran out of town.

At the summit, conspicuous is the Roman-porticoed, galleried, and domed Panthéon. Louis XV began it to replace old St. Geneviève Church. Mirabeau suggested it be used as a pantheon. He was the first to be buried in it. The second was Voltaire, his body exhumed for reburial with a state funeral. Both were later evicted for political reasons. Many another went in and out during the Revolution. With the return of the Bourbons the edifice was at last consecrated as a church, to be re-pantheonized.

The Panthéon is really a monument to French politics. In its crypt, Houdon's bust of Voltaire smiles and smiles.

The good thing on the Mount is St. Etienne, a church architecturally engaging. Begun in 1492, it kept getting this and that done to it in the latest style for a century. The interior is seignorial, with linking pierced-stone balustrades around the columns and an exquisite pair of Renaissance stairways. Lacking a church of her own, St. Geneviève has a gilded coffer here for a shrine.

The Rue Mouffetard, a market bedlam from early morning until noon, runs down the hill south. Houses lining this street have passages into courtyards with numerous branch passages, doorways, staircases. Exploring, you've decided you have wandered into a slum, when suddenly a glimpse through an open window reveals paneling, book-lined walls, a stone fireplace. They say Mouffetard is to be modernized. Angels and St. Geneviève defend it!

St. Germain des Prés, west of the Latin Quarter, developed in the shadow of a Benedictine abbey. A reminder is the Rue de l'Abbaye, one of the streets cut through its ruins.

The Place St. Germain des Prés is the heart of the Left Bank —Latin Quarter and all. On it are the cafés Deux Magots and Flore, and the political brasserie Lipp's. The Flore cradled Existentialism, as the hangout of Sartre and Simone de Beauvoir. In the 1920s and '30s all this area was holy ground to Hemingway, Scott Fitzgerald, and their fellow expatriates from post-war "normalcy."

In the tumult of traffic and hustling waiters, the old abbey church of St. Germain stands like a high-shouldered shrug. It dates from the eleventh century, and its little garden is the only memory of the fields which St. Germain was once of.

Between the square, Boul' Mich, and the river lies a quadrilateral of poke-about streets. The highlights are Place Furstemberg (very small, charming, although it has lost one of its four trees) and the curious Passage du Commerce. Entrance to the Passage is Boulevard St. Germain 130, opposite Danton's statue. It's an interior street lined with very old small houses. At No. 8 Marat printed his inflammatory newspaper. At No. 9 a German carpenter made for Dr. Guillotin the first models of his machine. Danton lived at No. 1. Halfway along is the picturesque triple Cour de Rohan, behind iron gates. Sainte-Beuve kept a love-nest there for his affair with Victor Hugo's wife.

From St. Germain to the Luxembourg is still a different Paris, one of fading gentility. Its St. Sulpice is the Left Bank's wealthy church. Here Camille Desmoulins married his pretty Lucille, called Loulou. He'd come a long way in a few years to afford a St. Sulpice wedding. His best man was Robespierre. Four years later, his best man having become his worst, he rode to the guillotine clutching a tress of Loulou's hair. A bit farther on is the Carrefour de l'Odéon, looking like an eighteenth-century stage-set for the Odéon Theater.

In the seventeenth century Dumas' Musketeers, Athos, Porthos, Aramis, and d'Artagnan, lodged in this district, within easy reach of Musketeer headquarters, which was at the corner of Tournon and Vaugirard, just across from the Luxembourg Palace.

The Luxembourg was made by Marie de Médicis, both to outdo her aunt's Tuileries and to keep herself out of political mischief—she was drawn to plots against her son, Louis XIII. Her palace now houses the French Senate, but the fifty-eight acres of garden are public and lively or dreamy with Parisians taking a variety of leisures. The beautiful part is the English garden at the west.

In the Luxembourg one day—the French-garden area, with those *allées*—we watched a stout little boy run about while his mother sat in a chair reading an English newspaper. The child suddenly crashed on the dirt-and-gravel *allée*. It hurt. We felt it. He let out a howl, and Mama quickly ran to him. As he opened his mouth wide for a still more emphatic howl, she got in first. "No 'ouch'!" she commanded. "No 'ouch'!" He closed his mouth, and opened it again—in a wide blond smile. It was completely, serenely wonderful.

ENVIRONS: A PALACE—A HOME—A CHURCH

In August, 1661, Nicolas Fouquet, finance minister, threw a housewarming party in his new chateau of Vaux le Vicomte. Of his six thousand guests, 5,999 were enchanted. The house and its gardens were superb, the entertainment delectable.

The guest not amused was Louis XIV. He left early. Nineteen days later he had Fouquet arrested.

At twenty-three, the Sun King had just begun to rule. Quietly subservient to Cardinal Mazarin, he had gone in patches while Mazarin lived like a king. But Mazarin had died this very year, in March. "I loved him, and he loved me," mourned the King. And believed it. All his secret rage and envy spilled out over the luckless Fouquet, and the Palace of Versailles was the result.

He hired Le Vau, Le Brun, and Le Nôtre—architect, decorator, and gardener of Fouquet's chateau. He stripped Vaux le Vicomte of everything that pleased him, including statues, tapestries, and a thousand orange trees. But the site he chose for his palace was, as described by the diarist Duke of St. Simon, "the most dismal and thankless of places, without vistas, woods or water, without soil even, for all the surrounding land is quicksand or bog." The air was putrid. Workmen died of sudden fevers and their bodies were carted away at night. One widow went berserk and called the King a tyrant. "Who, me?" he cried in astonishment. He had her whipped.

With Versailles, Louis XIV, architect of absolutism, created a legend of exquisite beings who lived like gods in fabled halls and gardens. In simple truth, 25,000 people were packed into a gilded, malodorous hive where the drains were faulty and water often failed. The palace was so vast and their precious little duties so many that the great lords and ladies of France were constantly on the run in shoes with three-inch heels, in whalebone corsets and stiff stomachers and heavy, elaborate wigs. Which is something to remember when, on your guided tour, you feel an ache in the small of the back or a twinge where a corn is blossoming.

André Le Nôtre fashioned the land and the landscape. You'd never guess it now but millions of pots, each carrying soil under a precious bit of vegetation, made the great park of Versailles. While the King was disciplining his court into the rigid formalities of Etiquette, Le Nôtre was disciplining nature.

The *pièce de résistance* is the Hall of Mirrors, where Le Nôtre and Louis XIV clasp hands. This is a grand gallery, beautifully pro-

portioned, under an arched and painted ceiling. The great mirrors reflect not only the room but in the windows Le Nôtre's park,
his patterned terraces and cool sheets of water spreading in
artful, falling levels to the horizon. It is as if you're standing on a
gold-and-glass platform above a Euclidean paradise. Here alone
the legend lives—you feel like a god offered a landscape for a
present.

Malmaison, Josephine's house, is a wholesome antidote to
grandeur. It was an unfashionable country house, well away (she
hoped) from gossip. She bought it while Napoleon was in Egypt
and moved in with a lover. Although Napoleon was enjoying a
mistress, this did not prevent him from going into a rage when he
got wind of his wife's affair. He came home determined to divorce
her.

The news flew to Paris before him. Josephine hurriedly rode
out to meet him. Unfortunately, she took the wrong road. Finding her away, Napoleon locked her out. He waited in torment.
She came. She pleaded with him. She screamed and sobbed. She
beat on the door like a madwoman. At last he opened it. So she
won him back.

With Josephine, he accepted Malmaison. Life was informal
there. He teased and pinched the ladies, cheated at games, had
small hunting parties, and strolled on the lawn with an arm
around Josephine's waist.

Years later, when he did divorce her, it was to Malmaison that
she retired, and there she died.

There are many portraits of Josephine in the Louvre, including
one by Prud'hon showing her in the park at Malmaison. They all
reveal a woman not beautiful but devastatingly feminine. One
would like to see her move, laugh and talk, even cry. She was
ornamental. The remarkable thing about her was that she did not
change. Nobody but Josephine could have been carried so
high—from adventuress to empress—and remained her pleasant
self.

The long, low house of soft-colored stone is furnished to the point of clutter in Empire style. Everything looks as if the servants have just cleaned up and Madame in her bed is sipping chocolate while looking out at her rose garden and wondering what to wear among those dainty high-bosomed dresses that flow with the lines of her elegant figure. Malmaison and Josephine are waking together.

It's a house that does not, could not, put on airs. She chose well.

Chartres is a town with a cathedral that stands on a hill "high above the clustered houses, making of their red-roofed agglomeration a mere pedestal for its immense beauty" (Henry James). Magnetic, it draws pilgrims and secular admirers from all the world.

The hilltop has always been holy ground. The Druids held rites there in a sacred grove around a well. The Romans, to break the cult, raised a temple to the mother goddess. Fourth-century Christians, destroying the Roman cult, built a church to the Virgin. Through every change the well was cherished.

The present church is the fifth of the Christian era, except for the crypt, which belongs to an earlier century. The extensive Romanesque crypt has a Virgin known as Our Lady Under Ground, and the ancient well, set in remains of Roman walls.

In 1194 a fire destroyed the upper church. It couldn't have happened at a better time. A new style had appeared: Gothic. Paris was peacock-proud of its new Notre Dame. As one man the Chartrians flung themselves into rebuilding their own Notre Dame. They'd show Paris! The blaze of excitement is still there in the soaring stone, the windows, the sculptures, for Chartres has been little damaged or altered.

The windows are sheer poetry. They concentrate on blue to such an extent that you seem to be floating through an eerily glowing dusk, like a fish in a pond. The touches of red are flamelike.

Our Lady Under Ground used to be the prime object of veneration. She has been superseded by the Virgin of the Pillar in the upper church. The shrine, opposite the window of Notre Dame de la Belle Verrière—a Byzantine Virgin and Child—is like a bazaar because of the crowds of the devout and the candle-selling around it.

Our own memory of Chartres will always be colored not only by the stained glass but by the poor elderly couple, he matchstick thin and palsied, she with a dreadful fungoid growth on her face, discussing in urgent whispers what price and size of candle they could afford.

CHANTILLY

Every woman worthy of the name knows black Chantilly lace and whipped cream Chantilly. But you don't have to leave Paris to see or taste them. What draws French and foreigner alike is the double chateau with its art treasures, the park and gardens, the fantastic stables where horses, hounds, and grooms are pampered to death, and the famous race track. As an extra fillip, the golf course is reputed the best in France.

And what a history the place has!—as voluptuous as the cream. But that can wait.

The two chateaus, Grand and Petit, are crammed with extraordinary collections now owned by the Institut de France. The most precious are the Raphaels, and the forty fifteenth-century miniatures in the Grand; and the library, or Cabinet des Livres, in the Petit with its illuminated manuscripts, especially the famous *Très Riches Heures* of the Duke de Berry. The walls are hung with hundreds of paintings of all the painting centuries except the twentieth, barely leaving room for statuary, woodcarvings, rich paneling, a celebrated Salon des Singes (Chinese-style decorations featuring monkeys), gems, and tapestries. The jewelry is seeable Sunday afternoons only, since the Grand Condé rose diamond was stolen in 1926. (Is this owing to a belief that no self-respecting thief would loot on the Sabbath?) Luckily, the stone appeared unexpectedly after several months of fruitless search, buried in a hotel apple.

The pictures are hung higgledy-piggledy, not according to schools or periods, as in most museums, but as the owners hung them—wherever they fitted the wall space.

The Renaissance-style Grand Chateau is little more than eighty years old, being the fifth erected on this site in two thousand years. The first one, probably a palisaded wattle-and-daub hut, was put up in Gallo-Roman times by a chief named Cantilius, whose name became attached to the locality.

The somewhat beaten-up Petit Chateau is true sixteenth century. The handsome park and gardens and the ingenious water complex, all of which Louis XIV envied, are the work of our indefatigable friend Le Nôtre, without whom, it seems, France would be garden-bereft.

Having the river Nonette at hand, Le Nôtre made a canal and water-scaped the grounds formally and informally, providing not only for future baths and bidets, but a moat for the chateaus; basins, lagoons with islets, cascades, a fish pond for Sylvie, and a winding stream for the hamlet. This last is the original example of contrived rusticity so popular at the time, in which Rousseau and Walt Disney seem to meet. The grounds are part French-dignified and part English-disheveled. Geometry is relieved by parterres, a flower garden, stairways and balustrades, statues, a play-chateau among the beeches for Sylvie, an eighteenth-century *jeu-de-paume* court now harboring a minor museum, two sixteenth-century chapels, a Temple of Venus, and an Isle of Love.

Between canal and big chateau are Philosophers' Walks named for Molière and other classic authors, for whom a spare bedroom was always ready.

Love too had its innings, as the Temple of Venus and the Isle of Love proclaim. Charming as Chantilly is, it doubled its interest for us when we read up on it before a second visit. Its history is at times preposterous. For example, the episode of the "Last Passion of an Aged Roué."

Our heroine's name is Charlotte de Montmorency, daughter of the lord of the place. Only fifteen, she is so adorable that the villain, fifty-four years old, falls violently in love with her at first sight. True, she is the sweet, innocent child of his highborn host. But our "heavy" is not a man to be balked by the code or to shrug off an obsession, for he is none other than Henri IV, the Vert Galant. He bides his time—in another year the girl will be all the riper for the plucking. Meanwhile he looks about for a weak and pliable youth to marry her to, and pitches on Henri de Bourbon-Condé, who in spite of a proud name is afraid of his own shadow.

They marry, while in the wings the Ever-Green Lover caresses his beard. But the boy and the girl know their king; those hot looks have not gone unappraised. The next morning they hightail it for Brussels, then the Spanish monarch's satrapy.

How Henri fumes, curses, and stomps when he discovers the empty nest! How he pleads one moment and threatens the next! It is a European scandal; even for kings he is setting a new low. When all else fails, he calls on the Pope to help him get his girl. The assassin Revaillac puts an end to his passion and our heroine's peril.

The king is dead—long live the king! Charlotte and her man return to the chateau and live happily ever after, making love in the love-cottage old Vert Galant had commanded to be built for his own sport—the one subsequently named the Maison de Sylvie.

Who is Sylvia, what is she? She is the chateau's next-generation beauty. The second de Montmorency married her. Her name was Marie Félicie Orsini, and she was lovely, good, and intelligent, so rare a combination that two poetasters celebrated her under the name Sylvie. But her husband led a revolt against Richelieu and died in battle of eighteen wounds, and she spent the rest of her life in a convent.

Next on the program is the story, "A King Comes Calling." We petty bourgeois, perhaps you as well, who make much ado of a score of friends for a cocktail party, go round-eyed with wonder as we glimpse in memoirs the palatial entertainments of a prince.

A royal messenger gallops over that bridge across the moat, steed all afroth. The clatter brings out the Condé's *bouteiller.* "From His Majesty, under royal seal, a letter!" The Grand Condé is drinking mulled wine with Mrs. Condé. He tears open the missive: company's coming! Not just folks, but the most exacting and expensive guest in the world, Louis the Grand Monarque. "P.S. Am bringing 5,000 friends."

Do the Condés blench? Do they send for the Grand Bookkeepers to see what assets they can liquidate, such as pawning a few emeralds or selling a Raphael or two? Not they. They hold 600 fiefs, own 130 chateaus and four Paris town houses, and he pockets the salaries of a dozen high offices for which his menials do the work.

So, on an April day in 1671, Louis XIV and 5,000 courtiers descend upon the chateau to test for three days the hospitality, sport, and comestibles of the Grand Condé. In the time between messenger and monarch, quonset huts, Mansart style, have been erected in the park, and private houses and inns have been taken over. Carpenters have made beds, upholsterers stuffed mattresses, and the province for twenty miles round has been denuded of chamber pots. Thousands of partridges, pheasants, and quail and hundreds of deer and wild boar have laid down their lives for the kitchens.

The man who carries the heaviest load is the Condé's Controller-General of the Mouth—his grand chef and commissary, the famous Vatel. He hasn't had a night's sleep since that letter came. According to Madame de Sévigné, by the time the Sun King arrives Vatel is a mental and physical wreck. He fears the worst. It happens. On the first evening the roast runs out before the last two tables are served. In the privacy of his cabinet Vatel knocks his head on his desk and weeps. Next day the fish for 5,000 mouths fails to arrive. It is too much! He has failed his prince and his king. Vatel says a prayer and runs himself through the heart.

Chantilly's 15,570-acre forest served for centuries as a hunting ground of royalty and nobility and the seat of the Captain of the Royal Hunt. According to François Cali in his beautifully illustrated book, *The Wonders of France*, the hunt killed here in a thirty-year period:

Hares	70,750
Rabbits	587,460
Partridges	116,574
Quail	86,196
Wild boar	1,942
Roe deer	4,669

or about a million living creatures: 202,770 birds and 764,807 animals. (And, at the time of Louis' visit, one overconscientious chef.)

You will understand, then, the importance of the Grandes Écuries or Super-Stables, veritable palaces of horse and hound and their attendant grooms, vets, ostlers, gillies, whippers-in, gamekeepers, and coachmen. The stables have room for 240 horses, 140 staghounds, 120 roe-deer hounds, 160 wild-boar hounds. They are as large as the two chateaus and stand just west of them.

The Hippodrome was made in 1834 when the rage for racing horses was caught from England. The Diane and Jockey Club prizes are galloped for in June, at which time the village of 7,100 is jampacked with racing fans, touts, high society, low society, and the merely curious who come for the concerts, fireworks, water fêtes, and anything that's exciting. Then the chateau is shut as tight as a drum, either because the track fears the museum may draw away business or because the staff wants to have fun too.

TOURAINE: THE CHATEAU COUNTRY

Touraine is the name of a province of Old France centering on the Loire Valley. It sings of love; the word "romance" was born there with the *Roman de la Rose*. It speaks of Agnes Sorel and Diane de Poitiers, the most beautiful of royal mistresses.

The region is one of soft climate, white houses and gray towers, lazy rivers, wine, good food, and the good life. Two lusty eaters and drinkers, Rabelais and Balzac, were born in Touraine.

Blois and Tours are the main towns. Many villages are shyly picturesque. Here and there the quiet loveliness declines to prettiness. Among the roses and magnolias, the palms, cedars, and fig trees, no ugliness hides.

Only the past is violent in Touraine, and that is handsomely petrified in the form of chateaus.

The medieval castle, built for defense, was a stone pile about as comfortable as a burial vault. In the fifteenth and sixteenth centuries the high and mighty of France, excited by Renaissance Italy, began to transform their fortresses into palaces. The change occurred under the Valois kings. Having fled to the Loire during the Hundred Years' War, they lingered there when the danger was over, learning how to live like kings.

Both as a word and an object, *chateau,* which is simply *castle,* put on glamour in Touraine.

More than a hundred chateaus dream or exclaim on the lyric landscape. They range from fortresses and pleasure palaces to manor houses. They are museums, or stately homes, or ruins. The tourist hazard is confusion, as testified by the dialogue we overheard:

He: All these places begin with "ch"—Chambord, Chaumont, Chinon—

She: But there's Amboise, dear.

He: Anyway, we've seen so many I can't keep them apart. Chenonceaux's the only one I'm sure of, because it straddles a river.

She: What about Chaumont, where that girl was so nice, with thick walls—

He: What I mean, I'm fed up. You can have this Bloys thing—

She: It's pronounced Blwah, dear.

He: Well, you do Blah by yourself. I'll just mosey round town.

The "Bloys-Blah thing" was the Sound and Light spectacle in the chateau of Blois. We saw it with his wife after dinner and are sure as can be that wherever he and she are now, he's still being reminded of what he missed.

Blois is a tranquil town of two hills and a humped bridge on the Loire. It has declined (or risen) from a secondary royal capital to a primary asparagus capital, retaining a courtly air that may be responsible for the Frenchman's conviction that more than ordinary chlorophyll flows through the veins of the Blesois vegetable.

From the main street the chateau of Blois looks like an Italian palazzo, complete with loggia. A ramp leads up to the Place du Chateau, where Joan of Arc had her troops and banners blessed in 1429 before riding off to battle. Here the chateau shows a different face—red brick with white stone trimmings. Except for the right-hand corner, which belongs to the thirteenth century, it's the work of Louis XII. There he is, riding a horse in the Gothic-canopied niche. He's going off to wars in Italy, and will come back beaten but bringing Italian masons.

In the interior courtyard, with the chateau rising all around, you're struck by the variety of architecture, from the Gothic thirteenth century to the seventeenth's late Renaissance. But the striking feature is the spiral staircase of François I, who succeeded Louis XII. It's an open stone cage girdled by sculptured balustrades. It becomes more beautiful the more you look at it, particularly at night when lights and voices are enacting the ascent of a man to his death.

It took place in 1588—the meticulously planned assassination by Henri III of his archenemy, the Duke of Guise. "The best political murder ever made," remarked Henry Adams, seeing it as pure theater long before it was staged by Sound and Light.

Henri, Duke of Guise, was at the head of the extremist Catholic League. At twenty-two, he had helped Catherine de Médicis plan and execute the terrible St. Bartholomew's massacre.

Sixteen years later he was again plotting. For some time it had been apparent that Henri III ruled only so long as Guise let him. At Blois even the Queen Mother—obese, gouty, slowly dying —awoke to the fact that Guise aspired to the throne.

Suddenly it was an open secret that one Henri would have to do away with the other. When warned, Guise shrugged. "He wouldn't dare!" He was a giant of a man in the prime of life, successful in war, intrigues, and love. Henri III, in contrast, was effeminate and cowardly, a collector of lapdogs and pretty young men, weakly vicious, responding to humiliations with no more than snarls. Guise despised his sovereign. "He wouldn't dare!"

Early on a rainy December morning, after a pleasant night with his mistress, the Duke crossed the courtyard and mounted the stairs to keep an appointment with the King. Doors closed quietly behind him. Armed guards were everywhere. All went like clockwork. In the antechamber of the royal apartment, the King's chosen men fell upon him with swords and daggers. So great was his strength that although mortally wounded he dragged his killers across the floor, expiring at the foot of the royal bed.

Henri III came out from an inner room, exclaimed, "My God, how big he is!" and fearfully kicked the body. Then he ran down the stairs to his mother's chamber to boast of what he had done. "Today, I reign!"

"My son," she said, "God grant that you are not left king of nothing."

Next day he had the Duke's brother killed. A few months later it was the King's turn to fall before an assassin's dagger. He was the last Valois. The throne passed to another Henri, the first Bourbon, and the great days of Touraine were done.

From Blois, Henry Adams (still another Henri) passed this judgment: "The Valois kings were true artists, and they never did anything artistically half as brilliant elsewhere as to build the Chateau de Blois in order to murder the Guises in it."

The Chateau of Chambord, only ten miles from Blois, is islanded in a plain which is surrounded by a forest. Odd is the experience of coming upon it, the fantastic whole of it, long after you've passed through the gates and just about given it up. One moment there's nothing but grass; the next, a vast white palace with plump towers, ornamental insets of blue-black slate, and an incredible superstructure of chimneys, cupolas, pinnacles, and stone whatnots. It began in 1519 as a royal hunting lodge and ended as the largest of the chateaus. It has 440 rooms and its caretaker is the master of 819 keys.

Like the later royal egomaniac Louis XIV, who played in much the same way with the hunting lodge of Versailles, François I (of the Blois staircase) went at the construction of Chambord in a frenzy of fun. He ran the realm close to bankruptcy in the process. He wanted the Loire diverted to make a moat for his gigantic playpen. The engineers shook their heads and he had to make do with a tributary stream which subsequently choked up.

As at Blois, the grand staircase is the showpiece. Here it's a *double* spiral. Using one you catch glimpses of anyone on the other, but never the twain shall meet. Lords and ladies played hide-and-seek up and down the double spiral, and on the roof among the verticals. Everywhere are gaily carved F's and salamanders, the insignia of François.

Chambord's noteworthy event was the premiere of *The Bourgeois Gentleman,* which Molière wrote and produced for Louis XIV. The Sun King sat in an angle of the stairs. His courtiers watched the play a little and their sovereign more. In the second act the King was observed to relax his lips, whereupon smiles broke out on every sycophantic face. Molière worried, but two days later the monarch told him he had greatly enjoyed the play.

Only a small part of the tremendous Chateau of Amboise is still standing on the rocky hill above its town and the Loire—the great tower with interior ramp, the adjoining King's Quarter, and the beautiful Gothic chapel of the Queen's Quarter.

Here the Renaissance began in France.

The man behind the civilizing impulse was young, romantic-minded Charles VIII, who for no sufficient reason decided to conquer Naples. He brought back a considerable loot of paintings, furniture, even utensils, and an army of masons, sculptors, gardeners, tailors, cooks, servants, artisans. He was a man who had discovered a new world. In the very year that Columbus set out on his first voyage, Charles began work on the old castle, his birthplace and favorite residence. Impassioned and imperious, he kept his men laboring night and day, winter and summer, for six years, until the day when, running to call his wife to watch him at tennis, he forgot to stoop under a low stone door. He was twenty-eight when his chateau unromantically killed him.

Louis XII, his successor, let work go on but was more interested in Blois. François I, who was brought up in Amboise, did more and gave the place its best days with his brilliant court and round of lively entertainments. He lured Leonardo da Vinci from Italy, and here Leonardo died and is buried—in the chapel, some say, but the truth is that no one knows where.

Leonardo lived in the town, François having given him the small manor house of Close-Lucé. You find it on the Rue Victor Hugo. The house, much altered and privately owned, contains models of some of Leonardo's machines, apparatus, and engineering projects.

This lost place where a blazing genius died in 1519, far from home, to be buried and forgotten, made us sad. As we walked back in dark silence under the white sunlight, we spoke simultaneously out of different minds.

"At the very least," said Sylvia, "they could have named the street after him. There must be ten thousand Rues Victor Hugo in France!"

Lawrence said, "If Leonardo were alive today he'd be a Sunday painter and a full-time inventor of sophisticated weapons systems."

Crossed thoughts en route to a battle royal? Then Sylvia said, with an air of surprise, "You could be right. He'd be working for General Dynamics, and painting *The Last Supper* weekends."

"All the same," Lawrence agreed, "they should have named the street for him."

Other chateaus are masculine; Chenonceaux is *la belle dame sans merci.* She makes a perfect picture reclining on the sleeping Cher and mirrored in it.

This chateau was built by a woman, the wife of a royal treasurer, in 1512. François I appropriated it, but it's associated with his son, Henri II, who gave it to his exquisite mistress, Diane de Poitiers. Anything having to do with that strange love affair seems fabled. At fifteen the dark and somber Dauphin appointed himself the champion of a widow twice his age. His attentions never wavered. He won her nine years later, and loved her until he died in 1559, when she was sixty and considered more beautiful than ever. Her best portrait is in Chantilly, painted by Clouet. It shows her in her bath to display her perfect breasts, which were said to rival the famed bosom of Agnes Sorel. Goujon's sculpture of her as the goddess Diana is in the Louvre.

Loches, in contrast to Chenonceaux, is a great fist. It rises above the banks of the Indre in the most winsome valley of all this region—a brute of a stronghold on the crest of a medieval town which is in itself a fortress. When the same noun, *château*, can tag both a small palace like Chenonceaux and a castle like Loches, it is being stretched too far. Loches is what in German is called a *Burg*, a powerful, self-contained fighting unit, with a fortified town under it.

The compact little town is filled with photogenic medieval survivals: old walls, the gates of Picoys and the Cordeliers, the St. Antoine belfry, the Hotel de Ville, the Chancellery, and many another fine old house. It nourishes a delightful park embraced by two arms of the Indre. Great gardening is in the tradition of the Indre-et-Loire, the old Touraine.

The scowling chateau, half-ruined, occupies an eminence surrounded by a wall more than a mile in circumference. There's a lower, first-defense wall in the town. On the west stands the menacing great keep, the Donjon. At the other end are the royal lodgings and the church of St. Ours. The Royal Gate, in the middle, is the castle's only entrance.

It looks impregnable, but Richard the Lion-Hearted took it by surprise in the record time of three hours.

The best part is the half-furnished Logis Royaux, which command views of town and valley. Agnes Sorel's tomb is in the round tower. The golden beauty of the fifteenth century was the first royal mistress to be officially recognized as such. Her lover was that sorry creature Charles VII, and it is said that Agnes continued Joan of Arc's work of propping him up to look like a man.

Troubled by conscience, she went in for charity, the money coming from the royal purse and being channeled through the clergy of the eleventh-century church of St. Ours. When she died the canons refused to let her be buried in holy ground until the King said, "Bury her elsewhere, and her bequests go with her."

She was painted by Jean Fouquet as the Virgin (of all personages!) with one perfect breast exposed. Antwerp has the original painting. A copy hangs in the chateau.

She died in 1450. Came the Revolution, and an exquisite irony— republican zealots, mistaking her tomb for that of a saint, damaged her effigy and scattered her dust.

The Chateau of Saché is a pretty country house in a beautiful countryside. Balzac stayed here with the Margonne family, writing *Le Père Goriot* and creating the setting of *Le Lys dans la Vallée.* His room is kept as he left it when he laid aside his pen and his coffeepot, without either of which he couldn't write.

Chinon is a medieval town beside the river Vienne, not as well preserved as Loches, careless about its notables. Richard the Lion-Hearted died in a house on the Grand Carroi now occupied by a bakery. Joan of Arc on her arrival was put up for two days at an inn on the same square. Rabelais was a native son.

The town is dominated by a ruin. High above it the long, broken profile of the castle covers an abrupt flat-topped hill. The ruins are hallowed. Here the first great act of St. Joan's glory and agony took place.

For France, 1429 had dawned as a year of black despair. The English held all the country north of the Loire and were unhurriedly besieging Orléans, key to the south. Charles VII, un-crowned half-king, was very busy in the Chateau of Chinon —daily confessing himself, attending three masses, praying and consulting soothsayers and astrologers. It was a time of omens and prophetic utterances. Among the prophecies was one that France would be saved by a virgin from Lorraine.

And here she was, armed with purity and an Excalibur, ele-ments of ancient magic.

How can it be true, the marvelous tale that begins as Cinderella in armor, and ends as Greek tragedy at the stake? This episode, like the murder of the Duke of Guise in Blois, is history acting like romancer Dumas. She came in February, accompanied far across country by six armed men. She left for Orléans in April by way of Tours and Blois, leading an army exalted by a wild hope under a banner embroidered with lilies.

You cross the ravine that served as a moat, by the stone bridge replacing the drawbridge. You pass through the imposing gate tower, and look for the royal lodgings. In the Great Hall the Maid met her sovereign.

The hall itself is gone. All that is left is the fireplace of its antechamber and a few steps of its staircase. The inner eye must reconstruct the confrontation scene.

The tapestried hall was ablaze with torches; the courtiers glit-tered with jewels as for a gala. Everything had been arranged to dazzle and confuse the peasant girl. On the throne, in royal regalia, sat a courtier who looked kingly. Somewhere in the brilliant throng was His Majesty, the least kingly of men. It was a test which only credulous minds could have thought up. They wanted to believe in her, but— The archbishop stood ready with his cross to ward off evil.

They brought her in, a sturdy girl of seventeen or eighteen with a plain, honest face. Some say she showed not the slightest hesita-tion, that after one look at the man on the throne her eyes searched the crowd, and she made her way straight to the man she had come to serve, and knelt before him.

"God send you good life, gentle Dauphin."

You can see the keep where they detained her virtually as a prisoner while debating what to do. Weathered stone, green grass, blue sky, peacocks strutting before the W.C.'s, and far below, the rooftops and the ribbon of river. There's nothing more to be seen. But it is enough.

With Chinon you have completed a circuit of time. With Joan of Arc the Hundred Years' War draws to a close. Next comes Charles disporting himself at Amboise to begin the gay era interspersed with dalliance and murder.

Read Shaw's play *Saint Joan* before visiting Chinon. It's a classic, and the confrontation reads like a report of what must have happened.

One of these chateaus is actually a home. Cheverny near Blois has been lived in by the Vibray family since it was built in 1630. The present Marquis de Vibray is one of the most entertaining personalities we have met.

We dropped in without notice or invitation and in some trepidation, for such conduct was hardly etiquette. Our progress through its park toward the front door was announced by joyous yelps of all twenty hounds of a hunting pack. Out popped a man who, after one look, cried, "You are Americans! Come in, come in!"

A servant gave us to eat and drink, we hardly remember what, for from then on conversation never flagged. "I like Americans," declared the Marquis. "I have had here as my guest your President Truman, a man after my own heart. How we talked, how we laughed! I have also been host here to the leaders of NATO."

"But the Vibray Americanism is no new thing. It goes back to your revolution against George III. An ancestor of mine fought under General Washington. Let me show you my most valued treasure. This, framed on the wall, is that Vibray's certificate of membership in the Order of the Cincinnati, signed by Washington himself!"

No wonder he and Harry Truman got along hilariously; this blueblood is a French variety of a direct, outgoing man. Talk hardly paused for breath. The Marquis told stories with such vigor, hunching himself forward, taking his chair's cushion with him, that he and it spilled over to the floor. Paying no attention to this tumble, he kept talking from his seat on the carpet. Regaining the chair, he did it over again. When we hoped aloud that he had a better seat on a horse, he roared with laughter.

The chateau is a hunting center. The Marquis took us through his museum, the principal feature of which consists of 2,000 deer antlers along its walls, the trophies of more than a century of a sport of sorts.

In Touraine the grand houses are mostly empty shells. Few are lived in. Cheverny, however, is not only lived in. Its interior is comfortably furnished with one lively, unpretentious, and wholehearted aristocrat, whose greatest pride is that a forebear fought against a monarchy, helping a rebel general to establish a republic.

ITALY

Italy is the land of ancient stones and spry people. Stones first, because that is what travelers think they have come to see in the form of ancient, medieval, and Renaissance monuments. But in the long run or the brief vacation it is the live Italians who triumph over the evocative past.

Italy was the prime goal of yesteryear's Grand Tourists. It still holds place among the Big Three with England and France. For here is where western civilization flowered, and here, even after Rome fell, the western spirit experienced its rebirth. The long boot-shaped peninsula from Venice and Verona to Naples and Sicily constitutes a vast museum of art and history.

"Museum" suggests custodians—a title that fits the natives the way "musician" describes the operator of a hurdy-gurdy. Italy is a grand opera house on whose stage struts that born buffo and tragedian, the Italian. No man or woman of other nations can make so much comedy and drama out of so little. The Italian is no less a spectator and appreciative critic of his own roles. His love of music includes a passionate enjoyment of the sound of his own voice. His body is a flexible *opera d'arte* on which are hung arms and hands that speak. His mouth is an instrument capable of soft liquid tones and of machine-gun staccato. His shoulders and eyebrows are likewise eloquent.

An unprivate man, he loves crowds, for his histrionics demand chorus and audience. He lives his life in public, revealing his soul even as his new-washed linen, dangling from every balcony and window, reveals the intimate secrets of his wardrobe.

For years now the authorities, shamed by visiting foreigners, have been waging war against public din. In vain do they stretch signs across main thoroughfares, like the one above Corso Cavour in Verona:

> CAMPAIGN OF STREET EDUCATION
> NOISE IS UNCIVILIZED
> SILENCE IS AN INDICATION OF CIVILIZATION

Not noticing that their government had declared them barbarians, the Veronese increased the decibel count by gathering in crowds under the banner to discuss it. On this note ends the campaign, in Verona and other towns and cities. For on the following day and all the days thereafter they no longer notice the bannered admonition. Noise is something they do not hear. Like gregariousness, it is their necessary backdrop for the full life.

Nor can the visiting foreigner do anything about it, for protest itself is so much noise. In Naples one Sunday we were awakened at an unripe hour by the dishpan tintinnabulation of a bell. It was a maddening bell, toneless and insistent. Vespas snorted by, chairs scraped and tables crashed as the dining room below was readied for breakfast, shouts of welcome greeted deliverers of wine and collectors of garbage. Through it all sounded the clangor of the bell.

Having taken so much punishment, we went out to discover the source. It turned out to be a school-size bell, a makeshift attached to the façade of a small church undergoing repair. From it hung a long rope which an old man kept pulling like an automaton, jingle-jangle, jangle-jingle-jangle-jang.

"Ha!" cried Lawrence, charging to do battle. In three furious strides he confronted the enemy. He delivered his entire Italian vocabulary of abuse. The ancient's face lighted up, broke into a crinkle of smiles. He replied as one reciting Dante, but never ceasing to pull the cord. He concluded with a courtly flourish of his free arm, inviting the stranger to enter the church.

Lawrence retreated to where Sylvia was leaning against a wall, weak with laughter. She pulled herself together. "What did he say?"

"It sounded like 'Signore, God is waiting for you.' What can one do with people like that?"

"Only—just love them."

ROME

I

Frowsy and battered by all the living done in it, insanely noisy, traffic-mad, dubiously perfumed by mingled odors of sweat, exhaust fumes, and sanctity, the Rome that wasn't built in a day, the Rome that all roads lead to, is an awesome mess—unplanned result of 3,000 years of birth, decay, death, and renewal.

How grasp it? Well, consider first the river.

To say that London is on the Thames and Paris on the Seine means something. Those rivers are important characters in their cities. The Tiber is only a wet brown furrow through Rome's stone acres that you cross to visit the Vatican.

Well, how about the seven hills Rome was built on? Ha! The time we spent looking for them!

It was a Rome older than ancient that was built on seven hills—the archaic Rome of Romulus and Remus, half-fabled kings, and people living in crude fortified villages well above the river and its malarial marshlands. They fought until the king of one hill conquered the others, drained a marsh, and laid out a *forum* where everyone could get together for worship, government, and business.

When the growing population began to feel intolerably cramped, the rulers engineered the topography, lopping hilltops,

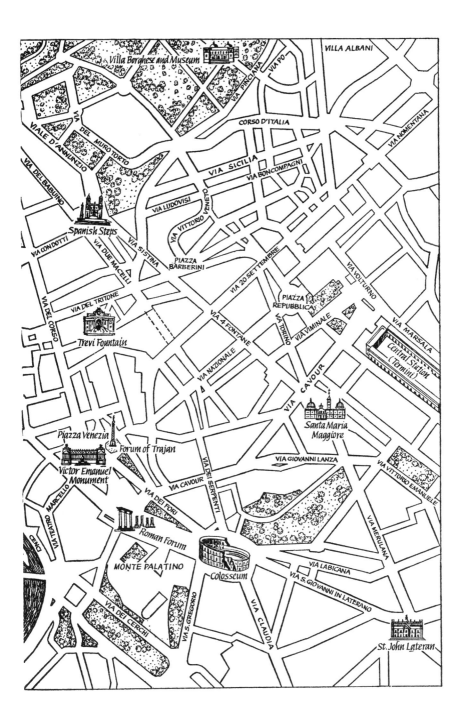

Villa Borghese and Museum

VILLA ALBANI

VIA PINCIANA

VIA PO

CORSO D'ITALIA

VIA NOMENTANA

VIA SICILIA

VIA BONCOMPAGNI

VIALE D'ANNUNZIO

VIA DEL BABUINO

VIA DEL MURO TORTO

VIA LUDOVISI

VIA VITTORIO VENETO

Spanish Steps

VIA CONDOTTI

VIA SISTINA

VIA DUE MACELLI

PIAZZA
BARBERINI

VIA 20 SETTEMBRE

VIA VOLTURNO

PIAZZA
REPUBBLICA

VIA DEL CORSO

VIA DEL TRITONE

Trevi Fountain

VIA 4 FONTANE

VIA TORINO

VIA VIMINALE

VIA MARSALA

Central Station
(Termini)

VIA NAZIONALE

VIA CAVOUR

Piazza Venezia

Forum of Trajan

Santa Maria
Maggiore

VIA MARCELLO

Victor Emanuel
Monument

VIA DEI FORI

VIA CAVOUR

VIA DEI SERPENTI

VIA GIOVANNI LANZA

VIA VITTORIO EMANUELE

VIA CRNO

VIA VITERBO

Roman Forum

MONTE PALATINO

Colosseum

VIA MERULANA

VIA LABICANA

VIA S. GIOVANNI IN LATERANO

VIA DEI CERCHI

VIA S. GREGORIO

VIA CLAUDIA

St. John Lateran

slicing off ridges. Some of the original seven humps disappeared. Meanwhile, the city spread over outlying hills and then inched over more marsh-drained land. It has crept out now over still another hill, this one crowned by a Hilton hotel by way of a temple.

If the natural fixtures of a river and hills don't help to make head or tail of Rome, does anything?

Yes. The Piazza di Venezia.

This is a square that works hard at being grandiose. When you enter from the Via del Corso you're so transfixed by the huge white (wear sunglasses) monument to Victor Emmanuel II that you hardly notice the battlemented building on the right which named the square. It's the Venetian Palace, built for a fifteenth-century Venetian cardinal. Mussolini bombasticulated from the little balcony. Under his eyes was not only the pompous pile corresponding, in marble, to his own public personality, but Trajan's Column—ancient Rome's finest glorification of a foreign conquest, and a dramatic example of the city's casual way of juxtaposing unlike centuries.

The piazza and the Victor Emmanuel lunacy facing it mark the clear divide between two different cities. Back of them rises the Capitoline Hill, looking down on the discouraging remains of ancient Rome. In front of them stretches the moiling metropolis that began with churches and feudal strongholds, was overlaid by wave after wave of building, incorporates here and there a pre-Christian relic that escaped burial under tons of masonry—and contains, somewhere well within it, your hotel.

II

Around to the right of the Victor Emmanuel are stairs and a ramp. The ramp offers the easiest climb to the Piazza del Campidoglio, set in a depression of the Capitoline hilltop. Designed by Michelangelo, it is like an elegant balcony fixed between space and time. Above, on the hill's high point, stands the church of Santa Maria Aracoeli on the site of Juno's temple. Below lies the Roman Forum.

The piazza centers on curly-haired Marcus Aurelius riding a fat horse. This famous Roman statue graced St. John Lateran for five hundred years in the mistaken belief that the horseman was Constantine, the emperor who made Christianity safe and respectable. The three government palaces (two are museums) were built only in part from Michelangelo's design. But the side forming a balustraded terrace above Michelangelo's stairway carries out the cool and measured Renaissance conception. On each side of the stairway the marble twins Castor and Pollux restrain stylized steeds. They were hero-divinities of the Roman legions.

The Capitoline, which has contributed "capitol" to English, was Rome's acropolis. It had two summits—one given over to Jupiter, the other to Juno Moneta. Juno's title of Adviser or Admonisher came to mean "money" because the mint was in her keeping.

Smaller temples crowded the slope facing the Forum. Processionals wound up from the Sacred Way. People from the Empire's four corners climbed this hill to visit its shrines of looted ivory and marble, bronze and gold—all to be relooted or destroyed in a shattering future. The nave of Santa Maria Aracoeli is supported by twenty-two antique columns. Sitting among them one day in October, 1764, an English tourist named Edward Gibbon conceived the book which was published in due time as *The Decline and Fall of the Roman Empire.*

"We will now mount the steps that run along the whole length of this portion of the Sacred Way, and visit the Basilica Julia, the largest in the Forum," directed the master booklet we had bought on entering. We mounted the steps, stared blankly, and read the next sentence: "It has been almost entirely destroyed."

There's the problem in a nutshell. The ruins of ancient Rome are exceedingly ruined. They're further complicated by the fact that there is not just one forum but five Imperial Forums in addition, each built by an emperor to relieve midtown congestion and at the same time glorify his name.

A broad avenue slices through the area, ending at the Colosseum, which rises above everything like a monolithic wrecked ship. The excavations on each side of the road look like dry moats thickly strewn with lesser wrecks—columns, arches, traces of streets, pieces of flooring, outlines of foundations. Here and there a church rises upon the substructure of the building it devoured.

Cats stroll, play, or doze on something Cleopatra admired, Augustus inaugurated, Horace touched. Tourists wandering through the desolation feel wonderfully refreshed when they come upon laborers who have laid down offerings. We enjoyed with them the spectacle of a clowder of cats dining on spaghetti, the remains of a proletarian lunch, a kitten tentatively pawing, chewing, then sitting back in a puzzled way: "This *must* be good. Well, let's try it again."

Trajan's Forum, the last and most magnificent of the Imperial Forums, is easily seen from the wall above it, just off the Piazza di Venezia. Built in 114 A.D., it had a known architect—Apollodorus of Damascus. Much of it is still below ground, under two churches across the street. Trajan's Column, now at one end and solitary, was near the center. The brick arches along the side are the remains of curved buildings containing two or three stories of shops. There are pieces of marble flooring where the basilica stood. On top of the column a small statue of St. Peter has replaced the colossal gilded figure of the Emperor, who had also an equestrian statue at the other end. Nobody shopping or strolling here could forget for a moment the name of Trajan.

Here, as in all the forums, everything—columns, arches, statues, buildings, shrines—was marbled, brightly painted, or gilded. How imagine it today, when the broken scene is dun-colored? Modern Rome still paints itself, but its colors are unappetizing: mustard yellow, brown, or dried-blood red.

III

Five palm trees in a row, buildings painted brown or red, a fountain that looks like a gravy boat, a stairway with flower stalls at the bottom and a church high up at the top—this is the Piazza di Spagna. It is Rome's most welcoming square. The Barcaccia Fountain, made by the father of the Bernini who baroqued Rome, is modestly endearing and its rim is much sat upon. The steps ask to be sat upon as well, and are usually draped with more or less beautiful young people.

Oh and ah! the Spanish Steps—rippling, flowing, cascading down the Pincian Hill! In stairdom there is nothing more gay and graceful, even at night when they look like a stage-set waiting for the cleaners and tomorrow's performance.

When you stand facing them, the house on the right is where Shelley lived and Keats lingeringly died. In the house on the left Babington's, founded by two Englishwomen in 1893, still serves the best teas. If it goes, gone too will be an oasis of warmth and intimacy for foreigners in Rome.

Where but in Rome would you find a fountain too large for its square, too noisy for its neighborhood, and starting out from the flank of a quiet Renaissance palace? No other art city of Italy could have perpetrated such a civic misdemeanor. But then, Rome isn't an art city. It's a city filled with art, which is something quite different.

Part of the Trevi's attraction is delighted surprise. It's an improbable thing. From a stately house, into a static piazza, Neptune, balancing on a winged chariot and flying a piece of drapery like a sail, drives his plunging steeds through the thick of a roaring cascade that tumbles over rocks into a shallow pool. He's assisted by two muscular Tritons. The lively scene is being regarded by Health and Abundance, two ladies in niches.

It's great fun.

The architect was one Salvi but the design was by—you've guessed it?—Bernini. For more of his water works, seek out the

Fountain of the Rivers on Piazza Navona. The square itself, enclosed by baroque churches and palaces that are mellow if you like them and moldering if you don't, is considered the most "typical" in Rome. This means that to the usual appearance of the grandiose in leisurely decay is added a feeling of intimacy and neighborhood.

IV

Hadrian's is the bridge on which you cross the Tiber to Vatican City; Hadrian's too the astonishing structure on the other side—a huge drum with an angel on top—called Castel Sant'Angelo. Then comes St. Peter's, with a dome that is a world landmark. Third on everyone's itinerary this side of the Tiber is Vatican Palace.

To us there are few buildings in Europe as curious and fascinating as Sant'Angelo, the tomb that became a castle.

Hadrian began it in A.D. 135 as an imperial mausoleum. It was finished a year after he died and his waiting ashes were brought here.

Resting on a square base, Hadrian's Tomb was an enormous cylinder 210 feet in diameter, faced with marble and surrounded by a colonnade with statues. At the top was a cone-shaped garden, Babylonian style, and there a gilded Hadrian-Apollo drove the chariot and horses of the sun. From the entrance a spiral ramp and transverse passage led to the burial chamber which held the urns of cremated emperors from Hadrian to Caracalla.

In ancient Rome burial was not permitted within the city. Tombs of the wealthy lined roads outside the walls and cemeteries (catacombs) spread behind them. The cemetery beyond Hadrian's Tomb was near the scene of Christian persecutions by Nero. In it lay a martyr named Peter. There were mostly non-Christians. Whole streets of pagan tombs lie under St. Peter's church.

The transformation of a mausoleum into a castle began about 130 years after Hadrian. During an invasion of Goths the Romans hurled the statues and whatever else they could down on the enemy. Bereft of its roof garden, colonnade, and statues, the tomb in shape and solidity was a natural keep. But castle fixtures had to be made.

The work, begun by Aurelian, continued under the popes. They made the ex-tomb their fortress-residence, complete with luxurious apartments and loggias for airy promenades, and a covered passage for speedy flight from palace to castle.

In 590 Gregory the Great was leading a procession of supplication against the plague. While crossing the bridge he saw, on the castle's roof, an angel sheathing a flaming sword in sign the plague would end. So Hadrian's Tomb got the name Holy Angel Castle.

Sant'Angelo is a wonderful place to explore when the visiting crowds aren't too shoving. It has been well restored as a tomb, a citadel, and a medieval-Renaissance papal palace. You begin the climb to the top by way of Hadrian's ramp and carry on by winding stairs, passages, unexpected courtyards. There are fifty-eight rooms. They include sets of "penthouse" apartments, beautifully decorated, made for this pope and that. Clement VII's bathroom is exquisite. The flat roof under the angel offers a grand view over Rome.

Tradition says that from the time of his burial a memorial of some kind marked St. Peter's grave. In 319 Constantine hurriedly built a basilica over it. A mere thousand years later this old St. Peter's was getting shaky. It was decided to rebuild, and work began in 1452. Hesitantly. The hoary church was so venerated that unless it fell down it would take a daring pope to do anything drastic. The daring pope materialized as Julius II, who dismantled a good part of the old church and began on a design with his architect Bramante, nicknamed the Ruinous. Later popes and their architects kept changing designs. St. Peter's must have seemed the eternally unfinished church of the Eternal City. It was consecrated at last in 1626. Among its architects were Fra Giocondo, Raphael, and Michelangelo.

The persistent inspiration, oddly, was the pagan Pantheon, built by Hadrian and combining a Grecian portico with a Roman dome. In his own time the builder-emperor won the jeers of architect Apollodorus of Damascus as a bungling amateur. But the Pantheon still stands. Trajan's Forum by Apollodorus is a ruin.

Unforgettable is St. Peter's setting—the Piazza San Pietro. It is embraced by two great curving arms of colonnades, four columns deep, carrying precise files of statues. In the middle an obelisk and two fountains are fine unobtrusive piazza furniture.

This geometrically majestic square is the major work of Lorenzo Bernini, the last of the basilica's architects. The only trouble is that nowhere from his piazza can you get a full view of Michelangelo's dome.

Within the church stands the object that launched Bernini on a career of fifty years as dictator of the arts. It's the baldaquin over the high altar—four fatly whorled bronze columns decorated with gilded laurel branches, holding the tasseled canopy ninety-five feet above the marble floor. When unveiled in 1633 the baldaquin was a sensation. It is sensational still, in a barbaric way, as if intended for Baal.

If Bernini's life span is represented in St. Peter's, so is Michelangelo's. In the first chapel at the right is his tenderly young *Pietà*. He was only twenty-two when he began it. He was seventy-one when appointed chief architect of St. Peter's. He was afraid he would die too soon to see his dome finished; and he did. Another tragedy was the great tomb for Julius I which he had planned for this church. It involved him in years of petty difficulties and ended up, incomplete, in another church. So it is to San Pietro in Vincoli that you must go to see his *Moses*.

St. Peter's is imposing, rich, sumptuous. In size it is a mountain. Behind the pseudo-Greek portico is a church built to so grand a scale that you'd have to be twelve feet tall to feel at home in it. You walk through marbled immensities under a ceiling-heaven coffered and gilded. Statues sixteen feet high seem of natural size; anything smaller is lost. With popes as with emperors, gigantism may be an occupational disease.

If we'd known beforehand that the Vatican Palace consists of many palaces linked together, built from the fourteenth century on; that it covers more than thirteen acres; and that 1,400 of its rooms and galleries constitute the world's largest museum—if we had known, would we have had the courage to plunge in? Do you?

Most visitors proceed at a smart pace through the endless corridors to the Sistine Chapel to see Michelangelo's frescoes on the ceiling. What with these, other ceiling paintings, and the handsomely decorated ceilings of miles of corridors, ideally one should be wheeled reclining on a chaise lounge.

Among the sculptures are the *Apollo Belvedere* and the *Laocoön*. Are all those male nudes still fig-leafed? One can't help noticing. Remarks overheard: "How do they attach them?" "Wonder if they've got a special man for that?" "Don't look now but—"

V

The Appian Way, dating from 312 B.C., ran more than 350 paved miles from Rome to Brindisi, with branches to Naples, Bari, and other ports. Roadside tombs solidly lined it for some ten miles out of Rome.

Now you take the ten miles in an excursion bus (or drive-yourself car) out from Porta San Sebastian (best of the remaining gates in the Aurelian wall) to the San Callisto Catacombs.

The Appian Way is narrow, quiet, lined with cypress, crumbling tombs, and farmhouses. Here and there are stretches of the ancient paving stones. A church called Quo Vadis Domine marks the traditional site where Peter, hurrying out of Rome, met Jesus going in the opposite direction, and asked, "Lord, whither goest thou?" And the Lord said unto him, "I go to Rome to be crucified again." And Peter returned to Rome. . . .

There are some fifty catacombs around Rome, one Jewish. When the popes reburied thousands of early Christian bones in Hadrian's Pantheon and in church crypts, catacomb pilgrimages stopped and the catacombs were forgotten until accidentally discovered in the sixteenth century.

San Callisto was among the largest and most important, with its tombs of St. Cecilia and the early popes. Visitors are escorted in parties by a priest speaking their indicated language—usually imperfectly. Closely following his dim light and pronunciation, your group descends into a maze of rough but well-constructed and well-aired narrow passages lined by tiers of burial niches, with here and there a pagan family chamber or a martyr's chamber ornamented with the beginnings of Christian art.

San Callisto goes down very deep and if laid out horizontally would cover eleven miles. You're taken through only a small part, the most historical and pictorial.

In spite of all the others with you, stepping on your heels, pushing, and someone's occasional facetious remark in a misguided attempt to cheer his soul, it is an eerie experience, incomparable for the swift and powerfully evocative transition from your own century into the third. To come up then, drive back, and be embraced by Rome's clamor and passions, is resurrection.

VENICE

I

We are children in Venice. The canals, humped bridges, carpeted gondolas, candy-striped mooring posts, frosted-cake buildings—aren't these the stuff fun fairs are made of? Delight wells up and we hold hands as we set out to see something that we won't find, to find something we didn't expect to see.

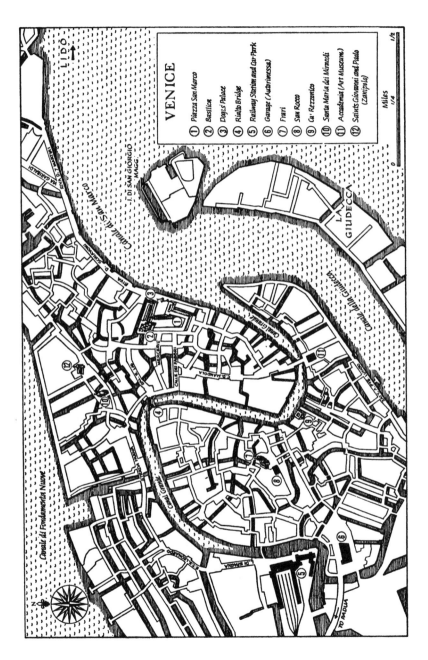

VENICE

1. Piazza San Marco
2. Basilica
3. Doge's Palace
4. Rialto Bridge
5. Railway Station and Car-Park
6. Garage (Autorimessa)
7. Frari
8. San Rocco
9. Ca' Rezzonico
10. Santa Maria dei Miracoli
11. Accademia (Art Museum)
12. Saints Giovanni and Paolo (Zanipolo)

Miles
1/4 · 0 · 1/4 · 1/2

LIDO

I. DI SAN GIORGIO MAGG.

Canale di S. Marco

RIVA D. SCHIAVONI

LA GIUDECCA

Canale della Giudecca

Canal Grande

Canal Grande

Canale di Fondamenta Nuove

TO PADUA

N

We are lovers in Venice. Entwined, we walk into a sunset that makes the Lagoon pearly and the city jewel-toned. We are sated with marvels, drunk on vino and visual pleasures, and it is enough now that, lost for the umptieth time, we have each other, here in this city of enchantment.

We are at home in Venice—that is, we know how to get from our hotel to Piazza San Marco without asking. On this wet and windy day we find that the sea has come up and flooded it. On flimsy boardwalks churchgoers balance and totter, slapped by the wind, laughing. Hardy young tourists slosh about barelegged. Rubber-booted porters convey customers to and from Quadri's in restaurant chairs on hand trucks, spectators cheering each load. Everything shines in a fresh sun that still has rain in it.

We talk to a porter. "The floods come now more and more often. In Rome they have voted the money to save us, and they sit on it and argue. For years. And now I think it is too late."

As we look at each other, troubled, he says lightly what people here always say when there's a fatal illness in the family: "That's life."

Some day you may come by ship. It was always the best way to meet Venice—watching her rise out of the Lagoon, domes and towers hung on the sky, the campanile and the Doges' Palace resting on a wafer. Careful. A breath might blow her away. A blink might blot her out.

Some day you will come by water because there will be no other way. Domes, towers, and all the art and artifice so long enjoyed will be more or less under the sea, and you will float among them in glass boats or bubble submersibles.

Even in her slow death by drowning Venice will put on a show.

There is still time. How much time, no one knows. Expect to be jostled by people from everywhere who are flocking to the lingering enchantress for last glimpses, handclasps, memories. Expect to pay heavily as Venetians scramble to earn perhaps the last good living of their generation. But go.

There is only one Venice. There will never be another.

II

The Queen of the Adriatic is composed of some 115 islets linked by 500 bridges over a maze of canals. Each islet has its own square *(campo)* and complex of little streets and passages. Transportation is primarily on foot; secondarily by water bus, motorboat, and gondola. Main street is a water-boulevard, the Grand Canal, crossed by three bridges and eleven gondola-ferries.

Venice permits only one *piazza*—San Marco—but gives it a right-angled *piazetta,* where St. Theodore and the winged lion oppose each other on antique columns.

In 828 two audacious Venetian merchants stole St. Mark's body from a church in Alexandria. Until then Venice's patron had been Theodore, a minor Byzantine saint puzzlingly coupled with a crocodile. St. Mark's familiar was the much more satisfactory winged lion of Ecclesiastes.

If you'd arrived in St. Theodore's heyday, your first sight of Venice would have been a castle, watchtower, and church —nothing unusual, except that their island was still being patched together from straggles and dollops of Lagoon land.

The Venetians, a vigorous race of shipbuilders and merchants, had become notoriously bad Christians by trading with the infidel. St. Mark did not reform them but he did inspire them to build, to show off their wealth. The castle gave way to the Doges' Palace, the church to the Basilica, the watchtower to the bell tower (campanile). Some canals were filled in and an orchard leveled. In short, by 1300 Venice had created the world's most magnificent public square.

It is still unsurpassed.

Stepping into the piazza from an archway at the back is like entering a grand ballroom that begs for sky-suspended chandeliers—instead of clouds of pigeons. It is enclosed on three sides by arcades sheltering expensive shops and the two veteran cafés, Florian's and Quadri's, with their rival orchestras and encroaching tables.

The open end frames a five-domed Byzantine extravaganza

likened by no-nonsense Mark Twain to "a vast warty bug taking a meditative walk." This improbable edifice is the Basilica, begun in 1063. On a balcony above the main portal stand the piazza's guests of honor, four bronze horses looted from Constantinople's hippodrome. They were part of the fabulous spoils of the Fourth Crusade (1204)—the only one the Venetians joined, to their great and immoral profit. Their canny old Doge, Enrico Dandolo, led the crusaders against Christian Constantinople, which they sacked.

Above the arcades on the left is a blue-and-gold clock tower. On the right the master of ceremonies, the soaring red-brick campanile, watches over piazza and piazetta. And beside the Basilica is the Doges' Palace with its exquisitely patterned façade, Gothic arcades, carved capitals, arabesque loggias, crenellations, and Bridge of Sighs. An architectural freak. And beautiful.

The Basilica, gaudy enough today, is nothing to what it was in its prime, as you can see in Bellini's painting in the Academy. Then it glittered. Gold, gold, gold. The Venetians were all Marco Polos—gold was the stuff! They gave their doge a golden ship, a golden stairway, a golden umbrella. They had a Golden Book for inscribing the names of their nobles. Gold adorned their palaces; one is called Ca' d'Oro—House of Gold.

Within, the Basilica is darkly splendiferous, all mosaic and marble. Its greatest treasure is the Palo d'Oro, a solid gold altarpiece studded with gems and Byzantine enamels. Don't fail to climb up to the galleries—marble-balustraded passages, crooked with age, affording bird's-eye views into the dust-dancing, gleaming body of the church.

III

Behind the piazza's blue-and-gold clock tower begins the meandering Merceria, the main shopping street. Taking it to the Rialto, you are following the historic route from the political to the business center of town.

Rialto is the bridge over the Grand Canal and the square on the other side where the old Church of San Giacomo admonishes merchants to be honest. The famous humped bridge is disappointingly lined with drab shops. But you can lean on the parapets, as you can't on Florence's bridge, watching the lively floating traffic. About two hundred "palaces" line the Grand Canal, most of them originally the homes (with warehouses on the "water" floor) of leading merchant-bankers and shippers. All the luxury goods of the East passed through the hands and ledgers of these palace-dwellers. Their banks were at both ends of the bridge. On Rialto square traders and money-changers transacted business.

A few banks are left, and a few goldsmiths. The shops once crammed with marvels now constitute a drygoods arm of the market. But glamour still hangs about the bridge, like a scent of spices in an empty warehouse.

IV

How much is enough when sightseeing? There comes a day when we say, "We've had it!" Besides, it's raining hard. What to do?

Our hotel windows overlook a junction of canals. We pull up our chairs and elbow-prop ourselves on the sills. Some kind of donnybrook, Italian style, always seems to be going on below.

Just now three garbage scows have tied up, clean barges modernly equipped with devouring chutes. Householders and hotel porters pop out of doorways and passages, heavily burdened. A humped bridge is in the way and containers on wheels are bump-bump-bumped up its steps on this side, down on that. (What does this feel like, we wonder, to those Venetian babies brought up in the luxury of prams?)

Arguments erupt. "No, your *rifiuti* are not for us—over there's your boat." "My garbage is as good as anyone's, and what are you here for? Your beauty?" Pedestrians under umbrellas stop to observe, comment, advise. Two barges have pushed off and the third is about to go when on-stage waddles the obese dishwasher from the trattoria, embracing a huge sack. Hoots and jeers greet him. "Too late again. She is gone. Until tomorrow, Luigi, guard your treasures well.—No! No!" For now Luigi, with a heave of desperation, has flung his spilling load on the clean deck and is scuttling back to his kitchen.

The two civic boatmen, actually speechless, can only agree with heroic palms-up gesture: "What is life but to suffer!"

Refreshed, we are ready now to search out the best of the eighty churches—the Frari, San Zanipolo and Santa Maria dei Miracoli. Instead we will probably find the Academy, or the Ca' Rezzonico where Browning died. Or maybe those four ancient lions of the Arsenal. One of them, brought from Piraeus, is deeply scratched with eleventh-century Runic writing which has been made out to be names: Harold the Tall, Haakon, Ulf, Asmund, Asgeir, Thorleif, Thord, Ivar. Norse mercenaries saying, across the centuries, "Kilroy was here!"

PADUA AND VERONA

I

Padua has:

Streets of narrow, irregular brown arcades, like cowled corridors.

Giotto's finest frescoes and Donatello's greatest statue.

A palace of justice containing the largest merry-go-round horse ever made.

The Ox and the Saint.

The last two come first in importance. The Ox is the local name for the University, the Saint for the Basilica of St. Anthony. They're the two poles round which the city revolves.

The University, Italy's second, began in 1222 when a band of dissident professors and students shook the dust of Bologna from their shoes. They established themselves in Padua at the Sign of the Bo (Ox), an inn occupying part of three joined and fortified mansions.

Meanwhile, a Portuguese missionary who had been ship-wrecked in Sicily en route to North Africa was stirring the faithful and working miracles throughout Italy. Destined for sainthood, this Anthony died in 1232 in a monastery near Padua. A year later the town, proud possessor of his remains, began building its great church around them.

Pilgrims—tourists with a religious motivation—thronged to the Saint, scholars to the Ox. Good business brought a building boom. University, basilica, and Padua grew up together.

The University is scattered, but the part you want to see is in the center of town and is called *The* University, colloquially *Il Bo*. Incorporating the old inn, the medieval mansions, and in its bowels a Roman bridge and mole, it would make a fascinating study for a detective-architect. In the fifteenth century a Renaissance plan was drawn up to create order and elegance out of a confusion worse confounded by private shops, storerooms, and merchant halls that had grown into the complex. The plan was worked out in spurts through centuries and completed in—1948. Only then was the last merchant diehard dislodged.

You find a medieval bell tower in one corner, modern frescoes in the newest wing, a Renaissance façade, a neoclassic courtyard, passages, rooms, and nooks cut, shaped, and decorated by a variety of centuries. Yet there remains an all-enveloping atmosphere of tradition and hoary age.

The gateway brings you into the beautiful old Court, two-storied, surrounded by Doric and Ionic pillars, its walls displaying the coats of arms of rectors and councillors. On one of the stairways stands a charming statue of the first girl graduate; she took her doctorate, this Portia, in 1678. Above are more than twenty-five halls and chambers, richly decorated. The alumni of the colleges include Thomas Linacre, Francis Walsingham, William Harvey, and Oliver Goldsmith—all men who have achieved space in encyclopedias.

Most famous and impressive is the ceremonial Aula Magna. The college when Galileo joined the faculty, it was turned over to him as the only hall large enough to hold the crowds he drew to his lectures and demonstrations. In an adjoining room stands the crude platform-pulpit his students built for him, a short man not easily seen by standees. An intimate monument.

Up a steep stairway into the roof, you find yourself in what seems to be the interior of a funnel of circular tiers of narrow galleries above a rectangular pit. This is the Anatomical Theater, built in 1594 and the oldest still existing. Why so cramped? For many centuries dissection was regarded as unchristian and had to be practiced in secrecy on the bodies of criminals cut down from the gallows in the dead of night. The dangerous illegal object was raised to the pit from the cellar, and since not a glimmer of light must show outside, the theater was lit by torchbearers. Elbow to elbow the students leaned over the galleries watching the anatomist. Guards were posted. On the alarm the corpse was lowered into the cellar, and the police would find a board covered with a green baize cloth and an anatomical model, and a professor professing.

The information clerk-guard at the desk, first floor left of the main stairway, is your guide unless otherwise occupied. Better to inquire first for a special guide at the Tourist Office. But don't expect English to be spoken.

Diagonally across the street from the University you see, you hail, you make for, Pedrocchi's Café, one of Italy's handsomest. It's an institution. From the time in 1831 when it didn't open its doors (it was originally built without any, to be always open), it has been the haunt of writers, artists, students, politicos. Here in 1848 the students began the uprising of the Risorgimento which ended in establishing modern Italy. A descendant of the founder presented the historic café to the city. It is still a multiroomed social center, and a godsend to weary tourists.

South of the University, at the end of Via del Santo, rises a Byzantine mountain with outcroppings of domes and pyramidal towers, set off by a piazza on which thirteen booths in a wide semicircle do a brisk business in candles and religious trinkets.

The Basilica is so eye-filling that you actually have to survey the square to discover Donatello's huge equestrian statue of Gattamelata. This hero's real name was Erasmo da Narni. His nickname, " Honey-Cat," was probably the word for a breed of wildcat. He was a *condottiere,* one of those self-made captains who led and hired out armies to the highest bidder. Donatello happened to be in town when he died, working on bronzes for the Basilica, and Honey-Cat's widow—known as the Lioness—commissioned the statue. Donatello took it on as a challenge, for not since ancient times had a horse-and-rider been successfully cast. What he produced made a sensation, but the sculptor wailed, "I need the criticisms of my Florentines, not the praises of the Paduans."

The face—the prizefighter's nose, strong mouth, dimpled chin!—of Gattamelata is too high above the ground for easy viewing. Opera glasses or binoculars come in handy, both for statue and Basilica.

In spite of Gothic touches the interior of the church seems almost Arabic. There's a vertical mile or so of small painted decorations in warm colors, imitating inlays and mosaics, and as sybaritic as the musky smell of incense from the bronze censers which glow with ruby-red lights in the semigloom.

We arrived on a Sunday night as a service was about to begin. Little by little, lights sprang up—for the altar, for the central dome, as in a theater. Worshippers scurried to rent folding chairs from banks of them at the sides, and settled themselves (scrape, scrape, scrape) in the vast nave. Others moved in a steady stream to the gold-and-marble shrine of St. Anthony. We followed those who went round to the back. There the devout pressed their palms against the back of the shrine, the marble wall of the sarcophagus, murmuring prayers. Some used new handkerchiefs or scarves to pass on to friends or relatives a touch of holiness. When we came on weekdays we would see them pressing packages against the shrine. For some reason Padua's St. Anthony is insurance against the loss of articles through the mail.

Donatello's crucifix and candelabra are on the high altar. The church Treasure is displayed between choir and apse—jeweled reliquaries containing some grisly holy relics, such as the saint's jawbone and tongue. This is a church close to the dark, medieval soul. Yet it celebrated its seventh centenary with an international auto rally.

Outside, at the left, you find the small Oratory of St. George and the Scuola di Sant'Antonio. Both have frescoes. Three in the Scuola are by Titian. They are numbers 1, 12, and 13.

Giotto's frescoes fill the Scrovegni Chapel in the park called the Arena because it's spread around the remains of a Roman amphitheater. There are thirty-eight panels in three bands, a bounty. Thanks for them must go to a Paduan named Enrico Scrovegni, who built the chapel and ordered the paintings to win salvation for his father, a usurer booted by Dante into his Inferno.

The Palazzo della Ragione, built for affairs of justice, is a long Romanesque structure dating from 1219, sandwiched between the vegetable and fruit markets. Upstairs the Salone, or Great Hall, claims to be the largest without interior supports. One long wall is decorated with fading frescoes—someone counted four hundred—by followers of Giotto. In a floor area large enough for a football gridiron stand two lonely items. One is the colossal wooden horse made in 1446 for—Paduans insist—a merry-go-round, and long attributed to Donatello. The other is the Vituperation Stone, where debtors sat accepting the vituperation of their creditors.

Padua's main street debouches at the south into an enormous space called the Prato della Valle, where a cheap market is in possession of arcades under minor palaces. Across an avenue as inviting as a desert lies an immense round platter of formal garden, girdled by a canal, entrance-bridged at mathematical intervals, and geometrically adorned by balustrades with seventy-eight statues on the circumference. One empty pedestal was earmarked for a stone likeness of John F. Kennedy; Padua was hoping the United States would foot the bill.

II

Verona is like a thumb thrust out into the Adige River with a city wall across the joint. Six bridges span the river, and on the other side wider walls bring into the town's orbit an expanse of green hills, the deceptively mild beginnings of the Alps.

All things here are shapely—the hills and the looping river, the castle and the Roman arena, the streets, squares, and antique buildings. There is space and light.

This is one of Italy's handsomest towns. Its romantic appeal made the story of Romeo and Juliet popular well before Shakespeare wrote his version. It had to oblige Renaissance tourists with a Capulet house and Juliet's tomb. Modern tourists are no less enthralled, even though the honest town claims no authenticity for either the tale or the mementos.

To get that matter out of the way—

"Juliet's House" is on the Via Capello in the center of town, where no wheeled traffic is permitted. Its plaque says: "This is the house of the Capulets where Juliet lived, for whom so many tender hearts wept and poets sang." In the courtyard is literature's dearest balcony. The so-called tomb is in the monastery church of San Francesco. To American novelist W. D. Howells it resembled a horse trough, perhaps was one. The monastery's lovely cloister is the real literary shrine. If it had nothing to do with true love, why does it look like that?

"Romeo's House," on Via Arche Scaligere, is a thirteenth-century dwelling with battlements, near enough—about three city blocks—to Juliet's to have made courting easy for the lad. The way to it lies through the market place, the narrow, irregular Piazza delle Erbe, and once you get tangled in the market and its surroundings you may never find Romeo.

Ye gods and graces, ye oranges and lettuces! There are more things in the Piazza delle Erbe than ever a tourist dreamt of. The Lion of Venice presides over the teeming market on a tall pedestal, reminder of the era when Verona was subject to Venezia. At the bottom of the rectangle stands the small Visconti column, raised when the Visconti of Milan were the masters. You have to work your way into the press of booths, people, and protective canvas umbrellas to see the two other interesting objects. One is a stone pavilion called the Capitello, in which mayors and governors took their oath of office. The last is a two-tiered fountain on which stands the "Verona Madonna," a Roman matron with a thick neck and flat head wearing a spiked iron circlet, the Lombard crown.

Of the four civic emblems, the "Madonna" is the most truly Veronese. The lady was probably a Minerva made by the best available native talent when this piazza was the Roman Forum. With all her imperfections she is a symbol of the rough, vigorous northern spirit that has survived all foreign occupations. Her fountain is one of many contributions of the Scaligeri (the Della Scala family), a dynasty that ruled for more than a century and introduced elegance. It was during the Scaliger reign that the Romeo-Juliet story took root, one of the two good things that came out of the senseless Guelph-Ghibelline feuds. The other? Dante's epic.

All around the market are exciting structures (some in crying need of municipal loving-kindness). Among them is a medieval clock tower, the crenelated Merchants' Guildhouse, and the Old Town Hall with a tower which begins with narrow stripes of yellow tufa and red terra-cotta, continues with red brick, and ends with marble—a composite of Verona's famed local building materials.

The market square is the anteroom to the Piazza dei Signori and other wonders. The way is through the balustraded archway called the Arco della Costa, from which dangles the rib of a prehistoric monster. La Costa, the fossil rib, is a public possession almost as highly prized as the Madonna.

The Piazza dei Signori is a square at once lordly and intimate, rather like a quad at Oxford. Archways with balustrades and statues lead to courtyards and other squares, each asking to be explored. In the middle poses a thoughtful Dante. He belongs. Exiled from Guelph Florence, he was embraced by the Ghibelline Scaligers, and paid them back with a place in his Paradise.

This fine square is enclosed by a fascinating variety of buildings. The most striking is the airy, graceful Loggia del Consiglio by Fra Giocondo (1476) with its exquisite marble colonnade, soft-yellow panels of frescoes, and touches of pink at the windows. The Scaliger Palace at the bottom of the square dates from the twelfth century and demands attention: four stories tall, each story slightly different; arcades at the bottom, crenelations at the top.

Entrance to the Old Town Hall is first on your right as you enter the square. It has had many things done to it since it began in 1193. The cobblestoned courtyard is powerfully medieval. It's enclosed by striped brick-and-tufa buildings with Romanesque arcades punctuated by iron-studded doors. Famous is the stairway on the right, the Scala Ragione, red marble with a balustrade mounted on arches, leading to a carved Gothic doorway.

Sheltering from rain in this Town Hall's portal, we discovered a tablet on the wall in the form of an open mouth with an etched face around it and the words, in Italian: "Secret Denunciations against Usury and Contracts of Usury and Usurious Contracts of Any Kind." We recalled in Venice's Doges' Palace the letter-box mouths for informers on everything, not only usury. Dante would have been pleased with this one. He plunged the early capitalists into his bottommost hell.

Go through the archway beside the Scaliger Palace, follow the joggle, and you come out on an astonishing sight. In a small open space, enclosed by a wrought-iron fence but otherwise open to weather and admiration, is a princely burial ground of elaborate marble-carved tombs—the Scaliger Tombs. Two are Gothic canopies soaring with towers and pinnacles to a flat summit like a truncated pyramid, on which the incumbent is immortalized as a fully accoutered knight on horseback. The grander of the two is that of Can Signorio, who murdered one of his brothers and successfully plotted at least one other murder on his deathbed.

Can Grande, greatest of the Scaligers, is apart. He rides a horse above the portal of the small, pure Romanesque church (1185) at the side, Santa Maria Antica, the family chapel. It had no room for tombs. Instead of preempting space in a larger church, the Scaligers got the novel idea of a private-public graveyard adorning a downtown corner of their city.

From 1260 until 1354 the dynasty occupied the Piazza dei Signori, when for greater security they built, on the riverbank, the Castelvecchio. It is a handsome brick fortress-palace with a massive keep and a fortified bridge flung like an armed gauntlet across the river to the Arsenal. Only thirty years after the castle was completed, the Milanese conquered Verona and the Scaligers passed into history. The keep is in use as an art museum of Veronese and Venetian paintings and sculpture. But the castle's most picturesque exhibit is the long battlemented bridge that, its three arches being of different size, lurches across the Adige.

The Roman Arena is of the first century A.D. and second in size only to the Colosseum. Nothing can compare with that one, but Verona's is so well preserved that summer festivals are held in it. One can only guess at its ancient magnificence; barbarians and local builders helped themselves to the marble facing.

Experts acclaim San Zeno as one of the finest of Italy's larger Romanesque churches. It is built of yellow tufa with ornamental touches of pink marble, shows a rose window and a portico upheld on each side by a column resting on the back of a red marble lion. It was once the church of a fortified monastery. The sculptures over the main door and the bronze reliefs are marvelous examples of Christian art from between the ninth and thirteenth centuries. Before their desperate sincerity, sophisticated Renaissance work pales.

There's a red-and-white duomo with strong, crude twelfth-century reliefs on the façade, pink marble apse, and an "Assumption" by Titian in a chapel.

The hilly left bank affords views over the town from the Giusti Gardens, the terrace of the Roman Theater which predates the Arena, and the heights of St. Peter's Hill. It was on St. Peter's that Verona began, around a fortified camp.

As for the Theater, they perform here in the tourist season *Giulietta e Romeo* di W. Shakespeare set to music. W. Shakespeare also wrote *Two Gentlemen of Verona,* but Verona does nothing with that. Or with Catullus, the great lyricist of love, born here in the eighties B.C., who had a passionate affair with one Clodia and told all.

TUSCANY: FLORENCE—SIENA—PISA

I

A funny thing happened in Tuscany on the way to modern times. It is called the Renaissance.

Florence was the birthplace of the "Rebirth."

The quickest and easiest way to meet the Renaissance is to stand face to façade with the Strozzi Palace on Via Tornabuoni. You can't miss it.

There's no mistaking this gigantic cube built of beveled stones, the ranks of windows marching across a stone desert, the cornice as flat and tight as the lid of a money box. It has been copied often and in many places. In Manhattan, at 73rd and Broadway, for instance, the Central Savings Bank is in imitation.

The Strozzi, like the Medici, were a great banking family when Florence was financier to the world and tossed off such proverbs as, "Twenty-five percent is nothing at all; fifty percent will pass the time away; one hundred percent is interesting."

We have a soft spot for their old home because of something

the Strozzi themselves never knew. In April 1489 a shopkeeper took his four-year-old son to watch the construction and later wrote in his diary: "As he had a bunch of Damascus roses, I made him throw them down [on the foundations] and said, 'You will remember this, won't you?' He answered, 'Yes.'"

That's the way to remember Renaissance architecture—when it was still so new and exciting that you would sweeten its stones and your child's memory with a gift of roses.

The style began with the Medici Palace. In 1440 Cosimo the Elder—the man who set the Medici seal on Florence—commissioned a protégé, Michelozzo, to build a grand house that wouldn't look grand. It must project his image of a man of the people. The plain-man effect, called "rustic," is in the rough stones, which in the Strozzi Palace are smoothly beveled.

The Medici Palace was altered by later tenants. You go there now mainly to see the delightful frescoes in the chapel, by Gozzoli. On all the walls the Medici, with friends and retainers, ride or stroll through a fairy-tale version of the Tuscan countryside to the Adoration of the Child.

Across the Arno River is the biggest palace of them all. Cosimo the Elder and Luca Pitti, of another banking family, were fierce rivals. Seeing that Cosimo had chosen a little-known architect, Luca hired the very best, Brunelleschi, for the Pitti Palace and ordered him to make the windows as big as the Medici front door. He was ruined before his palace was finished.

Florence's government square, the Piazza della Signoria, is ragged and inelegant, but on it stands the familiar Palazzo Vecchio—powerful, fortlike, with a jutting band of galleried battlements and a tall off-center tower—pre-Renaissance and looking don't-give-a-damn about it. As a teenager, Sylvia's first gift from an admirer was a box of chocolates with a color cover of this exclamatory edifice. When she saw the real thing she stood squeezing her husband's arm: "I'm here, I'm really here!" A great moment.

It rose in 1299 as the government palace of the proud new

republic. Stone dust was still in the air when Dante took his seat of office. The last to be elected never sat in it; after three hundred years of tumult the despairing Florentines voted for a king —Jesus Christ. Instead, Duke Cosimo I, another Medici, moved in.

Statuary is strewn about the square as if by careless centuries. Moving from left to right as you face the palace, you begin with Cosimo I on a horse, by Giambologna, and have had enough by the time you get to Cellini's *Perseus* in the Loggia where the civic fathers of an earlier day watched the burning of Savonarola. Michelangelo's *David* is conspicuous on the palace steps.

No less conspicuous is the worst of Duke Cosimo's commissions—*Hercules and Cacus,* by Bandinelli. In his strutting autobiography Cellini tells Bandinelli in abrasive detail what he thinks of it: "If one were to shave the hair off your Hercules there would not be skull enough to hold his brain. . . . "

Soon after this lively encounter Cellini is firing his furnace to cast his *Perseus.* Suddenly he takes sick, goes to bed, prepares to die. He is gasping his last when a workman runs in: "Benvenuto! Your statue is spoiled!" With a yell, dying forgotten, the master leaps out of bed. He refires his furnace to such a heat that it blows its top. No matter! Let the roof go up in smoke. Let all Florence burn, only save the statue! But the molten metal seems too thin. He rounds up his household pewter and feeds it to the fire. The *Perseus* is saved. So is Benvenuto, who sits down to a hearty meal.

And there in the Loggia, a beanbag's toss from the brainless *Hercules–Cacus,* is Benvenuto Cellini's masterpiece incorporating his "porringers, platters and dishes to the number of two hundred."

When you look down on the old brown city from the tawny hills across the Arno, Florence seems afloat around the huge bubble of her cathedral's dome. But in her streets the city is flat and so tightly squeezed by walls long gone that you don't see the Piazza del Duomo until you're on it, stunned.

It's a small piazza for what it holds—an octagonal baptistery,

Giotto's beautiful bell tower, and an immense cathedral. Each is coated with marble in large geometrical designs marked off by contrasting horizontal stripes. The baptistery is white and black; the duomo (cathedral), white and dark green; the campanile, white, green, and red.

Huddled together they look like an architectural harlequinade.

When we first saw them we hadn't met Siena but we did know Pisa's glorious trio of baptistery, campanile, cathedral. Pisa's duomo was begun in 1063. Its sculptured bronze doors of 1180, by Bonanno Pisano, were the first of their kind in Europe.

Florence was laggard. In Bonanno's day her cathedral was the baptistery. In 1330 she decided the baptistery must have bronze doors. She sent for Andrea Pisano. In the six years of this Pisan's work on the first pair, followed by five years with the campanile (Giotto having died), Florentine artisans studied and worked under him. It was the school thus established that sent Florence into her meteoric career in the arts which lasted three hundred years.

There was no specialization then, not even the concept "artist" as it is known today. An *arte* was a guild. Many artists came out of the goldsmiths' guild. They could do anything from decorating dowry chests to painting frescoes. Botticelli painted trays and boxes, such as you buy in the city's market today. He also painted cloth with designs guaranteed not to fade.

Florence's cathedral is disappointing. It was begun in 1296, in the flush of republican pride that also built the government palace. Both money and pride ran out. Brunelleschi's dome, the first great dome of the Renaissance, wasn't finished until 1434, and not until the nineteenth century did this duomo get its marble suit.

Young Giuliano de' Medici was stabbed to death somewhere between door and altar, while his brother, Lorenzo the Magnificent, only just escaped by closing himself in the sacristy until help came. But there's no sign or hint of drama anywhere in the big church. The interior is blank.

There are many important churches in Florence but the beauty is out of town, high up on a hill. San Miniato, dating from 1018, is one of the loveliest of small churches. Its roof beams are gaily painted. Light shines pinkly through alabaster windows in its raised choir. Beautiful antique pillars support the vaulted crypt. The rich marble flooring, the Tabernacle of the Cross with its blue-and-white Luca della Robbia vault, and the tomb of the Cardinal of Portugal with its charming Madonna in medallion —these are so right that they seem to have grown up with the church.

All is light, cool, and clear—marbeloid, marble-inspired. Down below, in town, anything may lie behind a marble façade. Here the promise is fulfilled.

Grand Duke Cosimo I found both the Medici Palace and the Palazzo Vecchio too small. He had government offices (*uffizi*) built between the Palazzo and the Loggia. Then he took the Pitti Palace across the river for his home. The Ponte Vecchio, bridging the Arno, was the traditional precinct of the butchers. The fastidious duke ordered them replaced by jewelers. He also built a covered passageway connecting the Uffizi with the Pitti Palace. You can see it still, on one side of the bridge above the jewelry shops—a puzzling feature until you know what it is.

The Uffizi and the Pitti Palace are now among the world's greatest museums, storehouses of Medici art collections. Yet they're not the only great museums in this city. Smaller but very rich are the Accademia and the Bargello. Then there's the Cathedral Works Museum, and the art of the churches.

When your feet burn and eyes blear, think of the artists. There were, in the Great Age, more artists than subjects. (We counted seventy-eight Madonnas in the Uffizi alone.) You think you have a hard time just looking? Eavesdrop on a typical scene in Renaissance Florence.

A dispirited *maestro* comes home and sinks with a groan into his chair. His wife, feeding the baby, inquires placidly, "Trouble, dear?"

"Maria, for love of Heaven, get the brat out of my sight!"

"Giovanni!"

"Forgive me. It's only that the Frescobaldi are getting a new chapel and have ordered another Madonna and Child."

"Oh, no, not another! And in dead of winter!"

You may interrupt to protest that great canvasses are not painted in so negative a mood. Right. The story is not finished.

Brooding in the warm kitchen, Giovanni sips a reviving cup of wine. Suddenly he smites his head. "Maria!"

She half-turns, soup ladle in hand, the bambino astride her hip.

"Good. Shift our beautiful son a little—so. No, hold the ladle." He stares at her, groping for his tablet. "Maria, do you love me?"

"Ah, *caro mio!*"

"So." And watching her face with the lovelight on it, smiling to himself, the master sketches like mad.

They will call it the Madonna of the Ladle.

II

Siena is a handsome walled town of the Middle Ages. Making esthetic use of its three hills, it forms a composition as pleasing and surprising as its guileless paintings.

Main street is lined with palaces (Renaissance overlaid with Gothic) ornamented with slim pillars and arches. The prevailing tones are of orange-brown stone and red brick. The prevailing lines are curves.

The grand mansions rose in the thirteenth century when Siena was a city-state rivaling Florence and allied to Pisa. It rivaled Florence in turbulence too. Great families like the Tolomei and the Salimbeni hacked at each other with murderous vigor. Class rose against class. Factions splintered.

Through riots, revolts, and wars the arts flourished. Why? we wondered, as we stood on the piazza's rim nibbling carefully—so as not to lose any teeth—on that Sienese confection called truthfully *pan forte.*

For Siena created a civic masterpiece in its Piazza del Campo, which fills the deep hollow where the three hills flow together. It forms a vast scallop shell, like the one Botticelli's Venus floats on. It is "shell-paved" as well—the flutings of red brick, the ribs of white stone.

All its lines converge on the Palazzo Pubblico, the government palace. This bears a Tuscan family resemblance to Florence's Palazzo Vecchio but is older by ten years.

High on the wall of its Sala del Mappamondo the condottiere Guido Riccio da Fogliano rides in profile to the siege of Montemassi. Against a deep blue sky he and his steed move through a bare war-and-winter landscape from a miniature camp under a craggy hill to a miniature town on top of another craggy hill. Guido is young, with a full cheek, keen eye, aristocratic eyebrow. His voluminous surcoat is of a piece with the trappings of his horse—a rich orange cloth covered with a beautiful design of green leaves and black diamonds. The animal, through a hole in his costume (it covers even his ears), shows a lovely eye. The two are like a medieval fashion plate. At the same time they are heroic, invincible.

What was the siege of Montemassi? The one important thing about it was that Guido Riccio won it and Siena honored him in 1318 by having Simone Martini paint this wonderful fresco.

The same room displays a green-and-gold Maestà (Virgin in state) with angels and saints, also by Simone Martini. Here you meet the Byzantine-Sienese ladies of the almond eyes, shapely mouths, and long, boneless fingers.

The walls of the Sala della Pace display moralizing frescoes on "Good Government" and "Bad Government." They show a Siena older than the one we now know. People in medieval dress are going about their daily business under crowded towers and battlements, among narrow houses with overhangs of turrets, balconies, and eaves. Dante's Florence looked like this city of fortified tower houses. San Gimignano, near Siena, still survives as a town of tower houses. There was a time, it seems, when every man's home was literally his castle.

Siena's cathedral covers the highest mound of its tallest hill. We climbed, stopped to catch our breath, and stared. The offspring of a pink elephant and a zebra might well be more sober and credible than this marble duomo and its bell tower. The sides and the campanile wear horizontal black-and-white stripes. The façade, striped red and green, sports arches, triangles, medallions, mosaics, fancy pillars, three gables, two turrets, crunch-candy pinnacles, sculptured statues and animals, carved posies, and an angel. There's also a dome. The whole joyous fantasy stands on a stepped platform paved with geometric designs in colored marbles.

We had seen something like it. But where?

The interior too was vaguely familiar—light and spacious, richly furnished and decorated, flowing around black-and-white pillars and a sculptured frieze of popes' heads. For the superb pulpit, we were told, Siena had sent for Nicola Pisano to outdo what he had created for Pisa.

Pisa! That was where the inspiration had come from. All the same, Siena's cathedral is highly individual, showing off what Italy could do with Gothic. Unique is the marble floor incised with cartoons done by a collaboration of artists and marble-masons over a two-century period beginning in 1372. Our favorite is the sophisticated homily called "Fortune," featuring Lady Luck as a naked hussy balancing easily with one foot on the globe and the other on a boat.

There's a Cathedral Museum. Its prize possession is the altarpiece of Duccio di Buoninsegna, founding father of Sienese art. When he had finished the magnificent Maestà and the thirty-eight scenes from the life of Jesus, Siena proclaimed a holiday. The entire population escorted the altarpiece from workshop to cathedral. Church bells pealed. Trumpets sounded. People wept with joy.

That June 9, 1311, was a great day for Siena and everyone from Pisa to Florence must have known it.

III

Pisa is a sad, shabby city. Once it was a wealthy maritime republic. The sea, retreating, left it high and dry. Even its river looks unhappy; the fine old palaces along its banks were destroyed in World War II.

Plodding through dismal streets, you emerge from Via Santa Maria into the open. Here, on a groomed green meadow, stands the most glorious trio in Italy—in Europe:

The round marble-embroidered baptistery with breast-shaped dome;

The shining duomo with façade of colonnettes and a dome like an upended goblet filigreed all around the rim;

The campanile, rising in circular tiers of pillars and arches —dramatically, fearfully aslant.

Here they are, three variations in clearest marble on a decorative theme of colonnades inspired by the Levant, from which eleventh-century Pisan traders and plunderers brought back the inspiration for architectural poetry. Here too is the bizarre marble striping that excited Siena, Florence, and the rest of Tuscany.

The campanile is better known as the Leaning Tower. It brings four million tourists a year, most of whom glance at the other two colossal baubles and go straight to the tower, exclaiming in various tongues, "My, it does lean!" It dates from 1173 and until only yesterday people were permitted to climb up the top. Now the slant is so pronounced that pieces of marble are falling; you keep your distance with heart in mouth, waiting.

Alongside "the famous group which is without a rival on the earth" is a fourth wonder, the Camposanto. This "Holy Field," a cloistered cemetery, was created by literal-minded twelfth-century Christians who imported soil from Mount Calvary in fifty-three shiploads. The cloister's walls were frescoed. The frescoes were removed by a special process during the war and stored away from Goering's greedy eye. The removal resulted in an extraordinary find—the underlying cartoon sketches from which the artists worked. The cartoons as well as the frescoes have been restored and you can see, almost side by side, the preliminary sketches and the finished work.

NAPLES AND ENVIRONS

I

Naples—"See . . . and die!" To the modern ear no pronouncement of the local Cumaean Sibyl could be more ambiguous. A city of ambivalence, part slum, the rest chaos, tucked into an opulent natural setting. Visitors disagree about it with one another, and with themselves. Your own emotions are likely to run the gamut from disgust to enthusiasm, depending on the facet of its personality that happens to be up for judgment.

Built on a great curving bay and mounting the slopes of a line of hills, Naples forms an amphitheater of white houses on a green ground facing the blue Tyrrhenian Sea, a classic western reach of the Mediterranean. The air is as soft and languorous as a siren's lullaby. Palms, bougainvillea, and flowering trees grow where permitted, but permission is not readily granted. Naples tolerates nature.

To beat about no bush and mince no words: from a distance, from the sea, Naples is sublime, but close at hand—*mamma mia!* Yet the squalor, the chaos, are at least tempered and humanized by a million Neapolitans who represent the Italian species at its most vociferous, wily, cajoling, passionate, persistent, carefree, and warm-hearted. First and always a port, Naples is everyone's well-worn sweetheart, sharpening her wits on tourists while waiting to strip sailors down to their shorts.

Older than Rome, Naples *feels* older. It was an offshoot of Cumae, the first Greek settlement on the western mainland. In ancient times Via Roma, the main street, was the road to Rome. Down it came Augustus, Tiberius, and other Caesars en route to Capri, and wealthy patricians bound for a Floridian vacation in

Herculaneum before Vesuvius spat and extinguished it. Virgil loved the town, Lucullus owned a villa covering the offshore islet where medieval Castel dell'Ovo now dramatizes the view for the tourists of hotel row. This area at the ankle of the Italian boot has been a resort for two thousand years.

One doesn't descend on Naples for its own sake alone but for Capri, Vesuvius, Pompeii, the Phlegraean Fields, Ischia, the Amalfi Drive—and the National Museum.

Fed up with museums you may be, but this one you must visit, and if possible both before and after seeing Pompeii or Herculaneum. Much of the furniture and fixtures of those struck-dead towns is on view: wall paintings, statues, mosaics, jewelry, housewares. Unique is the extensive collection of murals taken from the walls of excavated houses. These paintings on themes mythological and from everyday life were the "wallpaper" of the ancients. Some are fresh and bright, some faded and scarred; some shine with artistry, yet even the amateurish, the downright bad, done for a household which hadn't the money to hire the best decorator, appealingly bring to life the first decades A.D. They reveal that keeping up with the neighbors is a time-worn anxiety.

Housed in a sixteenth-century palace, the museum is one of the richest in antiquities. Particularly in sculpture, in which department are many startling enlightenments, such as the bronzes with the painted eyes, the prevalence of fatty-feminine male nudes, and the weird Diana of Ephesus (Room 23, ground floor) in bronze and alabaster with breasts in festoon. This version of the old mother-goddess was the one known to St. Paul. For an idea of what he was up against, read Chapter 5 of Herbert Muller's *The Loom of History*.

Other objects not to be missed are the *Farnese Bull, Venus Callipyge* (Venus of the Buttocks), and in Room 31 the beautiful *Dancing Faun* and the *Drunken Silenus*.

The handsomest structure in Naples is the New Castle (Castelnuovo) on the Piazza del Municipio, dating from 1297, with a fine Renaissance archway between two massive round towers.

The midtown Galleria Umberto, a vast hall in the form of a plus sign, filled with shops and cafés, is everybody's rendezvous. A-cross the street stands the San Carlo Opera House, where the world's melodious throats still pour out song in the season. The red-and-gray structure adjoining, with façade and entrance around the corner, is the seventeenth-century National Palace. You can visit the "Historic Apartments." They remind you that from the Middle Ages to Garibaldi, Naples was capital of a kingdom ruled by a variety of foreign dynasties. Among its queens were a sister of Marie Antoinette and a sister of Napoleon. This palace succeeded the Castelnuovo as a royal residence.

Unless you have a special interest in churches you can rest content here with two. The Cathedral of San Gennaro enshrines the saint's blood, which liquefies on the first Saturday in May and on September 19—the city's most important holy days. The cloister of Santa Chiara is lovely on a sunny day when the vines overhead make shadow traceries on the walks, and the gay majolica tiles of benches and columns seem to bob in and out between sunlight and shade. For admittance, seek out a Franciscan in the church.

A Naples visit would be incomplete without some slumming up the narrow alleys off the Via Roma. Draped and bannered with the eternal family wash, twisting and climbing with rude steps and ramps, they swarm with life. The poor laugh, sing, and suffer in what look like caves—one-room, sometimes split-level, caves—bedrooms, dining rooms, and kitchen combined. The living room is the whole outdoors. The marvel is that they are kept fairly neat and clean.

There are three funiculars. From Piazza Montesanto goes the one for the Certosa di San Martino, a Carthusian monastery which is a many-sided museum interspersed with cloisters, and at its best in exhibits of local history. View from its belvedere.

To culture Naples has contributed pizza, "Funiculi-Funicula," and "Santa Lucia."

Traffic being heavy and driving irresponsible, the street sign on the Via Santa Lucia near hotel row is interesting as an invitation to suicide: "The pedestrian has the right of way."

II

The date is August 24, A.D. 79.

A smoky, gaseous pall hangs over the countryside, turning day into night, obscuring even the flaming mouth of Vesuvius. Some fearful ones have packed and left, some are getting ready, others have decided they can't get away. After all, there have been earthquakes before, but not within memory has the volcano hurt them. It will probably stain the heights with new lava streams and then subside.

Suddenly a tremendous explosion shakes heaven and earth. A torrential rain of hot ash and fiery pebbles floods Pompeii. A swollen river of lava rolls ponderously toward Herculaneum. The heavy rain that checks the outburst comes too late.

Sixteen hundred and thirty-two years later a peasant digging a well in his village of Resina struck his spade on carved marble, and Herculaneum was rediscovered. In 1748 canal-diggers nine miles away uncovered bronzes and sculptures: Pompeii. A wave of excitement swept over the world. Vesuvius had hermetically sealed two ancient towns from time and change. It had preserved life as lived, death as died, on that remote afternoon in August. Excavations are still under way.

Pompeii was a commercial town of 20,000. Herculaneum, with about 5,000, was patrician-residential—a Palm Beach to the other's Miami. Herculaneum's petrified mud makes digging very slow, and the live town of Resina on top of it keeps it in part inviolate. Pompeii's grave of friable ash and cinders has been easier to dig out. As a result, most visitors go to Pompeii.

The ideal procedure is to go on your own and wander about with a map and pocket guide. Drawbacks: the extent of the remains, the fact that the famous houses aren't clearly identified, and the further fact that many are locked, their custodians unaccountably absent. Doors open for the guided excursion.

The tourist in a hurry finds the guided excursion easiest, but it too has a drawback—the willy-nilly stop, a time-waster, at a coral "factory" en route. The factory we were forced to visit consisted of two "front men" in a corner cutting cameos. It was a large, well-stocked jewelry shop where everyone has to twiddle his thumbs so long as any of the party is buying. But eventually you arrive at Pompeii, where your guide will take you at a brisk pace across the broken forum (earthquake-damaged years before the eruption) and along the wheel-rutted, stone-paved streets and the high sidewalks with intersection stepping-stones, to two or three of the best houses.

One of them is the House of the Vettii, with its glowing murals—those Pompeiian reds and yellows! A local artist is usually on hand painting copies of the delightfully whimsical cherub friezes. They have inspired a great variety of interior decorations since their discovery.

The Vettii is one of the houses with naughty pictures: a painted phallic figure beside the door, and a small room with some frank wall sketches. The figure is shuttered, the room locked. The guide whispers that for a small tip to the custodian the men of the group will be shown these forbidden treasures. On our trip Sylvia inserted herself into the stag party; emerging unembarrassed and uncontaminated, she advises other women to do likewise, discreetly but firmly. Equal right. These days, what men know about sex, women do too. But really, what Pompeii has to show is as nothing compared to today's porno movies.

Excursion guides are inclined to be slapdash. You should be seeing, besides the Vettii, the House of the Faun, that of the Golden Cupids, the Centenary House, the Silver Wedding House, and Villa of the Mysteries. The good guide will explain shops and signs. He will translate election notices: "Thieves and drunkards support X." "Vote for Y, he won't squander public funds." And other remarks—*sgrafitti*—painted or chalked on walls inside or out, such as the one in a dining room: "Don't put your dirty feet on our couch covers."

You'll appreciate why a character in a play by Plautus complains: "All my neighbors are witnesses of what is going on in my house by looking through my *impluvium.*"

The bodies you see (only about five, including a dog's) are plaster casts made from tragically clear hollow impressions.

The Last Days of Pompeii, a Victorian best-seller by Bulwer-Lytton, is still very readable though not strictly accurate. Forty-six (or so) years after the Crucifixion Christianity had not made itself at home in these parts. Also no Roman, no Pompeiian, ever put the date A.D. 79 on a letter. Our calendar was not established until much later. (Remember the gag about the man who had found a coin dated 29 B.C.?)

If you want to see Herculaneum as well, do it on your own, or hire a guide at the entrance (rates are posted). It's only five miles from Naples on the Autostrada, fifteen minutes by train by Circumvesuviana Railway, departures every half-hour. And by bus from Piazza Garibaldi every fifteen minutes.

There's a half-day excursion to Vesuvius. A chairlift provides grand views as it swings you up. At the top, if the lava is on the boil, looking into the crater is hypnotizing. People have thrown themselves in. Don't.

Sorrento, Positano, and Amalfi are, respectively, thirty-two, thirty-seven, and forty-four miles south of the city. These charming outriders of Napoli are picturesquely crowded between high ground and the sea. They swarm with writers, artists, escapists —folk who know a good place when they see it and make it home until the curious come in droves and force prices up. The transition is now well under way, commercialism blooming. But the Amalfi coastal road drive is spectacular. There are buses and excursions, boats, trains.

III

Capri is only a rock of dolomitic limestone 3.75 miles long by 1.5 at its widest—but how beautiful! A luxuriously flowering rock. It rises in sheer cliffs from the clear blue water, its high point Monte Solaro at 1,930 feet. The harbor of Marina Grande is a bite in the rocky north shore. A funicular now saves you the climb to the main village, also called Capri.

On the south side, at the foot of a precipice, is Marina Piccola, a beach foothold reached by the most hairpin-ish of roads, ordered and paid for by Krupp, the armaments man.

The second village is Anacapri (Greek *ana* means "up") in a crease 400 feet above Capri-town.

Two famous novels are set on this island: Norman Douglas' *South Wind* and Axel Munthe's *Story of San Michele*. Munthe's Anacapri villa may be visited.

That setting, the riot of growing things, the pretty houses, the rocks, the sea far below, the views of the mainland with Vesuvius hunched against the sky, the semiresidential third sex, the tourists of all nations, the tourist-stalking islanders, the colors—all combine to make Theater. In spite of too many of one's own kind, sirocco, and commercialism, Capri triumphs.

The most famous sight is the Blue Grotto. It's a sea cave of a lovely luminous color, a living blue, not seen elsewhere. You enter in a tourist-laden boat, one of many so burdened. You are rowed or chugged around briefly amid ah's and oh's, giggles and wisecracks. A beautiful moment, spoiled. The Grotto demands to be experienced alone, or with good friends, and quietly.

Other sights are the ruins of the Villa Jovis, built by Tiberius; the Certosa of San Giacomo, a monastery; and the ruins of Barbarossa Castle. But every acre of Capri has its charms, from the daily operetta of Capri-town's piazza, inland and upland in all directions.

Ischia, a volcanic island nearer the mainland, is larger than Capri, less spectacular, less embowered, less legendary. It has come into notice with Capri's overpopularity. As usual, artists and writers fleeing the crowds discovered it, and the usual evolution took place. Among its endowments are pines, orange and lemon orchards, hot springs, sandy beaches, and six settlements.

IV

Immediately west of Naples lies the strange country of the Campi Flegrei. It takes in a wealthy suburb, a bay, hot springs, seaside resorts, blighting factories, Greek and Roman ruins, a sibylline cave, two entrances to Hades, and a hot spot where the planet is visibly cooking: Flaming Fields. It was the heartland of Magna Graecia, the Greek colony in Italy. Conquered by Rome, Greater Greece proceeded to civilize the conquerors, and the two in combination shone through the Dark Ages to recivilize Europe.

Uncanny country. A tumble, jumble of things in a small area covered in a half-day excursion. Yet, a region to which is owed more than one can ever know.

Pozzuoli-bound, you pass through Agnana, a spa endowed with seventy-five mineral springs. Pozzuoli in its lovely bay was an important port. Its Roman remains include a six-story Roman bath and an amphitheater that seated 40,000.

A short drive inland brings you to the hot spot called the Solfatara. You walk through a wasteland of what looks like coarse sand. Steams rises from it. Here and there the sand is boiling, bubbling. At its liveliest point this elemental wound in the earth's crust registers a fever of 711 degrees Fahrenheit.

You are actually walking in the crater of a volcano half-extinct—better, still threateningly alive. It stinks sulphurously. What with Vesuvius smoking on the eastern horizon, you have every reason to conclude that Naples and environs exist precariously on top of hell itself.

So thought the ancients. They located two water gates to Hades near by. One is the Mare Morto above Miseno across the bay, a lake occupying a crater. The other lies ahead.

You go on to Cumae on its scenic hill of vineyards. Or what is left of it. This first of Greek cities in South Italy, mother of Naples, was founded in the eighth century B.C., and endured until its partial destruction by the Saracens 1,700 years later was completed by daughter Naples in A.D. 1207. Only scanty remains are here of an acropolis, temples incorporated into Christian churches, a Roman arch, a bit of wall of the fifth century B.C.

The high point of a visit to Cumae is the cave of the Cumaean Sibyl, long searched for and undiscovered until the 1930s. It is a deep tunnel pierced with air vents, leading to the chamber where the sacred prophetess uttered her oracles. Of the ten sibyls in various parts of the Greek world, the Cumaean was the greatest. Aeneas consulted her, and with her help descended into the nether world to consult with his father's ghost, going on from there to found Rome. Romulus and Remus were swept under the rug when Roman imperial glory demanded a Hellenic ancestor. In due time Virgil settled the matter to everyone's satisfaction by writing the saga of Aeneas. It was also from a Cumaean Sibyl that Tarquin the Proud bought the Sibylline Books, the basis for the state's merging of Greek and Roman religions.

In this man-made hole in the ground of Cumae two worlds met and were knit together.

Just off the Cumae-Solfatara road glooms a body of water that looks like melted lead. It is the cratered Lake of Avernus by which Aeneas went below. "Avernus" became a synonym for Hades.

The bay's western side is dotted with seaside resorts once famous, now charmless, dreary with poverty. Baia was a favorite of the Romans. The ruins of a temple of Venus stand beside the road, ankle-deep in water.

You're returning to Naples now, and suspecting that in the interests of tourism we're going to ignore a hell more modern than Avernus and more spectacular than Solfatara. Some may evade but we prefer to tell the truth and shame the devil—in this case the Italsider Metal Works at Bagnoli, a steel plant defiling the air. "A flaming town of fire and iron," an Italian writes ecstatically, "with roads black with rubble and hills of dross and debris among which shunting trains and elevator-cranes move." He belongs to the school of endeavor which sees Italy's future in more and more industry. Italsider gives the poor 5,000 miserable jobs, its owners profits, and the sightseer a stab of homesickness for Pittsburgh or Gary.

Last stop is high-hill Posilipo, suburb of luxurious villas and apartment houses, the necessary complement to slums. The views are splendid. It was here that a well-dressed boy of fourteen, frank and open of countenance, got into talk with us about his ambitions to be a great surgeon. Suddenly we noticed his hair move. Lice were having a field day atop that boy!

A symbol of Naples?

SWITZERLAND

Curiouser and curiouser! There are two countries to which Alice in Wonderland's exclamation applies: Switzerland and the Netherlands. Each is more curious than the other. Holland exists because the Dutch shoved back the sea and fenced off sections of its bed to lie on. Switzerland exists because a medley of people shook hands across those colossal obstructions, the Alps, building a country on and around the marching, melting glaciers.

Where Coleridge's Ancient Mariner bored the Wedding Guest with croakings about water, water everywhere and not a drop to drink, the two little nations built solidly on the wet stuff. Holland turned water into land, Switzerland turned it into electricity.

Where the Dutch revealed their character and brawn by converting seabed into rich farmland, the Swiss bored 673 tunnels through mountain walls and conquered peaks and plateaus with vertical transport, often on heights where no reckless ibex would try for a hoofhold.

Of Holland, elsewhere. Look now at the tangle of people and mountains that make up a country without a common tongue, running smoothly on four official languages and many dialects.

Its national hero, William Tell, is a myth.

Its national cement is the negative principle, laid down by a hermit, of keeping out of European quarrels.

The four ethnic groups—German, French, Italian, and

Rhaetian—have nothing in common but the puzzling fact that they're all Swiss.

With only 5½ million citizens (about the population of Michigan) and no standing army, Switzerland is the headquarters of peace and tolerance in an abrasive world. Swiss founded the International Red Cross, whose banner shows the Swiss cross with colors (red and white) reversed. They are constantly on call to run delicate diplomatic errands for nations not on speaking terms.

The Swiss manage without a Pentagon, FBI, or CIA, investing security in a militia to which every able-bodied male between the ages of twenty and fifty belongs, from cowherd to bank president. For two weeks each year 650,000 do their military training, during the rest of the year keeping their weapons and equipment in shining readiness at home. What other nations trust their people that far?

The Confédération Helvétique lives comfortably in two economies, pastoral and industrial. Its cheeses, chocolate, watches, and machinery issue from smokeless factories. The landscape is awesome and idyllic by turns, and the Swiss keep it undefiled. Their towns and villages seem to have sprung from a covenant with nature, for theirs is the handsomest country in Europe. They have no Louvre, but they have created an art of living. Among its triumphs are the Oberland chalet and the *sgrafitto* house of the Grisons.

Even the young are civilized—a near-miracle at this end of the twentieth century. The first time two schoolboys in Bern jumped up to offer us their seats in a crowded bus we felt offended. Did we seem that decrepit?

In Zug, capital of its canton, we met an American businessman who had found his tax haven. Over lunch we asked him to define a Swiss. He gave it a moment's thought, and said, "A Swiss is a man who doesn't discard his cigaret butt in the urinal."

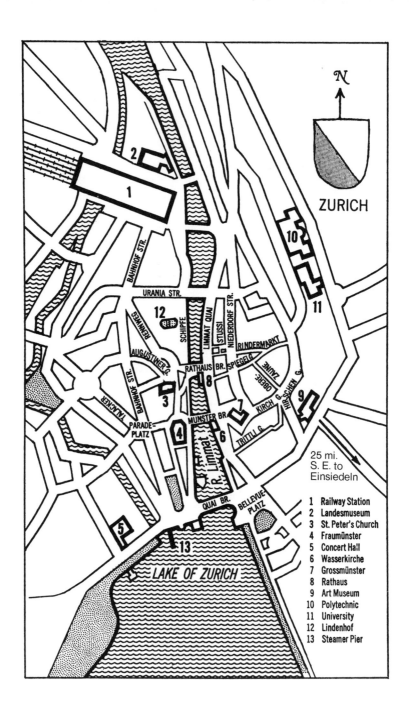

N

ZURICH

2

1

10

11

BAHNHOF STR.

URANIA STR.

12

SCHIPFE

LIMMAT QUAI

STUSSI

NIEDERDORF STR.

RENNWEG

RINDERMARKT

AUGUSTINER G.

RATHAUS BR.

SPIEGELG.

ZÄUNE

OBERE-

RATHAUS

BAHNHOF STR.

8

3

TALACKER

KIRCH G.

HIRSCHEN G.

9

7

PARADE-
PLATZ

MÜNSTER BR.

R. Limmat

6

TRITTLI G.

4

QUAI BR.

BELLEVUE
PLATZ

5

13

LAKE OF ZURICH

25 mi.
S. E. to
Einsiedeln

1   Railway Station
2   Landesmuseum
3   St. Peter's Church
4   Fraumünster
5   Concert Hall
6   Wasserkirche
7   Grossmünster
8   Rathaus
9   Art Museum
10 Polytechnic
11 University
12 Lindenhof
13 Steamer Pier

ZURICH AND AN ABBEY

A bishop of Norwich in England once wrote to a Swiss friend: "Even if only a dog came to me from Zurich I would hold him dear and never treat him like a dog."

To a Zurcher that's the right spirit. If you can't live in Zurich, the next best thing is to know what you are missing.

I

Zurich is Switzerland's metropolis—its largest and most prosperous city and its cultural capital. Handsomely modern, it has enough of the old to please the antiquarian. It is big enough to get lost in, but not too big for affection.

Basic anatomy: a river, a lake, and two hypnotic main streets.

Bahnhofstrasse, the modern main street, runs from the railway station (from which it gets its commonplace name) to the lake. Broad, linden shaded, and traversed by quiet baby-blue streetcars, this is one of Europe's grand shopping thoroughfares. Hotel concierges tell of tourists and wives of international financiers who do little in Zurich but walk up and down Bahnhofstrasse, absorbedly shopping the windows, or buying.

Lakeward the street begins to go dead, or at least anonymous, when the shops give out and the big banks take over. For Zurich is the financial capital not only of Switzerland but of Central Europe. We used to get a minor thrill out of entering one of these palaces of gelt to cash a $50 traveler's check, thereby making ourselves peers, in a way, of such as Onassis, the King of Saudi Arabia, and Thieu of South Vietnam. One day, perhaps, we will encounter a Gnome of Zurich.

Ruskin celebrated "the pale aquamarine crystal" of Zurich's lake. He was a romantic. Past the bank buildings, there's nothing to look at but a vast platter of wet stuff, faintly tinted. An excursion boat sits in it like a dumpling in thin gravy. Zurchers appreciate theatrical lakes like Luzern's and Thun's for visiting, "but you wouldn't want to *live* there!"

The city grew up along the river Limmat. Its riverside Limmat-quai is the main street of long ago. With gabled guildhouses, its own rows of shops, and the pepper-pot towers of the Grossmünster, it is the central strip of the Old Town, which lies on both sides of the linking Rathaus Bridge.

The Grossmünster dates from 1090, but not noticeably. Legend makes Charlemagne its founder. That is why he's sitting up there in the south tower, carved in stone. You can see him at close quarters in the crypt. Fifteenth-century, the original of the figure on the tower, he is crude and powerful, a grand old king and warrior. He holds a sword across his knees, wears a crown and curly beard. The protruding rusty nails that held him on his perch make him appear wrenched out of his proper century.

A different breed of warrior, Zwingli, preached the Reformation in this church, to make Zurich the first Protestant city in Switzerland.

Across the river stands the thirteenth-century Fraumünster (Lady Church), once part of a powerful conventual abbey. It has acquired windows by Marc Chagall. Its big square, the Münsterhof, is the one we like best in Zurich. An interesting polygon, it sets off two guildhouses, each the best of its period. The one with the wrought-iron gate and balconies is the Meise of the wine merchants, eighteenth-century and looking like a princeling's town house. The second, that broad-shouldered building all roof and windows, is the fifteenth-century Waage, or Weighhouse. All the guildhouses, with the exception of the Meise, have long been restaurants. Zurich likes to eat in style.

For urban explorers, the Old Town has secrets to be winkled out. Fairly easy to find are the cozy old Augustinergasse, St. Peter's of the big clock and deep-toned bell (rivaling London's Big Ben), the Weinplatz with its pretty fountain, and the Lindenhof, a park on a mound which once served a castle. But very few outlanders discover the curious riverside passageway called the Schipfe. Search for it at the Weinplatz.

The greater part of the Aldstadt slopes uphill from the Lim-matquai to the university, the Polytechnic, and the Kunsthaus (contemporary art shows of lively controversy). All those narrow openings between buildings on the quay are medieval lanes which lose themselves in others, become blind alleys, or open into unexpected squares. Niederdorf is the one fairly long street. It runs parallel to the quay, just above it, and once had a town gate. Road travelers came in that way, and Niederdorf was the street of taverns, singing, drinking, and brawling. It still is. There are a few drunks even in the morning, but it's an interesting street.

Stüssihofstatt, where you see the Königsstuhl's jutting oriel, forms a tilted square at Niederdorf. Here stands the city's one painted fountain, the Venner, a knight with a dog between his legs, facing a shop showing a gilded angel's head and the date 1599. On the corner the angled Haus zum Wind says, with wall writing, that it belonged to the Stüssi family, 1382–1462.

Farther up, Rindermarkt opens suddenly with (on the right) Leuengasse—a slit between bulging old walls held apart by an overhead buttress. Jerk that buttress away, and crash!

Narrow Spiegelgasse shoots in from the side. No. 14 is marked with a plaque. Lenin was living there with his wife Krupskaya when news came of the Russian Revolution. It was from Zurich's Bahnhof that he left in 1917 in the historic sealed train. On the platform milled pro-Bolsheviks and anti's, carrying slogans and shouting "Long live!" or "Death to!" As the train pulled out, the two groups began to mix it and the police moved in.

James Joyce lived in Zurich working on *Ulysses,* but he has no plaque; he moved at least three times. His framed photograph is over his table at the Kronenhalle restaurant, where he liked to sit drinking his (and our) favorite Swiss wine, Fendant de Sion.

The newest exile is the Russian poet and back-to-the-soil prophet Solzhenitsyn.

Among the notables Zurich has housed, we like best a memory of Albert Einstein, mathematician, physicist, professor at the university. At the Bahnhof one day he put down 20 francs for a ticket which cost 19 francs 25 centimes. "Give me twenty-five centimes," said the ticket man. "But I've already given you more than enough," Einstein protested. "Look," said the ticket man patiently, "you give me twenty-five centimes and I give you back one whole franc. *Nicht wahr?*" Einstein thought this over carefully. His face lit up. "*Gott,* how simple!"

II

Switzerland has some unabashedly gorgeous expressions of ecclesiastical Baroque. One is only twenty-five miles from Zurich—the Benedictine abbey of Einsiedeln, which has been drawing pilgrims for more than a thousand years.

We came by train and followed a group of monks, who greeted newly arrived pilgrims with a "kissing" of the crosses they carried. The town, which owes its existence to the abbey, climbs a long hill. We climbed with it. Abruptly, there was no street, no town. Out of sheer surprise we stopped short. We were at the edge of a vast open square. On it, and reaching down into it with a terrace, a graceful stairway, balustrades, crescent arcades, and a fountain, stood the church and abbey of Einsiedeln.

The perspective is so artful that with each step the pilgrims made toward the church, they receded from us by much more. Their progress was a dwindling. Meanwhile the church, between its twin towers and the long wings of its monastery, seemed to grow. When the last pilgrim, a toylike figure, was swallowed up by the church, we felt we had witnessed a performance.

Five times in its long history the abbey suffered destruction. This is the sixth on the site. It was built between 1705 and 1770, a period of superb harmony and lightness of heart.

It is astonishing to find such sophisticated beauty in a small, undistinguished Swiss town. "Amidst a savage scene of woods and mountains," wrote Gibbon, who was here in 1755, "a palace appears to have been erected by magic." The woods have been thinned but the "palace" is as magical as ever. The fine-grained stone gleams as though polished. All is grace and elegance.

The interior is an explosion of joy and caprice. It is white and gold, except for the deep reds of the paintings in the vaulting. The lacy wrought-iron choir screen is like a garden trellis. All around are airy balconies, plump cherubs leaning casually over space, athletically soaring angels, and a giddy wealth of decorative stucco. This church positively gambols in its adoration of a black Madonna.

More Baroque? St. Gall's cathedral and its monastic library are famous. That library is so beautiful it can make your heart ache.

BERN AND THE ALPS

I

The enchantment begins with a bong.

To be exact—as one should with a clock—it begins three minutes before the hour. That's when the figures on the Zytglogge come to life. The rooster crows and flaps its wings. The jester jiggles himself and his bell. Diminutive armed bears march out on parade. Father Time inverts his hourglass. A golden lion waggles his head. High up in the belfry, the shining bronze Duke of Zähringen bongs the hours.

The spectators sigh contentedly and scatter. Until three minutes to the next hour, the longest continuous show on earth is over. It was set off in 1530 when a journeyman blacksmith hand-made its cogwheels, pulleys and weights inside the tower.

With its performing clock, arcades, beguiling fountains, and its air of sedate good humor, Bern is the most delightful small capital in Europe.

We have lived regally at the Bellevue Palace, feeling remote from stern life; steeply below us, the swift green water of the Aar and on the distant sky the luminous Oberland peaks. We have lived more soberly in an apartment down by the river, neighbors

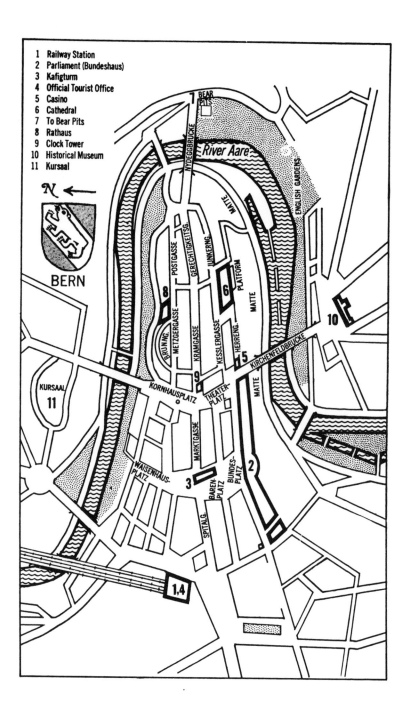

1 Railway Station
2 Parliament (Bundeshaus)
3 Kafigturm
4 Official Tourist Office
5 Casino
6 Cathedral
7 To Bear Pits
8 Rathaus
9 Clock Tower
10 Historical Museum
11 Kursaal

N

BERN

River Aare

BEAR PITS

NYDEGGBRUCKE

ENGLISH GARDENS

MATTE

POSTGASSE

GERECHTIGKEITSG.

JUNKERNG.

PLATFORM

MATTE

BRUNNG.

METZGERGASSE

KRAMGASSE

KESSLERGASSE

HERRENG.

KIRCHENFELDBRUCKE

MATTE

KORNHAUSPLATZ

THEATER-PLATZ

KURSAAL

MARKTGASSE

WAISENHAUS-PLATZ

BAREN-PLATZ

BUNDES-PLATZ

SPITALG.

8

6

9

5

10

11

3

2

1,4

7

to the woodland zoo. We've lived in an Oberland chalet with blue lake and white mountains in our windows—and Bern's proximity cherished like a homely fire.

"For rebirth," we once remarked to a Zurcher, "the place we would choose is Bern." Pierced to the heart of his complacency, he cried, "But you would be Mutzen!"

Legend says that when Berchtold of Zähringen founded this city in 1191, he decided to name it after the first animal he caught when out hunting. It was a bear. Familiarly called Mutz, a red-tongued black bear marches upward and onward along a diagonal yellow stripe on the city's shield and banner. He has a fountain to himself, and his cubs enliven other fountains. He decorates shop windows, cakes, and chocolates. Live bears have been kept in a public enclosure since at least 1441.

To other Swiss the Bernese themselves are Mutzen. You're told they are slow and lumbering, that they feel, act, and are bears as far as humanly possible. Fun is poked at them. "Don't tell a joke to a Bernese on Friday, or he'll burst out laughing in church on Sunday."

Mutzen or not, the Bernese feel a kinship with the ancient Romans. Theirs was a city-state sternly and shrewdly ruled. Less than a century after Berchtold they flung off feudalism and established a burgher oligarchy. It lasted six hundred years, became rigid and tyrannical, but left a tradition of zealous civic housekeeping.

The town is laid out in gridiron plan on a promontory defended not only by its clifflike height but by the fleet Aar, which makes a hairpin turn around its base. This tongue of land is cut into clean strips by four beautiful streets of arcades that form intimate shopping promenades under tall stone houses built to a fifteenth-century plan. They run the long way, or east to west. The Clock Tower was a gateway in Bern's first wall. The next hop to the west is marked by the Käfigturm (Prison Tower), and the third is bounded by the railway station. Bern moved west with architectural harmony.

On the street sides the arcades have benches and slanted cellar doors. The cellars are out in the open because of a decree to circumvent smuggling. Nobody was permitted an interior cellar door. Some of the deep roomy vaults are now little theaters. Scarlet geraniums march in window boxes along the white stone. Here and there stands a folk-tale sort of fountain, brightly painted and gilded. When the medieval banners of guilds and cantons dress these streets on the frequent festive occasions, you feel as costumed as they are, citizen of a happier century.

Bern's famous fountains are the ones featuring stone-carved figures on a decorated column. There are eleven of these and twenty others. Each of the eleven is a distinctive work of burgher civic art—as a collection, the best in Europe.

The first you're likely to see is the Zähringen Fountain on Kramgasse, which commemorates Bern's founding by raising on its pedestal Sir Mutz, in chain mail and helmet with visor, bearing a heraldic shield and banner. The fountain, the houses on each side with their buttressed arcades, and the Zytglogge form Bern's most photographed ensemble.

The child-eating Ogre is the most original of these sixteenth-century carvings. Justice, and Samson being very unkind to a lion, are stock figures but brilliantly done. The Bagpiper (we challenge you to say its German name of *Dudelsackpfeiferbrunnen*) has a livelier brother in Basel, but that one is said to have been designed by the great Holbein. The Messenger and graceful Anna Seiler are recent copies; you can see their originals in the Historical Museum. Then there's the Archer, the Musketeer, the Venner, and Moses.

By the time you've located them all, you know Bern—a little.

In the realm of statuary, however, there's nothing more captivating than the William Tell in the Historical Museum (that imitation chateau you see from Parliament Terrace, across Kirchenfeld Bridge). He's a sixteenth-century life-size archer, lean, muscular, cocky. He wears a parti-colored cantonal uniform, red, yellow, and black. He's sighting along his crossbow, one eye closed. Across the room, on chubby legs, stands his little son with a bright red apple on his head. "Come on, Pop, shoot!"

The museum displays guild treasures, mementos of the patrician past, period rooms, costumes, and the glorious booty won from Burgundy's Charles the Bold, beaten at Murten in 1476.

In 1405, Bern went up in flames and was rebuilt in stone. By now the Bernese knew their fresh, righteous strength. "God," they said, "has become a citizen of Bern." They built their houses with fortlike simplicity, but their new cathedral was to be worthy of the First Citizen.

The elaborate late-Gothic style caused a lot of controversy. Above the aristocratic door on the Kirchgasse side the architect slyly carved "Machs na"—meaning "Just you try to do as well!"

Over the main portal a Last Judgment is in lively progress. Saved souls in nightgowns are looking smug while the naked damned are being forked into hell by devils. A Bernese will show you the Lord Mayor of Zurich in hell, and in heaven the Lord Mayor of Bern. Within it are fifteenth-century windows, sixteenth-century stalls, and painted bosses.

Behind the church you find another of Bern's unique features. The Minster Platform is a gardened promenade, shored up by a tremendous wall rising from the riverside Matte. Two hundred years ago an English traveler excitedly reported, "This terrace, for its elegancy, has been compared to the terrace built by Solomon near his temple."

The Matte, sheer below, was a rip-roaring little port for river rafts that once traded far and wide. It retains some old streets with wooden arcades. Look sharp when strolling along upper Bern's southernmost arcades, and you glimpse tantalizing passages to stairs or lanes plunging down to the Matte. The Fricktreppe on Herrengasse is the one to take. You can come up without labor in the Minster Platform's nineteenth-century elevator, a ride of 99 feet in 45 seconds of the kind Solomon never knew.

Farther west along the river is the Marzili sector, where the riverside is trimmed into a park with public swimming pool, and the lower suburbs begin. It too has a nineteenth-century link to the upper town—the Marzili funicular, which carries you 120 yards in 90 seconds to (or from) Parliament Terrace. This terrace is still another of Bern's amenities, a grand landscaped balcony with views.

The Bundeshaus or Federal Parliament was built in the architecturally uninspired mid-nineteenth century, but in it assemble the Swiss House and Senate, and its Cabinet ministers. Their halls are worth visiting, speaking as they do of a small, brave, independent, and highly successful democracy.

The daily market is held on Bärenplatz, a long square extending from the Bundesplatz to the Prison Tower. Tuesday and Saturday are the big days, but country Mutz is no longer distinguishable from city Mutz.

To the east, at the tip of the promontory, Nydegg Bridge crosses the river to the bear pits, a major stop on the city bus tours. You lean over the wall and watch the antics in the double enclosure below. In one pit are the adult bears, expert in shameless begging tricks. In the other are the cubs.

There were seven cubs when we last visited, chasing one another, tumbling, wrestling, climbing. People of all nations packed the railing, laughing as freely as children. "Come on, Joe," begged an American wife. "The bus is waiting, everyone's on but us." "It's a good life," sighed Joe, blowing his nose and wiping away tears of laughter. Then, "To hell with the tour. You go on. See you at the hotel."

II

The sublime Alps shout "*Machs na!*" at the world from "Between-lakes," their dormitory town.

Interlaken consists primarily of one long street, the Höheweg, between the lakes of Brienz and Thun. Along it are hotels and a broad meadow which has been heroically saved by the community from speculators. Behind the hotels our friend the river Aar slips quietly by on its way to Bern. It begins in a glacier up there in the frozen white sea and will finally lose its name in the Rhine.

You stroll on the Höheweg and look at a macrocosmic stage-set, obligingly formed by nature. Across the meadow the foothills fall away to form a proscenium for the great peaks. The maidenly Jungfrau dominates. Her rugged courtiers are the Eiger, Schreckhorn, Mönch, and Wetterhorn.

Of the three ways to get here from Bern, the best is by train to Thun, thence by lake boat. The Thunersee, with its villas, chalets, and farmhouses on gardened shores, its castled towns of Thun, Spiez, and Oberhofen, and the snow-crested mountains piling up as you near Interlaken, is surpassed in beauty only by the Lake of Luzern.

Not to be missed (unless you have height ailments) is the train trip up the Jungfrau from Interlaken's Ost station to the Joch or Saddle at 11,333 feet. The line ascends by way of the Lauterbrunnen valley and returns via Grindelwald. By the time your day draws to a close you will have an excellent nodding acquaintance with Europe's most spectacular topography.

"No earthly object that I have seen," wrote Leslie Stephen, the English mountaineer, "approaches in grandeur to the stupendous mountain wall whose battlements overhang in midair the villages of Lauterbrunnen and Grindelwald."

Where he climbed tooth and nail, you ride in comfort and with some astonishment at the notion and achievement of running a railway into the high, hostile otherworld of glaciers. The terminus is at the end of a five-mile tunnel cut into Mönch and Jungfrau rock. A lift carries you to the Hotel Berghaus and civilization's welcome gadgetry. A passage in the mountain leads to the Ice Palace, sparkling chambers scooped out of the bowels of a glacier and embellished with ice carvings. That you are deep within eternal ice would be an intolerably awesome thought if it weren't for the Disneyland effect.

Scattered mountain villages—Grindelwald, Mürren, Wengen—where life was hard and simple a century ago, are now world-famous resorts. Their permanent populations are still reckoned in hundreds, but mid-winter and mid-summer they swell in population density to thousands. They are beautifully situated and equipped with a variety of lifts in response to man's curious counter-urges to climb and to slide.

While we were watching the awkward squad at first lessons on Grindelwald's nursery slopes, a tot of four or five Alpine winters tore past on baby skis, fetching the groceries in a rucksack to Mutti. Twelve heads swiveled in unison and envy.

A Wengen ski guide told us he had begun skiing at the age of three, on barrel staves.

LUZERN AND ITS LAKE

I

Like Zurich and Geneva, Luzern grew up along a river moated by a lake. Its setting is a superb apposition of the gentle and the savage. It spreads over both banks of the Reuss under soft hills and rugged mountains, dominated on the west by moody Pilatus. To the east rises the softer Rigi, and between these the clifflike promontory of Bürgenstock.

The leaping landscape performs on the lake's still waters. The city serenely keeps on the river's green tide.

On a ship returning from the adventurous round of the lake, everyone lines the rail to watch the towers, spires, and red roofs come up out of the water as the distance lazily narrows and the sky comes down. Luzern looks quite Venetian then. It is, however, medieval and Germanic. (That's why we stick with the German *Luzern* instead of the French *Lucerne*.)

A city wall forms a romantic skyline spaced by nine towers. This, along with the two roofed wooden bridges, are Luzern's indelible imprints.

The bridges are remarkable. The Kapellbrücke was built in 1333 as a fighting bridge. Spanning the river diagonally and with a zigzag, it is guarded at the zig by the octagonal Water Tower that gets on postcards. The interior—it seems odd to speak of a bridge having an interior—is decorated by seventeenth-century paintings of local history, set into triangular spandrels. The less theatrical Spreuerbrücke has paintings of the Dance of Death.

It is as imperative to visit the Lion of Luzern as to scale the Rigi. The Lion was designed by Thorvaldsen (1821) and best described by Mark Twain:

"The Lion lies in his lair in the perpendicular face of a low cliff—for he is carved from the living rock of the cliff. His size is colossal, his attitude is noble. . . . The place is a sheltered reposeful woodland nook, remote from noise and stir and confusion —and all this is fitting, for lions do die in such places, and not on granite pedestals in public squares."

The monument commemorates the Swiss Guards massacred in Paris during the French Revolution. It is still greatly moving, but no longer reposeful. The proximity of the Glacier Garden makes this corner of Luzern exceptionally touristy.

In 1872 a man was digging a new cellar when he unearthed an extraordinary pothole in rock bottom. Three years of excavation uncovered eleven glacier mills—deep cavities formed by stones whirled by the waters under a glacier. Each contains the boulder that scooped it out—a kind of nature-made mortar and pestle. (Trümmelbach in the Lauterbrunnen valley takes you right to the process; it's a glacial churning and outpouring within self-formed caverns.)

On the Löwenplatz, the stop for the Lion and Glacier Garden, a photographer was doing a brisk business with a huge sleepy St. Bernard for prop. A sightseeing bus pulled up. Last man out was a tour-tired boy of about nine who stood transfixed, staring at the St. Bernard in unbelief and adoration. The great dog came to life. With no apology to the client with whom he was being photographed, he shouldered his way through the adults and presented a giant paw. On the child's face, as he took the paw in both hands, dawned a look of sheerest ecstasy. None of the other sights, not even the Lion, could compare with this one.

II

Despite Victor Hugo's assertion, "The lake of Luzern resembles an eagle's crushed foot," that lovely body of water has no describable shape. From the south, at Flüelen, the Reuss flows in and manages to work its way to Luzern at the north. Meanwhile the land goes its own way—scalloped and shredded, bosomy and serrated. Some of it has snow on top, some is bare rock, but most of it is green. Everywhere, on improbable footholds, are resort villages.

We were idling in Luzern. All around, tourists were rushing off, returning in the evening tired but with the replete look of the tiger with the lady inside.

One afternoon we talked things over.

"Remember how we did those four English cathedral towns in one day?"

The other winced.

"But we felt good about it. We felt we Belonged."

"Umm."

"After that we could look any tourist in the eye, let him tell his paltry story, and then say modestly, 'How nice. Now this is what *we* did.' Remember?"

"Umm."

"Suppose we see how many places we can polish off in one day around the lake."

"Why?"

"Let's do it tomorrow. Just this once."

We pored over timetables.

We were shrilled out of slumber in the middle of the night—6 A.M.—and staggered to our balcony. The sky was blue, the east gold. The sun, struggling to get up, was going to succeed. The waiter arrived with beaming approval and our breakfast.

Lv Luzern   7:15

Arr Weggis   7:50

The steamer pulled out on the dot, carrying a mixed bag of nationals. Everyone, even the elderly British couple, looked bright and eager. We began to wake up. The air, unquestionably, was like wine—a good year. The water was blue-green, the steamer white, the red roofs rose on skirts and humps of moving shores. Tribschen, the villa where Wagner once composed, living luxuriously in sin with his best friend's wife, was dreaming among its poplars.

We all waved to another boat on our left that turned off for Küssnacht, an eastern arm of the lake. It was in the Hollow Way near Küssnacht that William Tell, hiding in ambush, dealt the tyrant Gessler his fatal arrow. And above stand the ruins of Gessler's castle. From Luzern the length-of-lake trip spells out the Tell story in reverse. It began at the other end, at Altdorf beyond Flüelen.

Our boat paused at Hertenstein to drop a Swiss couple. Queen Victoria slept here. After World War I the same hotel put up the Austrian Emperor Charles—last of the Hapsburg monarchs, sheltering in the land on which his dynasty had visited so much misery. The Swiss placed a memorial to him on the promenade. A forgiving people.

We disembarked nine minutes later at Weggis, one of the lake's most popular resorts. Its season begins early, ends late. The mild climate sends to Luzern its first spring vegetables. Weggis when we arrived was in the throes of an athletic tournament. We had coffee and a couple of sustaining *Gipfeln* on a hotel terrace, watched some flannel-trousered gymnasts warming up, and then the next boat was at the landing on schedule.

Lv Weggis   8:57

Arr Vitznau   9:14

Vitznau is home base for the Rigi funicular.

The Rigi is not as Old Man Mountainish as Pilatus, but bulky enough. Mark Twain and "Harris" (the Rev. Joe Twitchell) did it on foot at such a pace that the boy they hired to carry their coats demanded permission to go on ahead. "I'd like to get to the top while I'm young." The intending visitor cheats himself if he doesn't read the Swiss chapters of *A Tramp Abroad.* Also, Appendix D on "The Awful German Language." They're among the funniest pieces ever written.

Rigi's was Europe's first cogwheel railway. When the inventor, Niklaus Riggenbach, sought financial backing, people said he was crazy. Then the United States built much the same kind of railway up Mount Washington. On news of this, a banker tipped his hat to

Niklaus and hinted that in the matter of a loan . . . The inaugural trip took place in 1871.

Lv Vitznau Terminus   9:40
Arr Rigi Kulm (5,900 ft.)   10:16

No sooner was the boat moored than everybody poured out and headed for the red carriages of the waiting funicular. From Vitznau's church came a wedding party with its own band, and our ascent was accompanied by Sousa.

Whether the first or twentieth pitched ride up a mountain, it's a thrill. The low land falls away, becomes compressed; the air thins, becomes pure, cool, cold. The seats being so slanted that you sit normally, the mountains, the houses, every tree and blade of grass lean crazily.

Wild flowers star the slopes. Crocuses appear. Then snow. At first it looks sad, as if it wanted to melt but couldn't. Then it firms and thickens, puts caps and gowns on houses, forms fanciful drifts, becomes solid, unrelenting, blinding. A white world.

The summit! Everybody out! We stay put. We watch the wedding party making the short climb to the successor of Mark Twain's hotel. The band is floundering in the drifts. The young folk walk sedately. The boisterous elders throw snowballs. Down comes, half-sliding, a party of Americans. Rosy, laughing, they settle into the carriages. In winter the world below is a sea of clouds, while up here you gambol in sun above that wool.

The descent is even happier than the ascent. The glaring white world slowly recedes. Ah, the blessed relief, the joy, of green, of colors, of thickening air, earth-scented. Woods there are, and trails, and hikers singing. The panorama breaks into its component parts, the lake and low land rise to meet us.

And here we are where we started from, suddenly balanced and prosaic. But we have lived. We can say, "We did the Rigi. . . ."

Lv Vitznau   11:55
Arr Flüelen   14:15

The boat glides through a strait formed by two arms of land called the Noses. It's like a doorway into another room, the second third of the lake. We cross to touch at Buochs and Beckenried, then cross again to Gersau—another resort village, Rigi-sheltered, and with beach.

For half a thousand years Gersau was a republic of six square miles, Europe's smallest. It was sold to the Hapsburgs. The villagers saved their pennies and eventually bought back their freedom.

Tiny Gersau, fiercely independent, aroused the ire of big Luzern. Luzerners made a night raid and hung a straw man on Gersau's gallows—a sneer at the republic's claim to the right to try its own. The Gersauers responded by clothing the scarecrow in Luzern colors. The Luzerners flew into a rage and prepared to invade. Confederation counselors saved the day by delivering judgment: Gersau to remove the colors, Luzern to remove the straw corpse.

Gersau, once you scratch its surface, is full of stories. This one is probably of Luzern origin. That onion-bulb church held a silver bell. When Napoleon invaded Switzerland the Gersauers decided to hide the bell. But where? The lake, of course. A solemn procession of boats, led by the town fathers and the clergy, rowed to the middle of the lake and lowered the bell. But how to know where exactly it lay so that they could bring it up again? Easy. They marked the bow of the leading boat with an X.

We met similar stories in Brazil and Morocco. In the Moorish version, Zh'ha, the Moslem Peck's Bad Boy, goes fishing with a friend. Their catch is bountiful. Preparing to row home, the friend says, "Zh'ha, we must come back another day and catch more."

"Ah, but how will we find the same spot?"

"I know. We'll mark the boat." He leans over the side and chalks a big X on the bow.

Zh'ha says not a word but inwardly he laughs. "What a fool Mustapha is! How can he be sure that next time we'll be able to rent the same boat?"

Gersau now belongs to the Canton Schwyz.

Now our boat goes through another "doorway," the narrows between Treib and Brunnen, entering the Urnersee—Part III of Lake Luzern. The mountains look forbidding. The lake can be rough when the Föhn blows, as it blew for William Tell. An English party on the afterdeck stops singing. A chattering French group falls silent for the first time since embarking.

On the near shore rises a wall of bare rock, terribly wracked, twisted, striated. Geologic melodrama was enacted here. Along the cliff runs the Axenstrasse (the mountain is the Axenberg), that famous six-mile stretch of road blasted out of solid rock, showing open-windowed tunnels through which cars are moving like toys. It is a nineteenth-century engineering feat.

The engineer slows the boat as we pass a tooth of rock sticking up out of the water, inscribed (in translation) "To the Poet F. Schiller—the Original Cantons, 1859." The year before he died, Schiller, who never set foot in Switzerland, wrote its greatest piece of publicity, his drama of William Tell. Rossini, who did the opera based on it, deserves a little something, a rock of his own. Who hasn't been captivated by that Overture as a youngster, and been driven almost crazy by it as an adult?

This "Lake of Uri" is the inner sanctum of Swiss history and legend. We cross to the landing stage for the Rütli, a meadow in the woods where leaders of the three Forest Cantons met in 1307 to swear the Oath. It is to the Swiss what the meadow of Runnymede is to the English—the hallowed cradle of liberty.

Over now to the east shore, to Sisicon, a name among mountain-climbers, a training center for rock work. Veterans of the Swiss Alpine Club tune up here before tackling the really hazardous precipices.

And now Tellsplatte, where William, in the storm-tossed boat carrying him to Gessler's dungeons, escaped from his captors. The commemorative chapel has patriotic paintings.

We come finally to Flüelen, end of the water road—a long, quiet village with a handsome church poised on a hill. A bus is waiting.

Lv Flüelen   14:23
Arr Altdorf   14:31

Altdorf is the capital of the Canton of Uri. In the main square stands the statue of a burly, bearded Tell with a crossbow over his shoulder and an arm around his son, who walks beside him. The two are ambling through the mountains—represented by a chromo landscape painted on a square red-and-mustard tower behind them. (Men of Uri! Are you blind? Do something about this! Go look at the William Tell in Bern's Historical Museum!)

On this square was enacted the opening scene of the story. Here the great archer, having refused to bow to Gessler's hat, which the tyrant had hung on a pole, was commanded to shoot an apple from his son's head.

Everyone knows about William Tell and the apple; even the Communists love the story. In Budapest doctors had to warn the state TV director against repeating a thirteen-part serial on William Tell because wild-shooting little Hungarian Tells had sent twenty-five "sons" to the hospital for emergency head and eye operations. And Moscow's satiric magazine *Krokodil* mocked shortages with a Tell cartoon showing on the boy's head a sign, "No apples."

Many are the fictions so dear to people that they are cherished and nursed into pseudo-fact. In Verona you are shown Juliet's tomb and Romeo's house. In Tobago, Robinson Crusoe's cave. In Denmark, Hamlet's castle. In Henry Ford's synthetic colonial village, the wool of Mary's little lamb. But nowhere is there a legend so scenically documented as W. Tell's.

Misguided tower apart, Altdorf is an attractive little capital strung along a waggling main street with some eighteenth-century houses and inns. Good ironwork shows in overhanging signs—the Goldene Schlüssli's gilded key, the Schwarzer Löwen's swarthy lion standing with tail up and tongue out in a gilded floral frame—and in the older memorials in the terraced, gardened cemetery. A wooded mountain rises over the cemetery and there, above the serene graves, cows graze, clanking their bells. But most of Altdorf is quite new, having been rebuilt after a devastating fire in 1799.

Henry James was here, pausing on his way to Italy. He worked it into a short story, "At Isella," in which he writes of looking through gates at gardens and houses of patrician families—"longing plaintively, in the manner of traveling Americans, for a few stray crumbs from the native social board."

Now, if he had not aimed so high, and been content to look in at Hauger's—

On the tiny square near the old hospital we stop to admire the modern stone frieze above Hauger's bakery. It depicts the story of bread from the planting of the seed to the meal in the peasant's cottage. Then with noses pressed to the window we study the oddly shaped cakes and breads.

A white-and-pink maiden peers at us from behind them, and beckons us in. She identifies the Urner *Pastetli* with raisins, the big square Birnbrot, the even larger Maisbrot. Herr Hauger emerges from the back. We praise his frieze and he says the Haugers have been baking here for generations.

The white-and-pink maiden has been storing buns and pastries in a flowered paper bag. This she now offers us with a smile like a dollop of whipped cream. While we try to shape up a combined thanks and rejection, Papa Hauger comes forward with two family-size bars of chocolate. "No, no!" we cry, but it's no use.

This is Switzerland, where they keep trying to give you a piece of their country. And they thank you and wrap it in colored paper, and put a silken string around it, and tie a loop in *that* for you to carry it away dangling from your finger.

Lv Altdorf   15:56

Arr Brunnen   17:00

Luzernwards sails the white ship. We get off at Brunnen, the port for Schwyz and, after Luzern, the chief lake resort. The Axenstrasse begins here. Just across the narrows stands the fantastically decorated Boatman's House of Treib, a tavern much picture-postcarded.

Wagner's patron, mad King Ludwig of Bavaria, loved Brunnen. He'd row across towards Rütli and between the cliffs where the echoes really give, blow his 20-foot alphorn—a boy in a tunnel. And the people of Brunnen would wag their heads and say, "That Ludwig!"

We have only six minutes before the bus leaves for Schwyz. No regrets, Brunnen is mostly hotels.

Lv Brunnen 17:06

Arr Schwyz 17:26

The bus loaded with housewives, shopping baskets, and children deposits us in the Hauptplatz. In this little capital of the tiny canton that gave Switzerland its name and flag, 10,000 Schwyzers enjoy a glorious situation. On one side the two dramatic crags called the Mythen, on the other a chain of snow-clad peaks. Between the buildings, glimpses of orchards and flower-sprinkled meadows.

All this is visible right from the center of town. This enveloping beauty is your first impression. Your second may be that you have stepped into an operetta.

They have a Rathaus all painted with pictures. On top sits a diminutive bell tower which on this chesty building is like a brute of a husband putting on his wife's bonnet for laughs. They have a fountain, and the knight on it is knock-kneed. Dotted about are the small but stately mansions of the old peasant patriciate. A costumed chorus should dance, yodeling, out of the wings.

A burly man in a velvet jacket with embroidery does come down the Rathaus steps. He subjects the square to a leisurely survey. He scratches his head, tilting his hat with feather over one ear, and takes his long curved pipe out of the middle of his beard. Will he break into song? No. He walks to a tiny car, squeezes his bulk into it, and drives off out of the play.

They have a fussy church—Baroque. Entirely apart is a late-Gothic chapel with an upstairs and downstairs. The story goes that Schwyz and the Abbot of Einsiedeln had a dust-up. In consequence the Pope forbade mass to be celebrated "on the soil" of the canton. The Schwyzers dug a basement and went to mass *under* the soil.

Upstairs being locked and the tourist office gone home, we contented ourselves with the vaulted downstairs and its three grim skull-and-crossbones montages and Dance of Death windows.

The setting includes a twelfth-century tower with museum, and the Wysses Rössli, leading hotel and restaurant, with balcony on the square.

Schwyz is so quiet you can hear the sun purring.

To the Hapsburgs the Schwyzers were the most bristling, bellicose, and barbarous of the mountain men, and they seized with glee upon the name, which sounds close to the German for "sweat." They made it a term of contempt. Under the sting of this epithet the cantons fought so furiously that they ennobled the name. Six hundred years later the last Hapsburg was reduced to seeking asylum in a village eight miles away.

Lv Schwyz   19:15
Arr Luzern   20:02

We bus to the railway station of Seewen (Schwyz hasn't one of its own) in seven minutes. The train ride to Luzern is by way of Arth-Goldau, a main junction. We arrive in time for a leisurely wash-and-brush-up before dinner.

The *maître-d'* visits our table. For him we list our accomplishments. "*Voilà*, Fritz, we have polished off:

> One three-part lake
> One mountain
> Three lake resorts
> Two cantonal capitals—

between breakfast and dinner, using for locomotion—

> Taxi
> Lake steamers
> Mountain railway
> Bus
> Train."

"Ah, c'est brave, ça!" says Fritz.

Not only are we feeling *brave,* but our favorite dish, gnocchi, is on the menu. Our cup is—yes, wine, please—full. We have pushed Sisyphus' boulder to the top of an Alp and cocked a snook at the gods.

We return the smiles and opening gambits of the newly arrived Americans at the next table. Casually we put the question, "And did you have a good day?"

The husband gets out an itinerary that he unrolls like a scroll. The wife leafs through her leather-bound Travel Diary. The old gentleman extracts from his pockets envelopes of snapshots evidently made by one of those clever cameras with built-in laboratory.

"We left Geneva this morning, mopped up Lausanne, Montreux—"

"And the Castle of Chillon, dear—"

"Then—let's see—Aigle, the Diablerets, a Col-something mountain pass, Gstaad—"

"We met a real duke at Gstaad," the wife interjects, and the old gentleman hands us a ducal portrait.

"Spiez, Interlaken, a look at the Jungfrau, then over the Brünig Pass—and here we are!"

"And what did *you* do," the wife asks kindly.

Sylvia says, "We went up the Rigi, and—"

No use. They wear the glazed look of people who aren't listening. We hand back the duke. We could tell them how the ruling Prince of Liechtenstein gave us tea in his castle of Vaduz. But they are pushing back their chairs, getting up. "So nice meeting you. We're off for Zurich, Salzburg, and Vienna in the morning."

Lawrence fires a belated parting shot. "Well, you never got off the picture-postcard route, did you?"

SION

The Simplon Express tore shrieking through the Rhone valley, the Swiss Valais, like a demented thing. Orchards, vineyards, and villages flashed by. Mountains wheeled against the sky, their foothills rising and falling. Suddenly a rocky mound reared up like a petrified wave with crenellated crest. Advancing, it turned to present a sheer wall, man-made at the summit, slit with vigilant eyes. We sat up with a jolt. For an instant the towering fortress filled our window, looking as if it meant to annihilate our frenzied metal snake with a spit of flame. Then it was gone.

"What was that?" Out with the map.

"Sion?"

"On our way back we must certainly—"

We did.

There's nothing Swiss about Sion, capital and chief town of the Valais. Its ambiance struck us as Latin American semi-populated, half-forgotten. Side streets shabby. Gardens random. Weather hot and dry. It wouldn't have surprised us to see a crumbling adobe wall and an Otomi Indian riding a burro. People stared at us as they had in Tulcán and Arequipa. Our hotel reminded us of one in Managua. We had the same strange effect on the staff, who would spring up from siesta attitudes when we walked into the lobby.

And as in those strange hot countries between Mexico and Peru, there is power in Sion—the power to haunt.

A medieval plan leaps out. Three strong points—Tourbillon and Valère on rocky summits, and under them a fortified foothill, called the Majorie. A bisecting river. An encircling city wall, gone now except for the Sorcerers' Tower, a crooked thing of oddly wavering lines and roofs like witches' hats. A tower is a tower is a tower—but not in Sion.

Nor is a castle a castle.

When we climbed Valère to see the castle that had stared down at our train so menacingly, what we found was a church.

Sion had been an ecclesiastical stronghold and Valère its fortified cathedral. In the fifteenth century a new cathedral was built down in the city, leaving Valère bereft of title but still in use as a church and fort until the end of the eighteenth century.

It's a stiffish climb from the main stem, the Rue du Grand Pont. By car you can drive about three-quarters of the way. Entrance to the fortress is through a tower pierced by an outer and an inner gate, and up a ramp to a third gate, usually closed. Ring for the caretaker.

You're on top of the rock, in the courtyard of the castled church. Many people once lived here, protected by walls and warrior bishops. The living quarters of the guards and canons house a cantonal museum with Gallo-Roman bronzes and a re-markable collection of Romanesque carved coffers.

Now for the church itself.

Who ever heard of a church with a mill? This church has one, and also an arsenal—a chamber where molten lead was poured to make shot. Mill and arsenal are accessible from the nave. There are other rooms too (the caretaker lives in them) and there used to be many more—granary, kitchen, smithy, armory, stables— everything necessary for castle housekeeping.

The church proper combines Romanesque of the eleventh or twelfth century and Gothic of the thirteenth. It is surprisingly large, well-lighted, and lofty. On the capitals of the Romanesque columns, birds, beasts, and strange heads look out from luxuriant foliage, as if carved by a homesick Mayan. One of them has a weird horizontal man who ends in a snaky tail. Another depicts Jonah with his head in the mouth of—not a whale but a dragon, and the beast is too small for the swallowing job. We know it is Jonah because the museum's curator told us.

Everything has a touch of the primitive, naive and bold. There is much to see—frescoes, paintings, carved choir stalls, a fourteenth-century marble Virgin with Child (and apple), painted tombs, and Byzantine silks which were discovered in a cavity under the stone floor. And there's a fifteenth-century organ. Only Spain has an older organ, but it no longer works, said the curator. This one still does.

But see us in the church of Valère—

It is full of the soughing-whistling of winds outside, and we sheltered as if in Noah's Ark, riding high above the world. We have the honor of being escorted by the curator, a gentleman and a scholar who has served us coffee and liqueurs in his Louis Quinze living room, and now describes what we are seeing in polished, academic French. His voice is insistent, his manners are exquisite. We hope we are making our polite responses at the right places—which we take to be when his finely arched eyebrows go up. We fall a phrase behind. He looks distressed. We try harder. No good; we have fallen a full paragraph in the rear. We give up pretending and drift within Jonah's dragon, Noah's whale. He drifts with us, forlorn.

And suddenly a great swell of music lifts us up, carries us through vast pillared spaces, sets us lightly, gently, down. The organ is playing, the oldest organ in the world.

We look at our scholar, and he at us, across the barrier of language. He has done this for us—whistled to the winds, whistled up the organist? He nods, this fine-grained gentleman, and the glowing smile on his face is with us still, illuminating a strange and wonderful church on a rock in the Valais.

THE NETHERLANDS

Holland (properly, The Netherlands) is approximately the size of Maryland plus adjacent Delaware, with a population of nearly 12 million. All its western region and part of its northern is sprinkled with lakes and crisscrossed by canals and rivers. This area, best known to the traveler, is so flat as to seem concave and to have a disproportionate amount of sky. In the east, on the German and Belgian borders, one finds another Holland, of moors, forests, and above all, hills.

The Dutch are a small nation whose strength of character has given them important roles in history—and what is more important to the visitor, makes them a people interesting to know. For 600 years they have been creating their own country by fencing the ocean here and there, pumping the water out, then diking their new land. The process, which still goes on in the IJsselmeer in the north and the Walcheren district in the south, gives them the right to proclaim, "On the seventh day the Lord rested, but we carried on."

Thus, a considerable area of western Holland along the coast is below sea level, in some parts as much as 20 feet below. Amsterdam's Schiphol Airport is 12½ feet "netherland." The Dutch sense of humor, nearly always on tap, bids a man to suggest that if he dug a hole two feet deep in his garden he could establish a record for distance below the sea in his neighborhood.

Until the end of World War II the Dutch owned a piece of the planet several hundred times the homeland's size—the Dutch East Indies, now the Indonesian Republic. The loss of these rich colonies was a severe setback for the Dutch. Yet they could joke about it. When a fat hausfrau boarded the crowded platform of an Amsterdam streetcar, the conductor bawled out, "Madam, look out for your overseas possessions!"

There was a time, not long ago, when the sun never set on the Dutch flag. Now all that's left is Surinam in South America and some small islands in the Caribbean. Still, Dutch experts go to all parts of the world dredging and building harbors and, on call, putting their thumbs in other nations' dikes. And Dutch shipping makes Rotterdam and Amsterdam spectacular ports.

Yet the ideal of this world-horizon people is a trim little house set in a flower garden. Their domestic sport is an outing on the lakes and lagoons. Their magic word is *gezellig*—comfortable, homelike, cozy.

The Hollander is noted for bluntness in a business deal. But this directness, we have observed, seems to come from a desire to get it over with, the important business being general talk and sociability over beer or gin.

In this great little nation living on "repossessed" land, about ninety percent of the population speaks another language besides Dutch. The second language is likely to be English. Amsterdamers claim that nine out of ten of their citizens speak English; if so, this is a higher percentage than New York can claim.

Dutch is an engaging member of the Germanic family of languages. Like Swiss-German, it dotes on diminutives. The aa's, oo's, and ee's look like baby talk. There is a double vowel, "ij," pronounced "eye." And as the little girl remarked to her parents, "You know, I think 'het' is better than 'the'."

If in any street you hear the metallic siren's voice of the hurdy-gurdy, seek it out. It will be a gorgeous white-and-pink creation with gilt trimming, about the size of a grand piano up-ended on wheels. Like the Pied Piper it gathers dancing children. Parents lean out of windows. Pedestrians and cyclists stop to watch and smile and remember how, when they were little . . .

You will sooner or later wonder why so many narrow houses, especially in Amsterdam, have two doors side by side, taking up a good part of the ground floor. One of those doors may well be blind; it is there as a status symbol, from the days of the separate servants' entrance. Then you may see an apartment building with, absurdly, ten or twelve front doors. The explanation is either an overweening sense of decorum or a skeptical view of human morals. For what struck the Dutch when the multiple-family dwelling entered their lives was the easy access between apartments. To guard against the violation of a certain commandment, every household had to have its own door and lock.

On the other hand, where other people close themselves in against the street, the Dutch like to have their living rooms on display, curtains open and lights on at night until bedtime.

Certain eating habits are interesting. The Dutch are a herring people the way New Englanders are a codfish people and the English of East Anglia oyster-mad. At awninged herring-stands your true Hollander, for the pause that refreshes, dangles a herring above his mouth, dispatching it in the manner of a seal at the zoo. For daintier feeders the attendant cuts the herring into morsels and serves it in a bowl with chopped onion and an oversize toothpick. Best herring-time is April–May but the fish remains consumable until well into September.

The *broodjeswinkels* are (as you can easily translate) sandwich corners. Holland is one of the few countries where an honest pancake may still be had at various *eethuisjes* (eat-housies), and no nonsense of being served flapjacks or griddle cakes.

If you're lucky enough to have a boat-owning friend or business acquaintance, you may see a side of life important to the Hollander in summer. North of The Hague, among the polders, lies a labyrinth of canals and lakes, with Wassenaar as the vacation capital. Moving his family to a waterside cottage, hotel, or house-boat, Papa commutes between it and the office in town. Every family seems to own a boat or two, motor or sail, tub or sleek craft. It's a carefree communal life on the water under the widest of skies. You see a sail moving on a parallel course but apparently on dry land; you deposit the bridge toll in a wooden shoe swung at pole's end by the keeper; you pull up alongside a barge to buy fruit or flowers. You fish, you swim. Happiness is a Hollander on the water.

For local color there's no place like Amsterdam. On the broad terrace of the American Hotel we wrote duty letters home, while Piet, the garrulous waiter, stood by. Our last envelope sealed and stamped, Piet seized the lot and before you could snap out "Scheveningen" was in the thick of traffic in apparent pursuit of a streetcar. He ambled back to us.

"But what did you do with the letters?"

"The letters, they are already on the way to America."

"By tram?"

"Ja-ja, first step of the journey. That tram, you understand, goes by the post office, where a postman empties the letter box attached to the rear."

As Einstein remarked in Zurich on a different occasion, "But how simple!"

AMSTERDAM AND ENVIRONS

I

When you come by plane, west wind on its tail, it makes a sweep and lays out before your eyes the Venice of the North, a city spread over seventy-five islets within a cobweb of canals, at its base the larger waters of the IJ (pronounced "eye"), carrying ships, the North Sea Canal, and the islanded railway station.

As the plane loses altitude the midtown plan looms large. It is an open fan on the IJ harbor with a clearly defined nub into which the Amstel River penetrates from the side like a misplaced fan stick. The main canals are ranged in parallel semicircles around the nub, and everything is neatly woven together like basketry by streets and radial canals.

Another dip and turn, and Amsterdam rushes up with

thousands of brick houses, tall, narrow, gabled. They slide together in a jumble of steep roofs, glinting windows, shining strips
of water. You land at Schiphol, the airport built on the bed of an
extinguished lake.

An airport on a lake bed, a railway station on a handmade
island, a harbor lower than the sea—whether you come by air,
rail, or water, your introduction to Amsterdam is a novelty.
In some neighborhoods the North Sea is 14 feet higher than a
six-footer's head. A Mokumer will add that when the man steps
into a hole it will be 15 feet. The houses rest on a forest of piles,
some sunk 80 feet deep. The Royal Palace on the Dam sits on
13,659 of them emplaced in 1650. A while ago engineers dug up a
few at random, tested them, and put them back. Good for
perhaps another century.

The improbable city began as a settlement of fishermen in
marshes and peat bogs between the Zuyder Zee and the North
Sea at the junction of two rivers, the Amstel and the IJ. A wetter
spot on the globe would have been hard to find. In the 1200s,
either with vision or the determination to keep their feet dry, they
built a sea wall and with it a dam so remarkable that they became
known as the people of the Amstel Dam. When they had enough
of a town to be named, it was their dam that named it.

Atop the dam they laid out their main square. It is still called,
simply, the Dam.

The seventeenth was Holland's golden century, with Amsterdam the financial capital and richest city of Europe. Among the
far-flung trading posts founded in that time are two of the most
exotic places we have ever seen: Willemstad on the island of
Curaçao and Paramaribo in Surinam—Dutch communities in
the tropics half a world away from the Zuyder Zee. New Amsterdam may have looked somewhat like them before the English took it over as New York. Its lingering Dutchness led to
Washington Irving's Father Knickerbocker, and is recalled in
many a place and family name: the Bowery, Brooklyn, Harlem,
the Catskills, the New Jersey Oranges, Nassau, Van Rensselaer,
Vanderbilt, Roosevelt.

Old Amsterdam had long been fixed upon its platform between Amstel and IJ. Its outer limit was formed by a band of water from the controlled Amstel. This band was the Singel Canal, a water-street and moat backed by fortifications. With prosperity and a pressing population, the little port began to ripple out.

Through the years when the Dutch were winning the empire they have since lost, and challenging England's sea supremacy, Amsterdam built the crescent canals of Herengracht, Keizersgracht, Prinsengracht. With the all-embracing sinuous Singelgracht (not to be confused with that primary Singel), the Golden Century was over. It left an urban patter that Europe marveled at, and rows of mellowing houses.

"Mokum" is the Amsterdamer's pet name for his city. No Mokumer we consulted could explain what it meant, but its emotional content is powerful. In Mokum they would understand the cry wrung from the heart of Schnozzle Durante when he sighted home sweet home from the transatlantic plane: "Ah, Brooklyn, me Mudderland!"

The Amsterdamer is a distinctive breed of Dutchman. He is impudent, direct, more curious than his cat, and by turns contentious and tolerant. Pretensions he cannot abide. He has a vast contempt for gimmicks and *kitsch* and a weakness for quirks and eccentricity.

In Mokum the quality most prized is *gein,* or *geintje,* which has no English equivalent. It's a special humor bequeathed, they say, by the Jewish element, and is part of everyday give and take, much as in New York. Customer: "What makes it so expensive?" Shopkeeper: "The price." It must be friendly, interested, innocently confiding.

Who but a Mokumer would call a lowly stew (what the French and Spaniards would denominate "rotten pot") *sjopje-handele-mendele*—Chopin-Handel-Mendelssohn? Or irreverently christen seven churches: the Coal Bucket, the Parrot, the Bathhouse, the Sugar Box, the Incinerator, Sing Sing, and Our Dear Lord in the Attic.

Other Dutchmen are approachable but the Mokumer is more likely to do the approaching and, when he does, may take you home for dinner. Then you will learn the meaning of the word *gezelligheid*: a mixture of homemade comfort and human warmth.

Within the fan between the IJ and the Singelgracht lies most of what is worth seeing. The right first action is the boat ride. The "*Rondvaart*" lasts an hour and a quarter, navigating the most picturesque canals and invading the IJ for a look at the shipping.

For walks, the best canals are the famous inner four: Singel, Heren, Keizers, Prinsen; and the radial Reguliersgracht and Spiegelgracht. These *grachten* have the choicest *bomen, bruggen,* and *gevels,* i.e., trees, bridges, gables. The daily flower market is on barges in the Singel.

You will be puzzled by houses that lean forward. It's not that, being old, they're tired. They were built so, at a 2.5 slant from the perpendicular for every vertical meter, to save windows from risk of damage when merchandise was hoisted to the attic warehouse, or piano to the second-floor parlor. These were the homes of wealthy merchants, and many are now offices. About six thousand of the seventeenth-century houses are now protected from destruction.

But why so narrow? Because taxes were assessed on frontage, and no Mokumer would pay out more stivers in taxes than necessary, even if he had to build stairs as narrow as ships' ladders. Some stairways had a rope instead of a banister.

For an idea of how the merchant aristocracy lived, visit the Willet-Holthuysen Museum at 605 Herengracht, a furnished seventeenth-century patrician mansion.

On some bridges you'll see a hooked pole striped red and white. This is for hauling hats, balls, even people out of the canals. The absent-minded, the drunk, and children occasionally fall in —about two hundred a year. Police cars carry dry garments for such emergencies.

Opposite the railway station, on the quay, squats a small, round medieval tower, the Schreierstoren. Here the wives, children, and sweethearts of sailors wept as they waved goodbye to their men departing on, perhaps, a two-year voyage to the Orient. In 1609 they waved to the *Halve Maen* (Half Moon) captained by an English navigator in Dutch service. Sent to find the Northwest

Passage to the Indies, he found Manhattan Island instead and the river that bears his name, the Hudson.

The Royal Palace on the big, busy, unhandsome Dam began as a town hall. It is only a nominal palace. Royalty doesn't live there but comes for only a few days each year to keep Amsterdam happy in its nominal title of capital of the Netherlands acquired during the Napoleonic occupation. Hollanders always explain that Amsterdam is their capital but the Hague is the seat of the government. They leave it to you to make sense of this.

Two once-secret places reflect very different historic periods, one of them too close for the heart's peace. This is the Anne Frank House at Prinsengracht 263. Here eight Jews lived in hiding for two years until the Gestapo hunted them out in 1944. Otto Frank, the only one to survive, saved his younger daughter's diary, World War II's most human document. An international foundation preserves the house. You are shown the movable bookcase and taken up the tortuous stairway it concealed to the pitiful rooms above where two families lived on from day to fearful day, and where Anne wrote, "I still believe that people are really good at heart."

The second shrine is "Our Dear Lord in the Attic" on Oude Zijds Voorburgwal 40. In the 1600s, when Catholics were barely tolerated in this Protestant city, they were still permitted to worship privately. On this old street owners of three adjoining houses removed walls in their attics to make a chamber roomy enough for 200 clandestine worshipers. The curious three-attic church and one of the houses are preserved with their seventeenth-century furnishings. They form the Amstelkring Museum.

Amsterdam is inseparable from Rembrandt, from his paintings in the Rijksmuseum and his house (Jodenbreestraat 4-6) on the edge of the old Jewish quarter, his favorite neighborhood. A couple of blocks farther along the street is the fine seventeenth-century Portuguese Synagogue, from whose congregation a

young man named Baruch Spinoza was excommunicated at
about the time of Rembrandt's bankruptcy.

Rembrandt (1606–1669) was twenty-five when he came to the
big city, son of a miller of Leiden. He began his career with *The
Anatomy Lesson of Dr. Nicolaas Tulp,* a group portrait commissioned by the doctor. It was acclaimed. Orders poured in.
Rembrandt and Amsterdam appeared to be embarking on a
love affair like that of Rubens and Antwerp.

What happened? *The Night Watch.*

This was another group painting, done for a militia company.
Rembrandt had twenty-nine men to put on canvas. He got them
all in, but many are in shadow or blurred and others show little
more than an arm, hat, and shoulders. Everyone had paid his
share and posed in his best finery. They were furious. Moreover,
it was a strange painting. To many the darkness, the use of
browns, was repellent. Just as bad was the suggestion of action to
people accustomed to clear, static statements on canvas.

It was called *The Night Watch* in derision, and it ruined Rembrandt.

The Rijksmuseum resembles the railway station, and in fact
had the same bilious architect. But it owns the world's richest
collection of Dutch paintings, an abundance of glowing, vivid
masterpieces and of those gems rated minor works by the mys-
terious process that establishes great, greater, greatest. The head-
liners are Rembrandt, Hals, Vermeer.

Everyone makes for *The Night Watch*—just follow the crowd.
Another of Rembrandt's group portraits, *The Syndics of the
Drapers' Hall,* painted twenty years later, is the only other work
of this kind for which he managed to get an order. He gave the
six directors of the Cloth Merchants' Guild their money's worth.

In the 1960s two of this bankrupt's paintings came on the
market. One sold for $2,235,000, the other for $2,300,000.

Hard by the Rijksmuseum are two more—the sensational Van
Gogh Museum, which opened in 1972, and the Stedelijk, given
over to twentieth-century art.

II

As the Sunday sightseers crowded aboard the Volendam-Marken excursion boat, our Mokum friend muttered *"Kitsch."* Yet he himself took us there. Phony or corny they may be, but tourists and natives as well make the pleasant trip.

Volendam is a fishing village on the IJsselmeer and a Catholic enclave in Protestant territory. Its old livelihood came from catching and smoking eels. Sunday is visiting day because that is when the people dress for church, the men in their baggy britches, tall fur hats, and silver-buckled shoes, the women in billowy black skirts with striped aprons, and starched white lace caps. *Kitsch?* The eelers have their own private contempt for city folks, and a little for their neighbors whose fishing is for the tourist trade.

Marken was an island until 1957, when causeways attached it to dry Holland. Markenaars long ago left off fishing to devote themselves wholly to tourists. The argument about what is phony-folksy indicts Marken more than Volendam.

It is a village of tiny crooked streets with wooden houses painted black and white or blue and white. The men wear the baggy bloomer and round cap; the women, doll-like skirts and colored lace caps, their yellow hair in long ropes but with a stiff square fringe on the forehead. Up to the age of six the boys are dressed in skirts. Everyone wears wooden shoes. Centuries of inbreeding have produced some freaks and subnormals.

You are invited into homes. A tip is expected, and you give without pain because the interiors are worth seeing. They are painted blue or yellow and decorated with delft-blue tiles and plates. Copper and brass shine. The wall beds are curtained with hand embroidered linen.

III

Non-*kitsch* is Alkmaar, Holland's leading cheese market. The time to go is any Friday morning from May through September.

By rail there's a Cheese Express from Amsterdam and another from Rotterdam. As many Dutch as other nationals fill these specials.

"Wifelje, I have tomorrow off. What'll we do with it?"

"Oh, Piet, it's Friday! Let's take the children to Alkmaar and lunch in Haarlem."

"Great idje! Where's my camera?"

The cheeses, red or golden cannonballs, are set out in rows on the big square by the Weighhouse. Buyers walk about, hefting, sniffing, sampling. A slap of hands clinches a deal.

As each lot is sold the cheese porters spring into action. They belong to an ancient guild of four companies. All wear white, but each company sports a different color of straw hat, and their "sledges" are colored too. Having loaded a sledge, two porters harness themselves to it, one fore, one aft, and carry it to the Weighhouse scales. The weighing is done in public with a tally-man calling out the weight and registering it on a blackboard.

The porters then reload and carry their sledges to the buyer's truck or barge. In the final scenes the cannonballs are whizzing through the air, thrown swiftly to the vehicle, and you'd better not get in the way of a flying 4.4-pound globe of viscous-rigid cheese.

From Waaghuis Tower a carillon signals "Market Over," and strikes twelve with knightly automata. The view from the tower takes in not only the town and its canal pattern, but flower fields, dunes, the North Sea, and here and there a windmill. The foreground is dominated by the roofs of the fifteenth-century Groote Kerk and the medieval Town Hall.

IV

Haarlem, a mere twelve miles west of Amsterdam, is Holland's tulip capital. Its major event is the spring tulip show, climaxed by the Flower Fair.

Its more permanent attraction is the Groote Markt, the distinguished main square. On it stand the fifteenth-century Groote

Kerk, the many-centuried (it began with the thirteenth) Town Hall, the seventeenth-century Frans Hals Museum, and the Renaissance Vleeshal.

The most striking of these buildings is the Vleeshal (literally Flesh Hall), the Butchers' Guildhall, for its fancy stepped gables. Go round to the side for the full effect.

The Hals Museum was originally an *Oudemannenhuis,* and it is thought Frans himself was living there at age eighty-four when he painted the group portraits of the *Gentlemen Regents* and *Lady Regents.* These are black-and-silvery, very different from his brilliantly colored *Archers of St. George,* painted when he was thirty-six. Like Rembrandt, Hals died in poverty, but through his own improvidence, not in unmerited disgrace. Haarlem had awarded him a pension which he squandered.

The Groote Kerk of St. Bavo is Holland's grandest, remarkable for its length and height, cedarwood vaulting, the carving of choir stalls and screen, the organ, and ships' models. The ships are copies of the original models presented by the Dutch-Swedish Trading Company in the 1640s. The organ was immediately famous for its size, beauty, and tone when built in 1738. Young Mozart was proud to play on it, and today's organists are no less proud to compete here for an international prize.

The Flower Fields begin about three miles south of Haarlem and roll on for ten magical miles. In March the 30,000 acres begin to bloom: crocuses first, then narcissus, next hyacinth and tulips, followed by irises, carnations, gladiolas. Within the Fields, at Lisse, are the 62-acre Keukenhof Gardens, where the floral scene is at its loveliest.

Aalsmeer, eleven miles from either Haarlem or Amsterdam, is the greenhouse market, supplying cut flowers to florists at home and abroad. Between 8 A.M. and noon it holds public flower auctions on a canal (summer) or in two auction halls. The canal affair is the more Dutch. You sit in a stand, canalside. Bidders, each with a button at his desk, sit beside the bridge under which the flower-heaped barges float. Each barge stops under the great central dial on the bridge. A sample bouquet or two is handed the auctioneer. Bidding is by push-button; the dial's needle registers the price in Dutch pennies of a single flower of the bouquet. That lot sold, the barge floats on to discharge at the warehouse as the next barge drifts up to the bridge.

The open markets of Alkmaar, Aalsmeer, and Gouda, with bids and prices openly arrived at, mean that here big business gets along well with old burgher traditions of honesty, as against *Caveat Emptor*.

THE HAGUE AND DELFT

I

"The pleasantest village in Europe," wrote George Gascoigne, English poet and adventurer, describing The Hague of 1575. Built around a chateau of the Counts of Holland, it was a favorite summer retreat of noblemen who came for the good hunting in the forest. Its name is shortened from 's Gravenhage, the Count's Woods.

It became the national capital through an accident of weather which pains Mokum schoolchildren when they learn of it.

The summer of 1581 was so hot in Amsterdam that William the Silent and the delegates of the States General he had convened moved to The Hague. It was this body that proclaimed the break with Spain and founded a new nation on the astonishing principle that when a head of state fails his people it is their duty to revolt. Some years later the Pilgrims came to nearby Leiden; they took off from there for America, where their descendants acted on this principle against George III.

Today The Hague is a village still (of 600,000 inhabitants) because it has no town charter. The old patrician retreat is now its downtown and the forest is a woodsy park. Leisured and dignified, aloof from its swollen urban body, the heart of The Hague sets the tone of a sedate capital.

In the middle is the Binnenhof, the old chateau, on a placid lagoon called the Wijver which once encircled it as a moat. From the thirteenth to the nineteenth centuries it developed into the complex of buildings you see today, housing the Parliament and various administrative bodies.

The oldest part is the Knights' Hall (Ridderzaal), which with its two towers and rose window looks like a church. It was here that William and the States General sat when they fled the heat wave. It was their Independence Hall. Now it is the throne room where the sovereign opens Parliament in September.

The Hague's best building is the Mauritshuis, home of the Royal Museum of Art. It was the seventeenth-century mansion of a count of Nassau-Siegen, first governor of Dutch Guiana in Brazil. He was nicknamed The Brazilian, his house the Sugar Palace from the source of his wealth. It is early "classical Dutch," a mingling of cozily domestic and noble-formal, perfect of its kind.

The superb collection of 400 paintings includes about 15 Rembrandts. Here too are Vermeer's *View of Delft*, four portraits by Holbein, and a lovely Virgin by Quentin Metsys.

The promenade boulevard of the horse-and-carriage days, Lange Voorhout, planted with linden trees, has a center strip reserved for the monarch, who rides to Parliament in a golden coach drawn by eight horses. Every aristocratic family had a town house in The Hague. Most of these are now occupied by banks, insurance companies, embassies, ministries.

The Prisoners' Gate, on the Plaats, looks like a medieval house but was a prison and is a museum of instruments of torture.

The Peace Palace on Carnegielaan was built with Carnegie money and inaugurated a year before World War I broke out. Various nations contributed the furniture and fixtures—and some, later, also the war. It is the seat of the International Court of Justice.

Even if you are no longer a child, you must see Madurodam, a mile and a half from town center. This ingenious Holland-in-miniature is a special delight for children. More than 20 million large and small persons have visited this "city" of representative houses and structures from all over the Netherlands: canals, harbors, railways, airfields, all built to a scale of 1:25. Ships float, trains run, church bells ring, windmills turn. The winding route through it is two miles long, ending in a man-sized café. The toy Holland is run by a council of boys and girls elected annually by The Hague's school children. They in turn elect a deputy mayor and aldermen. The members share the responsibility for running the microcosm.

Leaving, we made for a white cart with gaily striped awnings; it was a hot day and we had ice cream on our minds. But when we came close we read the sign: EET PRONK'S HARING. We did not eet aany.

II

With towns, as with children, there is sometimes the undoubted prettiest. In Holland, Delft is the one with the big blue eyes and the naturally curly hair.

The pleasure it gives lies in its old-fashioned Dutchness: its cozy old houses, homelike shops, tree-lined canals, humped bridges, mellow tones of brick against freshly painted woodwork and flower boxes, and an overriding serenity in which the two big churches are like solemn shouts of hosanna. Here and there a grouping of houses or a view of water, red roofs, and a spire wring from one a sudden, "This is it—this is true-blue Dutch!"

This is the town of Delftware, the glazed porcelain, chiefly blue and white, originally inspired by Japanese pottery imported by the Dutch East India Company. Here the scholar Grotius was born, and here Jan Vermeer painted his rich, static portraits-with-interiors. Here William the Silent felt more at home—and here was forever silenced.

The Markt, main square, is a vast rectangle. The tall Nieuwe Kerk rears its brick hulk at one end, the low Town Hall sits at the other, impolitely turning its back. On the long sides, as if lined up in competition for a prize, are rows of seventeenth- and eighteenth-century houses with shops full of cool shining Delft-ware and more homely merchandise.

The Salamander Pharmacy near the Royal Delft Shop displays a *Gaper* (pronounced *Hah*-perr), the head of a man with his tongue stuck out, the doctor having just said, "Here, take your medicine." He's the old Dutch sign of a pharmacy, like the pestle-and-mortar elsewhere in the world. He isn't a stock figure. Each druggist used his own wit to produce his sign. The Salamander's is the best we've seen.

Shopping Interruption. The problem abruptly presented here has caused rifts in matrimonial harmony. It did in ours. He set off at a sightseeing pace. She, lagging to admire the blue plates, got farther and farther behind, disappeared into a shop, and had to be dragged out. "I was only a minute. Just looking." Travelers in connubial harness are advised, if one of them is a crockery lover, to separate temporarily.

This is the time to know that only one manufacturer, Porceleyne Fles, can call itself "Royal," and that only one shop, Reynders at Markt 45, is the outlet for Royal Delft, the porcelain with the hallmark collectors look for. Fles was founded in 1653. Its factory, in an old convent, may be visited.

The Nieuwe Kerk is fourteenth-century Gothic and a national shrine. In it is the marble-and-alabaster tomb of William the Silent, "the wisest, gentlest, and bravest man who ever led a nation."

It was Vader Willem the Delfters knew, a man prematurely old at fifty, the warrior-statesman they would call into their homes to adjudicate a family quarrel. The bronze image on his tomb, however, is that of the young Prince of Orange, who was high-spirited, elegant, far from silent. The sobriquet has its own story. His enemies called him *sluw*, meaning sly. This libel became translated into Latin as "taciturn," and reentered Dutch and

English as "silent." At young William's feet is Vader Willem's pug dog Kuntze that trotted at his heels through the streets of Delft.

You find the Prinsenhof, where he lived, on Oude Delft, a street of fine houses on the largest canal. The beauty is No. 167, a small Gothic palace decorated with coats of arms. It's the Gemeenlandshuis, seat of the dike-reeve and his court of aldermen. They are the guardians of the seventy-six polders of Delftland which (Delft included) lie more than three feet below sea level. No. 39, with stepped gables, was the Dutch East India Company, the giant conglomerate of its time. No. 199 is the Lambert van Meerten Museum, a nineteenth-century house built old Dutch style, notable for its collection of tiles.

Prinsenhof's gateway is No. 185. The old building was a convent until Delft went Calvinist. William first came here in 1572. It was a makeshift residence, shabby, bare, and drafty, and in the important winter of 1580 gave him a cold that almost carried him off. But he was up in time to get approval of a document comparable, in the sixteenth century, to the later American Declaration of Independence.

And it was here, on Tuesday, July 10, 1584, that William after dining, was walking down the stairs when a Catholic fanatic shot and killed him.

The medieval structure with its interior gardens is over-restored but lovingly so. It's in part a museum of local and national history and in part a social-cultural center of Delft, with art exhibitions, an antiques fair, a shop of modern crafts. Lively and friendly, it is the way William would have wanted it.

Explore, behind the New Church, the street, canal, and cobblestone quay Vrouwenrecht, with curved bridge leading into a short medieval lane. Then take canalside Voldersgracht, where gabled houses rise from the water. No. 7, adorned with a double stairway and a row of cows' heads, was the Butchers' Guildhall. No. 6 is a patrician house called The Peacock.

On Hippolytus, the Old Church raises a turreted, leaning tower and spire. Founded in the eleventh century, rebuilt in the thirteenth, it is a church of all architectural seasons. Should you want to see inside, you may have to arouse the caretaker who lives across the way on Holy Ghost Church Street.

Koornmarkt is an attractive canalside street with, at No. 67, the Paul Tetar van Elven Museum, furnished to give an idea of the kind of house and studio Jan Vermeer had. He was "discovered" long after his death, by which time his own house was gone.

Thursday is Delft's big day of the week with cattle and flower markets. The Event of the Year is Taptoe, at the end of August. When we saw the word on a poster we laughed—but came to in time to wangle tickets. It's a military tattoo, music by bands of many nations, with the New Church serving as backdrop with bells and illuminations.

ROTTERDAM TO GOUDA

Rotterdam is to be admired for its vast port and the Lijnbaan, a model traffic-free shopping area. But it is wholly modern and no place to linger—it makes you feel that you should be at the office.

I

On a bright, happy day we set out on a fifty-four-mile circle trip from Rotterdam to Schoonhoven and Gouda. It can be done from Delft in the reverse direction. Or, if carless, you can go by train from either Rotterdam or Delft.

Only do not say "Goodah." The name is pronounced "How-dah," as for the canopied seat on an elephant's back; and the more gutturally you begin, the better they like it.

After Ablasserdam you salute the first of seventeen windmills, the Molens Kinderdijk. Holland once had 9,000 such. Fewer than a thousand remain and these seventeen are the largest single concentration. They've been preserved for tradition's sake but may come into use again. The name "Kinderdijk" comes from the tale that in the flood of 1421 a cradled baby was safely washed ashore. A second passenger was a mewing kitten.

The road along the Lek River runs on top of a dike. At its base snuggle neat farmhouses. This region of polders and farms seems out in nowhere, the land insubstantial, the light watery, the wide sky aquatic.

The approach to Schoonhoven across the Lek is over a lift-bridge favored by sketchers.

Schoonhoven is a small, quiet town of 6,500 with an air of importance. It's at the junction of the Lek and Vlist, and for centuries from the fourteenth was a center of silvercraft. Examples are in the Hall of Handicrafts, that odd building with "ears" on the Haven.

The Haven, main street, is humped over a canal. The fifteenth-century Town Hall raises a complicated tower carrying a clutter of bells cast from the cannon of Olivier van Noort, half-pirate, first Dutchman to sail round the world. St. Bartholomew's, thirteenth century and with tower askew, has his tomb. Some interesting old houses stand about, among them the Weighhouse and the Archers' Guild.

Two human incidents occurred. Lawrence was filling his pipe beside Town Hall's fountain when a blue-smocked native thrust his own tobacco pouch at him: "Eggberrt—*gut!*" Lawrence offered his: "Daniels' Mild—*auch gut!*" Very *gut* was the feeling exchanged.

Later, gaping idly in a shop window, we heard two women talking on a nearby doorstep. Suddenly Sylvia stared, wild-eyed, at her husband. *"Mijn God!"* she cried, "I onderstand Dutch!" Amid yards of chatter she had grasped an inch: "My little Johnny had a fine seat on a bicycle at age two." *"Mijn kleine Jantje had een goed citje op de fiets toen hij twee jahr oud was."*

Out of Schoonhoven, north, a country road ambles along the Vlist. Go slow. There's only nine miles of it. In this green and flowery countryside every farm has its garden behind its little bridge over the channeled river. The houses, some with thatched roofs, are of generous bulk. Nearly every one of them has beside it a smaller—the Elder House. In it live the old parents who have retired in favor of a married son, leaving the young couple to run their own lives while not losing them or the family farm.

II

Flourishing, prideful Gouda is good to see at any time but particularly on Thursdays between May 2 and the end of September, when the cheese market is held. Be there on time. It takes place 9–10:30 A.M. before the Weighhouse, an eye-catching little thing by Pieter Post, who designed the Mauritshuis in The Hague.

On cheese-Thursdays the main square is decorated with the coats of arms of the thirty-two villages from which the cheeses emanate. Banners with fierce heraldic lions fly from the Town Hall. Farm wagons, trucks, and market stalls crowd the square. Shops are busy selling wheelbarrows, pitchforks, and other down-to-earth objects. Looking into the pharmacy we saw farmers buying items and quantities puzzlingly large. Then we recalled the animals-and-people pharmacy at Bulle, in the Gruyère country of Switzerland, with its list of cures in the window for a dozen or so ills that cows are heir to.

Gouda's cheese auction is a seasonal addition to its regular Thursday market, which includes a cattle market. Closing time is signaled by a carillon.

But in the end it's the permanent fixtures that steal the show—principally the square itself and Town Hall.

The Markt, in shape roughly elliptical, is Holland's largest. Its irregularities make it interesting even when nothing's going on. It sets off the Town Hall superbly.

The Town Hall is a character at once droll and strong.

It begins with a double stairway and a canopied porch half-hiding a Gothic portal and adorned with lions on pedestals holding shields. It mounts with arched windows, pauses to hang out two turrets that look like elaborate lanterns, and ends reluctantly with a two-story tower, pinnacled gallery, and spire. All this at the narrow front. The long flanks are strong and simple, with red-and-white shutters at the marching windows. Dormer windows nest in the steep roof, and the rear is finished off with crowsteps and a topping lion.

As if all this isn't enough, the eastern flank has a performing clock. On a platform under the clock stand doll-like medieval figures before a miniature red-striped double door. They represent the people of Gouda and two standard-bearers. On the hour the doors fly open, and the "people" turn to watch a puppet Count Floris V of Holland giving the good burghers of Gouda their town charter in 1272.

St. Janskerk, on the opposite side of the Markt, has a wealth of stained-glass windows, sixteenth century, and so highly prized that during the Reformation bitterness the iconoclasts spared them.

Gouda does not live by cheese alone. It is noted for its pottery, molasses, shortbread, and pipes. The DeMoriaan house on the Gouwve Canal has a pipe museum. The natives like to tell you that Shakespeare as a young man worked for a time for a pipe-maker of Gouda.

An out-of-the-ordinary municipal museum is the seventeeth-century Catharinahuis, which has a pretty garden and a gateway with a curiously sculptured and painted Last Supper represented as a gay banquet. The house was a hospice, welcoming travelers and promising good cheer. Within are a Dutch kitchen, the Surgeons' Guildhall, and a golden chalice which a fifteenth-century countess presented to the archers.

THE OTHER HOLLAND

Little touristed, to east and southeast are the Netherlands that aren't nether, which have woods and hills in place of canals and dikes. Two of its pleasantest towns are Arnhem and Maastricht.

I

Arnhem, on the Rhine, is a significant name to those who know or study World War II. Here in 1944 the British Red Devils and a Polish air brigade swung down from the sky. Their mission was to drive out the occupying Nazis and hold the bridge for Montgomery's advance. For ten terrible days the parachutists fought, expecting reinforcements that never came. Arnhem remembers. Near their graves in Oosterbeek cemetery it created the "Airborne Museum" of Doornwerth Castle to the memory of heroism.

Rebuilt, the devastated capital of Gelderland province is shining and prosperous, its factories practically invisible. It is *Urbs in Horto,* a city in a garden. The infiltrating Sonsbeek Park, whose lush greenery threatens the railway station, is a mile-long collocation of lawns, groves, rivulets, cascades, fountains, swan-furnished lagoons, an aquarium, a grotto, a deer park. Adjoining is the even more extensive Zijpendaal Park. Five more parks dot the town's semicircular perimeter. In them sit half a dozen swimming pools the size of small lakes, one with artificial waves.

The traffic-free shopping center is bordered by the Jansingel, a promenade among flower beds. From the Foermondplein, white steamers make excursions of the Rhine.

There's a touch of individualistic impudence on the Markt, where something new has been added to the very old church of St. Eusebius. In a cantankerous battle between the pastor and the sculptor, the sculptor had the last word. Look hard at the steeple and see if you can identify Disney characters: Mickey Mouse, Donald Duck, Snow White and her dwarfs—and the pastor himself in the guise of a dragon peering out from under a cloud.

The chisel man may have been inspired by the Town Hall. This was originally the palatial house of a swashbuckling character who wanted to gild his front steps. When the town fathers said no, he had fiendish faces mounted on the façade. Arnhemers dubbed it the Duivelhuis.

The Open-Air Museum, in a woodland park, is like a life-size

Madurodam. Its exhibits are authentic old farmhouses, barns, cottages, windmills, a double drawbridge, even a village street, collected from various parts of Holland, each typical of a time and place. Interiors are so completely furnished that they look as if the home folks had stepped out for a minute.

The zoo adjoins. It's one of those vast cageless affairs where the animals roam free and look positively fatuous. You'd swear the chimps are smugly saying, "It's better out here than in there." Not a zoo for weak human egos.

Arnhem is passionate about wedding nature to culture. Internationally famous is its Kröller-Müller Museum in the middle of a forest and game preserve, the Hoge Veluwe National Park. It owns 270 (at last count) Van Goghs. The steadily growing collection includes works of Seurat, Braque, Picasso, Mondrian, Maillol, older Dutch masters, Delftware and Chinese porcelains, and a sculpture garden which has inspired many another modern museum.

II

Remarkable. It happens time and again in Holland. Talk together in English in ordinary conversational tone, and the native citizen at the next table, who has been tentatively smiling when catching your eye, speaks up.

So the old-fashioned gentleman with the pince-nez dangled on a black ribbon joined us with his coffee after a preliminary exchange, and announced, "There are really only two great cities in Holland."

"Ah," we said. "And what is the other one?"

His chuckle was as good as a bestowal of the key to the city. "Amsterdam," he said.

"Why?"

"Because, like us, it has humor—and temperament."

The "great city" of Maastricht—you stress the second syllable—contains 100,000 burghers who consider it something special. And it is. Sitting at the tip of a 30-mile tongue of land thrust out like a rude comment between Belgium and Germany, it is 141 miles from Amsterdam, 95 from Arnhem, 20 from Aachen and Liége. By those figures, and the fact that it is as Catholic as German Aachen and Belgian Liége, what right has it to be Dutch?

The right of determination and a plebiscite.

For its stubbornness it has paid in blood, having been invaded and occupied by foreign armies nineteen times. Geopolitically speaking, its situation is nothing to laugh about.

Astride the river Maas, the French Meuse, Maastricht is the capital of the Netherlands Deep South. The region is called Limburg, which is also the name of the neighboring Belgian province. Each of these Limburgs happens to be the smallest province in its small nation. (No, the odorous cheese comes from a third Limburg, east of Coblentz in Germany.)

These Limburgers are gayer and more volatile than other Dutch. They're celebrated for their celebrations, particularly their Carnival. They like to make music; their many bands and singing societies are in constant demand.

No sooner are you in town than you detect a different kind of Dutchness. The houses are mostly stone, not brick, and look vaguely odd—neither Dutch nor French but something in between. The countryside is hilly, dramatized by chateaus and by farmhouses that seem to aspire to chateau-hood. There's not so much sky about, and it is feathered by trees. The people look stockily Germanic and act French.

Maastricht's secret is that it isn't Dutch, French, or Germanic. It is *Mosan*—which means, "of the Maas." That river made an ethnic and cultural crack in Europe long before present boundaries were fixed. It flows 600 miles from its source in France to its estuary in Holland. Along its middle reaches, where Maastricht stands, the Romanized Gauls developed their own civilization and an art founded on metalworking.

Mosan art in the early Middle Ages filled important churches as far north as Finland. It is rare and precious now.

The Mosans are all mixed up with the Walloons of Belgium. But the Dutch Limburgers form a Mosan otherland in remotest Holland. The name Maastricht signifies Crossing of the Maas. There was a ford the Romans prized—it linked their legions to Cologne. And of course Charlemagne was here.

The Romanesque basilica of St. Servatius is Holland's oldest church. A low, powerful, complicated structure, with square towers and a beautiful galleried apse, it was begun in the tenth century to supersede a small sunken sixth-century church built over the saint's tomb; he died in 384. No sooner was it finished than it had to be enlarged for the pilgrim business. Parts kept getting added, and the interior was fashionably Gothicized in the 1400s.

Since then unwise restorations have kept St. Servaaskerk from being a great church, but there is greatness in it, and much of interest: The eleventh-century buttresses on the west side with the little street, Onder de Bogen, that goes through them. The "Emperor's Hall." The twelfth-century choir and apse. The two lower crypts (the saint's crypt is part of the sixth-century church). The sculpture of the southwest portal and the Treasury door. And the pulpit's winged bull.

The priceless object is the Noordkist shrine in the chapel of the transept. This reliquary of St. Servatius, gold-plated and further enriched with cloisonné enamels and precious stones, is one of the finest works of Mosan goldsmiths. Its date is about 1180. There are lesser Mosan works in the church Treasury, and Byzantine relics.

Across a narrow street beside St. Servaas stands little St. Janskerk, Gothic, with a tall slender spire. Protestant, it was the basilica's baptistery. The two churches share a gardened mound—the top of a hill which the town's rising level has all but swamped.

Maastricht has still another highly individual church. Our first sight of Onze Lieve Vrouwekerk (Church of Our Lady) stunned us. It raises a stupendous cliff of brick flanked by two tall cylindrical towers. It is no-nonsense power. This grim, fortlike version of "I believe" is only a few years younger than St. Servaas but looks much older.

The interior is a letdown—nothing can surpass that incredible façade.

The Lady Chapel's portal is on the street, its great doors wide open. As we stood wondering why, a young woman rode up on a bicycle, her full shopping bag dangling from the handlebars. Propping her bike against her hip, she genuflected expertly, moved her lips in prayer, and sped off. In the next six or seven minutes, three more women awheel and three afoot stopped at the open doorway, crossed themselves, prayed briefly, and went on. A drive-up, drop-in chapel for busy housewives.

The municipal museum is in a narrow fifteenth-century Mosan building, the former town hall. Besides its complement of canvases by Rubens, Jan Steen, Van Dyke, and Breughel, it displays Mosan art, early medieval, moving in its strength of feeling. The new Town Hall, seventeenth-century, is on the Markt, which is liveliest on market Fridays. More popular is the Vrijthof, behind St. Servaas, a promenade with trees, cafés, hotels. Scattered about are the remains of town walls and towers, among them the camera-worthy gateway called the Helpoort and the thirteenth-century St. Servaas Bridge.

Maasland takes pride in its food. Specialties are asparagus, mushrooms, snails, trout, fruit pastries, beer classed as Old and Super-old, and a spiced alcoholic drink called Els. The out-of-town Chateau Neer-Kanne is a massive castle, every room converted to dining. It's on a rise on the Belgian border, three miles from town through gently hilly country with here and there a Limburger farmhouse built around a courtyard, chateaulike. We hope the restaurant is still in full swing, but if it isn't, the castle itself is worth seeing. For wine cellars it has frescoed corridors cut into the sandstone hill.

St. Pietersberg is considered the most spectacular item of all this region. It's neither a church nor a castle, as its name would seem to indicate, but a hill which has provided building stone since Roman times. St. Piet's, having been mined and quarried for so long, is a subterranean labyrinth of 200 miles of shafts, halls, and galleries. Nine centuries of workmen and visitors have scratched, chalked, or painted pictures or autographs on the walls. Your guide (you can't go in without one) will hand you a piece of charcoal so that you can add your name to Napoleon's. These cave-quarries have sheltered peasants and their cattle in many wars. In World War II they were again a refuge, both for people and for priceless art works hidden from the infamous collector Goering.

WEST GERMANY

The German Federal Republic is a truncated nation with one-half of its former capital, Berlin, in communist East Germany and its present capital in Bonn, a small town otherwise distinguished only as Beethoven's birthplace.

This halved Germany, with a finger down East Germany's gullet, is a bizarre appendix to the many Germanies going back to Charlemagne's of around A.D. 800. Karl der Grosse was the first unifying force of the tribal states that came to be called, loosely, German. His attempt at putting them together as the Holy Roman Empire (which, quipped Voltaire, was neither Holy, nor Roman, nor an Empire) failed.

As a nation, Germany is young. Its consolidation dates from about 1870, the work of Bismarck, the blood-and-iron Prussian Chancellor. Prussia was the largest piece of the Teutonic jigsaw puzzle of palatinates, duchies, principalities, electorates, and free towns, and as such became the hard core of modern Germany. To this the Iron Chancellor added, by conquest, lands he wrenched from Denmark, Austria, and France (Alsace-Lorraine).

Prussianly militarized, the new Germany introduced peacetime conscription, built a navy to rival the British, and threatened the European balance of power. World War I was the result.

In 1919, after the Armistice, Marshal Foch said with uncanny prevision: "Let the soldiers ground arms. The war is postponed for twenty years."

In 1939 came the war in which the Nazified Germans made their contribution to uncivilization, practicing genocide, massacre of civilians, slave labor, torture, and the destruction of countries they occupied. Planned evil on such a scale was new.

But the Good Guys won.

To put it more exactly: The Good Guys won, but . . .

In any country the people are a part of the tourist scene. What of today's Germans?

On the train from Belgium into Germany we became uneasy. The one of us who had been in a world war developed a grinding pain in the back of his neck, the other a headache. The immediate cause was the couple in the opposite seat. He owned a bristly blond crew-cut, a forehead low and square, eyes blandly blue, shoulders that strained his jacket. She was Brunhild to his Gunther, a magnificent animal. They could have modeled for a racist poster.

The passengers stirred, began to reach for coats and suitcases. The train was pulling into Aachen.

Suddenly "Gunther" towered over us. He spoke a mixed English and German from which we made out that there would be no porters—could he help with our luggage? "No, *nein, vielen dank.*" He shook off our protests and burdened himself while his Brunhild helped Sylvia on with her coat and said, shyly, "*Willkommen in Chermany.*"

The traveling body moves with comparative ease. The mind finds the going harder. A qualm, at the very least, is the psychic fee paid by the traveler entering Germany.

But he goes on to enjoy, for West Germany is pleasant and the people are as superficially human as the rest of mankind. Here in the scenic south, combining the nostalgic old and the postwar new, are the anciently more developed and cultural regions prized by the travelers, the Grand Tourists, of as far back as the seventeenth century.

AACHEN AND COLOGNE

I

Aachen (Aix-la-Chapelle) is a good introduction to Germany. It is Charlemagne's town. He was probably born here in one of Peppin's bivouacs. Although he spent as much of his life traveling, battling, negotiating, and pulling Europe together as any modern statesman, the grand warrior took time out to replace his father's crude house with a palace and a royal chapel.

As Emperor of the West he had many palaces, but Aachen was his favorite. Here he spent the last years of his eventful seventy. He died in the palace and was buried in the chapel in A.D. 814. There he rests to this day, semi-sainted, having been canonized by an anti-pope.

Aachen flourished as an imperial coronation seat. From 840 to 1531 German kings and Holy Roman emperors were crowned in Charlemagne's church. Industrially it flourished as well. Before trousers were, Aachen was. Since the eighth century the cloth guilds, now unions, have been known for their fabrics. It became a medieval fashion center. More prosperity followed the discovery of mineral springs. The people still consider themselves the best-dressed Germans. They also boast that theirs is the world's largest umbrella factory.

We have our own personal joke on Aachen, or it on us. In the days when we knew no German at all we came into town from Belgium and signed up for a room in a modest hotel opposite the railway station. The man at the desk asked, *"Ist das mit?"* We puzzled over this and finally said yes. He said, *"Gut."* Arrived in the room, we looked around. What was this *"mit"*? Opening the stand between the beds, we discovered a chamber pot. "Ha," we cried in unison, *"voilà* the *mit."* Next morning we discovered that *"mit"* meant "with breakfast."

Thanks to the generosity of a pope who gave Charlemagne an elephant and a tamed African lion, Aachen became the first

European city with a zoo. It has become a city of parks. Its love for public greenery would bemuse a realtor or speculative builder, for the serene lawn of its municipal park occupies a considerable quadrilateral—smack downtown. This and other parks hide the fact that it is an industrial town of 170,000 and a crossroads, a rifle shot away from the "Three Countries Corner" where Germany, Belgium, and Holland touch at the Europaplatz—a monumental traffic turnabout adorned with an artificial lake.

Between the cool, groomed greensward and the Münsterplatz stands a very unusual monument: the Dom or Cathedral. One look at this marriage of Carolingian Romanesque and Gothic and you know you are in for something special. The Dom is what happened to Charlemagne's chapel.

The chapel was an octagon. Wrecked by Norman invaders, it was rebuilt in the same form in 983 and became an important church. Not only did it possess Charlemagne's shrine; it had also acquired a precious job lot of holy relics: swaddling clothes of infant Jesus, robe worn by the Virgin, and the cloth on which John the Baptist's severed head had lain.

The church *had* to grow—the pilgrim and king businesses made that imperative. But the octagon could not be touched. So one part after another was tacked on during the fourteenth and fifteenth centuries.

Externally the Dom is exciting. It has a squared and spired front, a wedge-domed middle, and a rear like a galleon's poop.

Within, not a dull moment. The entire church seems to be in movement around the octagon. Wonderful are the things to look at: in the choir, for example, that silver-gilt shrine of Char-lemagne, and the high altar's facing of gold panels carved in reliefs—the Carolingian Pala d'Oro. And the extraordinarily beautiful pulpit. This marvel is wrapped around by a superb coffered wooden cloak which swings open on hinges to reveal a blazing golden ambo adorned with gems, fifth-century ivory sculptures, a jeweled cross, and a chair presented by a monarch crowned in 1014. The under-pulpit is usually displayed only on important occasions, but seek out the sacristan, tell him you've crossed an ocean to see it. And jingle some coins.

The octagon, decorated with inlaid marble and mosaics, is girdled three-quarters of the way up by a sixteen-sided gallery. Its eight-fold dome shines with gilt, and from it is suspended like a coronet a magnificent bronze chandelier presented in 1170 by Frederick Barbarossa.

The gallery is as spacious as a theater's. From this mezzanine generations of Europe's grandest notables enjoyed a prize seat on historic ceremonies. Charlemagne's marble throne is here, copied from Solomon's as far as Biblical description could provide the blueprint. The antique columns came from Italy.

Downstairs, look for the bronze lion's head on the west door. In its mouth is the devil's thumb. See if you can get it out. There's a reward if you do—unspecified and probably entirely spiritual.

Legend says that when money ran out, the devil arranged to finish the church in trade for the first soul to enter. Having kept his part of the bargain, he lay in wait. Naturally, no one dared to go in. How cheat his satanic majesty in this impasse? A burgher who was probably a lawyer shooed a wolf inside, the deal having failed to specify a *human* soul. Leaving in a rage, the devil slammed the door on his own thumb. In the entrance hall sits the wolf with a neat hole in his chest where his soul was wrenched out. Opposite is a huge pine cone representing the rejected soul. All this, we hazard, goes back to the time when the early church was luring into the fold followers of the Old Religion. Wolf and pine cone were pre-Christian symbols.

The Treasure of this cathedral is said to be the richest north of the Alps. It includes the exquisite Lothar Cross (about 900 A.D.) and the Shrine of Our Lady, one of the great reliquaries achieved by the Meuse-Rhine goldsmiths of the 1200s.

Under its French name of Aix-la-Chapelle, Aachen may be known to you since schooldays as the terminal point of Browning's celebrated dactylic dash, "How They Brought the Good News from Ghent to Aix." No one we asked had any idea what the good news was that had been worth the lives of two fine horses, the news that "alone could save Aix from her fate." One thoughtful citizen remarked that if something can save someone from her fate, it never was her fate. Another to whom we showed the poem proved to be an official of Aachen's international riding tournament. He gagged at the part where the narrator-hero pours down the throat of the surviving steed, Roland, still heaving and sweating from the 115-mile gallop, "our last measure of wine." "Is this good for a horse in such a condition?" he demanded.

Aachen was the goal of other historic dashes. When Prinny —Prince of Wales and heir to George III—was making violent love to the pretty widow Maria Fitzherbert, she fled to Aix, then (1783) a French possession. The Prince wrote her imploring letters, one of them forty-two pages long, and sent them by courier with orders not to spare the horses. After a bit of this the French, suspicions aroused, intercepted three of Cupid's messengers and jailed them.

II

Hardly were we out of Aachen than we were, psychologically, in Cologne-Köln. For our seatmate was a voluble, portly Kölner with a portly briefcase, homebound from Brussels. Herr Heimwärts was an umlaut Babbitt carrying good news (contracts) from Aix to Köln.

"*Ach, Köln ist kolosSAL!* You will see. Nine hundert trains a day! Ee-machin!" The auto traffic, it is *erstaunlich*, prodigious. The new airfield—*wunderbar!* Such a going and coming, 600,000 passengers a year! And the loaded barges on the Rhine! Kolossal Köln, crossroads of Europe, communications hub for Holland, Belgium, *und so weiter*, and the Red lands.

World War II's more than fifty bombing raids had reduced the city to rubble—but this was a blessing, a Wagnerian horn blast to rebuild. The result—overwhelming! Köln had even overwhelmed herself; so as not to stifle in her own growth she had to throw more bridges across the Rhine, dig a subway system, raise elevated pavements for pedestrians. More, bigger, better, higher, farther out, quicker; work, "chobs," production, sales, exports. Population: 1946, 400,000; today 860,000; tomorrow *zwölfhunderttausend!*

Knew we that Chermany faster than the United States progresses? Invests a greater percentage of its resources in industrial research and development? That, while *Vereinigte Staaten* is being a military spendthrift, a *Verschwender*, using up its best scientists and engineers in weaponry and chasing after the moon, "in our Chermany we build the future, no rockets that poof!— anoder hundert million gone . . . Look you out, Amerika!"

And Köln, the vanguard city, is the place where we would see all this. His pale eyes widened, his hands were busy with illustrative gestures, his voice quavered with boom-town patriotism. We were oversold. As the train made a sweep through Ehrenfeld suburb, and the highest spires (520 feet) of the largest Gothic church came into view, Our Man in Köln flattened his nose against the window and whispered, "KolosSAL!"

Crowds surged through the vast railway station and crowds swirled in the Platz outside. The Höhestrasse, a main shopping street where wheeled traffic has been *verboten* for generations, was thronged. The Rudolfplatz was crazy with people and vehicles. Every restaurant, café, *Bierkneipe*, was jammed with eaters destroying such native delicacies as Kölscher Kaviar (blood sausage on rye) and Hämchen (pickled pig's knuckles with sauerkraut and mashed potatoes). And washing it down with tuns of beer.

But the traveler does not come to contemplate economic miracles. He comes for the strange and wonderful. And Cologne's main attraction since the Middle Ages has been the great Cathedral of Saints Peter and Paul.

Wait, Herr Heimwärts!—But there he strides to his office in Unter Sachsenhausen where the big banks are, and it's too late to point out to him that even this Dom was once Big Business.

In 1184 the prince-archbishop brought from Milan the bones of the Three Magi. A golden coffer was fashioned for them by master craftsmen. This shrine became immediately a more lucrative enterprise than is brought to Cologne today in the fattest briefcase.

The church then in existence couldn't cope with the pilgrims. The present cathedral was begun in 1248, on a scale truly colossal. It was not finished until 1880, 552 years later. And just sixty-odd years after that, it was hit by fourteen big bombs, nineteen shells, and incendiaries uncounted, which left standing only the skeleton; but a stout one it proved to be. Blame those hits on the cathedral's fatal proximity to the railway station and bridge, prime targets. (Account how you will for the havoc wreaked on Cologne's many other churches, distant from military objectives.)

Restored, the Dom is in every way an awesome church. In dimensions it is one of the world's largest Gothic edifices: 472 feet long, 202 feet from floor to roof, with spire the height of a 35-story building. The climb to the sightseeing lookout in the south tower is more than five hundred steps.

The best places for admiring it *in toto* are on the other bank of the Rhine or the Deutzer Bridge. In the 1950s were added the splendid bronze doors with mosaic inlay (south transept) by Ewald Mataré.

Inside, the church is too vast for beauty, but that it is imposing no one will deny. The great columns seem almost fragile. The stained-glass windows (stored during the war) make a noble show, especially the five of the early sixteenth century in the north aisle. The shrine of the Three Magi is a marvel of medieval goldsmithry.

Spare time for the fourteenth-century choir stalls, the largest set of such furniture in Germany. It's not, however, the size that counts but the carving, its humor and scarcely inhibited delight in satire and the grotesque. The Treasury in the north transept tries to rival Aachen's. The St. Peter bell is a colossal 10½ feet in diameter and weighs 25 tons.

On the south side of the cathedral the war revealed the

Dionysus Mosaics, thought to have decorated the dining room floor of a rich second-century Roman. They are like an open invitation to cast aside decorum, clothes, and chastity.

Cologne contains at least forty-six smaller churches, nearly all formidably original. In our notes and memory three stand out as worthy of a visit:

St. Maria im Kapitol. Eleventh-century basilica resting on the site of a Roman temple. Excavators found cells dedicated to Jupiter, Juno, and Minerva. The architectural style is starkly Dark Ages. Most interesting feature: a population of images and pictures of the Virgin, some of them extraordinary. The most striking comes from Mechelen in Belgium: Mary and Joseph kneeling in a stable lovingly unglorified. This scene and theme has been done by a dozen of the world's great painters, but not with this utter sincerity.

St. Ursula. Medieval pilgrims came to the town mostly for the magic bones of the Three Magi but they also shopped this church, which was thought to house the bones of St. Ursula and her band of spiritual amazons. The Ursula legend is a horrific tale of ten, or a thousand, or eleven hundred virgins returning from a pilgrimage to Rome, slain by Huns "at or near where the church stands." Bones were dug for and discovered; an attempt was made to hide the fact that *male* bones were among those present.

Whatever the facts, the tomb is a fascinating artifact, with its gold-framed compartments containing bones, and a series of ten fifteenth-century panels picturing the legend for the illiterate. Also a chamber with bone decorations and two shrines.

St. Gereon. This basilica is a curious structure. Some call it a ten-sided nave. The nave is actually round but has various pockets north and south, plus an excrescent baptistery that bulges out of the south like a goiter. The choir area has a southern transept arm with lovely stained glass, which leads to an ambulatory with side-knobs.

This ensemble is fit to stop a thoughtful architect in his tracks. How did it come about? Blame it on Isis, the Egyptian goddess the eclectic Romans included in their Pantheon. Her temple was oval.

Fourth-century Christians pitched upon it for their own holy house, pushing it this way and that as their needs grew with time. It was fascinating before bombardiers rained havoc on it. Much is gone but it is still remarkable, and Treasury and crypt are intact.

Heavy are church demands upon sightseers. Apropos may be the remark we overheard by a precocious youth in the Cathedral, which was crowded with trippers: "Something odd has happened to religion when more people come to a church to stare than to pray."

HEIDELBERG AND ROTHENBURG

I

The "Student Prince" university put Heidelberg on travel itineraries. That school was a major port of call on the old Grand Tour from Renaissance times through the nineteenth century, when the visitors were mostly scholars and students. Founded in 1386, it claims to be Germany's oldest and largest university. Of the 12,000 students enrolled, many come from foreign parts.

Its main building is in the heart of the old quarter, and next to it is the Neue Aula (New Hall), a capacious auditorium built with the help of American dollars two years before Hitler took over. The great library owns important manuscripts, including the Minnesinger collection of 1200–1400.

The picturesque students' jail can be visited after a call on the Hausmeister next door at Augustinergasse 2. Unless you revere learning and are awed to learn that the university has produced almost as many scholars as dueling scars, you will probably opt for the jail, whose walls and ceilings have been frescoed by countless inmates. Its picture in colors is on postcards.

The fact remains that, although the red sandstone castle above the town is the main sight, it is to the university—as a romantic literary subject—that Heidelberg owes its tourist popularity. In the 1900s a novel about student life became a best-seller. A play followed, and finally the operetta *The Student Prince,* with Sigmund Romberg's music, including the often-bellowed drinking song. The musical has done for Heidelberg what Schiller's and Rossini's *William Tell* did for Switzerland.

There is really very little to see of this fabled school, its different disciplines scattered all over town; no campus-center of student life. Dueling is suppressed. It was never practiced by more than a small elite of "corps" members. The old tradition of the *Kneipe* or beer-binge is not much honored. The faded tintypes on tavern walls are pathetic relics of the golden age.

When we were first here, Lawrence as a young university professor was invited to sit at a fraternity table at the Red Ox, plied with tankards of beer, and obliged to sing his university song. He was not questioned about his saber record. On the north side of the Neckar the Hirsch tavern, which served as dueling ground, is still in business. About a hundred yards away stands the Scheffelhaus, setting of the operetta. A colorful touch that remains is the colored cap and sash of the five corps, each different.

Now for the castle, Heidelberg's most striking leftover and a boon to sellers of photographic film. This former grand residence of the Electors Palatine was begun in the thirteenth century and finished in 1688. It and the wooded hills between which Heidelberg lies in a quasi-gorge are the most appealing elements of the local scene.

The Schloss is 330 feet up, on a spur of the 1,830-foot Königstuhl. In shape it's an irregular square with round towers at the corners.

Its luck as a live castle has not been good. God and France's Louis XIV hurled thunderbolts. In 1689, just a year after its completion, the Sun King's cohorts captured it, found they couldn't hold it, and blew up as much as they could. Four years later they returned, wrecked more, and went on to destroy the town. In 1764 lightning made a direct hit. Much restoration was done between 1897 and 1903.

Well, what is left is a dramatic roseate ruin in a lovely setting, one over which Mark Twain waxed lyrical. There are greater crowds now than when he was here. On a Sunday the camera fans alone, with their tripods, special lenses, light meters, movie equipment, and girl friends to be posed, make as much *Geschäftigkeit,* tohubohu, and hurry-scurry as did the French when frantically tearing it down. "What exposure are you using?" is heard in a dozen languages.

With terraces at various levels, flowers, trees, and winding paths, the views on every hand range from pretty to noble—on the compact town below. On the Neckar, which enters upper left and disappears lower right. On the Heiligenberg and its Philosophers' Way. And far out over luxuriant plains to the hazy Hardt Mountains.

The castle's courtyard is thronged. Its fountain (snapshot favorite; they queue up for it) has four columns from some old palace of Charlemagne's. You like the octagonal bell tower and the Elisabethantor, an elaborately decorated gateway. Everywhere the native reddish stone has aged beautifully. Had the French and the Act of God tried deliberately to create a romantic ruin, they couldn't have done better.

Restoration has provided visitable rooms. The famous item is the Great Tun, a giant barrel capable of holding 49,000 gallons—we forgot to ask, "Of what?"

If the weather is right give yourself plenty of time. You'll want to linger—in the courtyard, on the terraces, and along the tree-shaded walks. You will be within a golf-iron shot of where Mark Twain said, "I have never enjoyed a view which had such serene and satisfying charm," and jotted it down on an old envelope and put it into the book he had begun writing.

From town a funicular takes you up to Schloss station, saving your legs for the walk down, which it would be silly to miss. The funicular goes on up to Molkenkur (woods and hotel, café with terrace) and on farther to the very top, which is not interesting.

Heidelberg's population is 120,000. The Old Town is only the eastern tail of the city, but it wags the dog. It's a narrow length about three blocks wide crowded between the castle spur and the Neckar, plus a bit on the other bank.

The sights are not many. The citizens are proud of the house Zum Ritter, the one fine building spared by the French, now a hotel. Its fancifully gabled and decorated Renaissance façade hints at what the wreckers have deprived you of. There are some good eighteenth-century houses, the Karl Theodor Bridge with its gate towers, the Karlstor gate, and the two squares, Kornmarkt and Fischmarkt.

The wooded hill across the Neckar is the Heiligenberg. By winding paths you reach a viewpoint tower, and climb past the modern festival amphitheater to the scanty ruins of a ninth-century basilica. Strolling along the Philosophenweg may not make a Kant or Socrates of you, but it does grant the handsomest views of Heidelberg and castle. It was in a rented house on this hill that Mark Twain began writing *A Tramp Abroad,* which contains, besides the swearing bluejay story and the essay on the German language, a chapter on the dueling custom.

On the flatland west of the hill are a small moated fourteenth-century castle, now a museum, and the oldest church, eighth century and consecrated to St. Vitus—whose name, by the way, is connected with the nervous disease chorea because medieval sufferers resorted to this saint to pray for deliverance.

You're bound to meet Uncle Sam's soldiers. Their headquarters occupy sixteen buildings on the outskirts. In front of the Red Ox we talked to an Iowan and a Marylander. They were pathetically bored and we couldn't help them. Their plaint was girls, or lack of them. The university men's competition was too strong.

II

Take the Burgenstrasse (Castle Road) from Heidelberg to Rothenburg ob der Tauber. The pleasant route follows the Neckar. On the hills stand castles in various stages of ruin or repair. A young thing on our bus exclaimed, "Oh, isn't it landscapy!"

The scenery of winding river, gentle hills, and rugged cliffs, of woods, clearings, and red earth, is happy. After industrialized Heilbronn the road leaves the Neckar and becomes more intimate. It passes the small market towns of Blaufelden and Schrozberg and rides along a declivity, the deep Tauber valley, spanned at one point by a fourteenth-century double bridge. Then, a few points off your port bow, you sight a hill with a silhouette that seems to have been taken from the cover of a child's fairytale book. Walls and towers become fixed in the unreal but true way they did when you were very little, and you seem to be riding right into the story.

Rothenburg ob der Tauber is one of Europe's most complete medieval walled towns.

With its walls and thirty towers (no two alike), its brightly painted houses of half-timber, gables, oriels, and individual touches at doors and windows, its surprisingly spacious streets with fountains and decorative shop signs, Rothenburg is almost too good to be true. It is so charming and right, spruce and trim, that a surly soul we met suspected it of having been built as a tourist trap.

The 12,000 Rothenburgers go about their business without a glance at the outlanders who have come to stare at their houses and clutter up their market square to watch the clockwork automata perform. No itching palm is thrust at you, no nudge to offer you a souvenir or postcard or sausage. Do you want a guide? Apply at the town tourist office in the town hall; it sends out a hasty call for an English-speaking student or teacher.

The town was born of a castle soon after 800 A.D. It grew in spite of tyranny, plague, famine, revolution, siege, war, and fire. In 1356 an earthquake brought down the castle; where it stood is a garden with views over the walls. In 1501 half the Rathaus was destroyed by fire; it rose from its ashes in Renaissance style beside the old Gothic remnant. The main church, damaged in an air raid in 1944, has been rebuilt. Thus, except for the loss of its castle, medieval Rothenburg is intact—its center unmarred by incongruous new building.

The town center is the Marktplatz backed by former guildhalls. Before them stands a fountain topped by a small St. George poking a dragon pup. The new (Renaissance) Rathaus fronting the square's long side has a portico raised on steps which tourists find handy for sitting on while waiting for the *Meistertrunk* to begin. It takes place on the façade of the Drink Hall Inn, club-house, and drinking hall of the patricians, the Hall was closed to them in 1504 because of a murder and is now municipal offices.

The story behind the show is an incident in the Thirty Years' War when Rothenburg was captured by the imperial forces of General Tilly after hard fighting. Angered by his losses, Tilly ordered the executioner to behead the entire town council, after which his troops would plunder and then set fire to the town. The women gathered with their children to plead with the soldiers, the councillors in the Kaisersaal to plead with Tilly. Moreover, the executioner balked at the wholesale job assigned him. Imperial messengers came and went between HQ and his little house on the street subsequently called Joy Lane.

Meanwhile, back at the Weinkeller, a brilliant idea struck the Cellar Master. Let Tilly be softened by the Imperial Welcome, wine served in a huge goblet made for the visit of an emperor who had failed to come. The cellar's best wine was poured into the precious goblet. Tilly drank. He mellowed. Smacking his lips, he made a sporting proposition. "The council and the town I will spare if there is among you a man great enough to drink down without stopping for breath the whole six and a half pints of this goblet!"

Burgomeister Nusch volunteered. He loosened the belt around his *embonpoint,* tilted the brimful goblet, drank, and drank, and drank, and saved the town. That feat is the *Meistertrunk.* It did Nusch no harm, beyond a belch or two. Seventy-four at the time, he lived on into his nineties.

Every day at 11, 12, 1, and 2 the shutters of the double window fly open and two half-figures stand revealed. Tilly at the left points his baton. Nusch at the right raises the goblet and tilts back his head. Tilly turns toward the spectators a face of wooden amazement. The shutters bang to and that's that.

Look next at the old Rathaus, around the corner from the new. Here is a severe, powerful façade with a steeply pyramidal gable out of which rises a watchtower. Pinnacles march up the gable. This structure of 1240 is considered South Germany's finest bit of Gothic. Look for the medieval measuring rods imbedded in the wall beside the massive oak doors. Cheaters were ducked in the St. George fountain. Weights too were available to check on millers and bakers.

When you face the Drink Hall, Hafengasse is on your right, Herrengasse left, and Schmiedgasse just behind you. These are streets to be explored almost inch by inch.

Hafengasse has a fountain lavishly planted with flowers, the squat Roeder Gate with its guardhouses, and the massive Markus Tower. They're popular with postcard makers and painters, all of whom have been blind to the bakery with the amusingly regal crest of the bakers' guild over its door—two gilded lions holding a crowned pretzel. The pretzel rules all bakers, but this one is the most elaborately worked.

Herrengasse, which developed behind the castle, is a street of patrician houses and a fountain featuring a grotesque merman, two-tailed, sitting at ease with a tail in each hand. You can walk into the courtyard of No. 15, which has been cut into apartments. Across the street the yellow-painted Staudt House, still owned by the Staudt family, has an entrance fee. The street passes under a gateway and the lordly thirteenth-century Burgtor to the gardened promontory once occupied by the castle.

Schmiedgasse, with its overhanging signs, old houses in great variety, merman fountain, and climax of the Plonlein, is the most captivating of the medieval streets. The second house on the left, with the stone figures, was built for himself by architect Leonhard Weidman, who built the New Rathaus (1572) and carved under its oriel his self-portrait.

The modest house next door with the curlicue gable belonged to the beloved patrician mayor Heinrich Toppler, who died mysteriously of poison in 1408. They say that his New Deal for the humble was considered by the aristocrats treason to his class. Mayor Nusch of the *Meistertrunk* lived in the house opposite St. John's Church (which is part granary). Beside the Goldener Hirsch, a short stubby lane takes you to a platform with the best long view, and stairs down to lazy, inviting, sanded paths in the valley.

But the Plonlein is just ahead. This is a forking of streets. A very old half-timbered house stands at the parting of the ways, and each street has its own thirteenth-century gate tower. The lower is the Kobolzellertor, with double roof and dormer window. The upper, the Siebersturm, has a red-and-blue clock. Half-hidden stairs and passages connect the two towers. Color-washed houses follow the two lines of movement. Here is where the quaint in the medieval-urban scene becomes high, unselfconscious art. Every visiting artist tries his hand at the Plonlein.

Spitalgasse, beyond the Siebersturm, leads to the Spital bastion, where you can mount the stairs of a tower to walk on the wall. One side gives intimate glimpses of back gardens, kitchens, roofs; the other, open countryside framed in the defense slits.

North of the Marktplatz the town clusters around St. Jakobs-kirche, the important church: 1373, Gothic, recently restored. Its side portal is called the Marriage Gate because weddings took place there at the time when the Church was weaning the folk from common-law marriages in order to claim the sole prerogative.

This church is built across a street, Klingengasse; that is, the street goes through the church by means of an archway. Klingen Tower, at street's end, was the key to Rothenburg's water supply. Foreign engineers were imported to devise the system of pumping water up to certain towers and from them to the fountains. In a siege, water supply was vital. Tradition says the engineers were killed to preserve the secret.

Judengasse intersects. One of Toppler's reforms protected the

Jews. But they weren't permitted to gable their houses. It's interesting to compare the gabled and ungabled. The long house on the left bears a memorial plaque in Hebrew. The street has a fountain with a friendly lion.

Nearer the church is Deutschherrengasse, lined with fourteenth-century houses. Here too is Joy Lane. The executioner lived in the little blue house, bottom right.

South by train and road are Dinkelsbühl and Nördlingen, smaller Rothenburgs. Less gladdening, they gain by being less touristed.

NUREMBERG

Nuremberg is spawn of a castle planted, no one knows when, on a rocky rise that cried out for a stout tower. The town spread out below the Rock. From the tangled history of town and Kaiserburg it seems the town built its bastions against both outside enemies and the castle. Which explains, perhaps, why they are so strong that not even the bombs of World War II could lay them low. The medieval girdle of walls and towers is still complete, even though missing a spur or tower here and there.

The city flourished, became rich and beautiful, in the fifteenth and sixteenth centuries. A canny trader between northern Europe and the East, it was also Germany's foremost manufactory of arts and crafts. At the height of that golden era, to keep up with the Joneses, whether in Venice or Antwerp, you cultivated "Nuremberg Taste" in furniture, silver plate, tiled stoves, musical instruments.

Ingenuity's name was Nuremberg. Its armorers produced spare parts so that a gentleman readying himself for tournament or battle and in need of steel gloves or greaves didn't have to buy a whole suit. One Nuremberger invented the pocket watch, another the geographer's globe.

Albrecht Dürer was Nuremberg's great artist. Born in 1471, son of a goldsmith, he was one of those rare, happy mortals not only supremely gifted but universally loved—except by his shrewish wife. He bought a fine house below the Rock, and everyone who mattered in Europe came to see him. When Maximilian I couldn't pay him for three years' work, Nuremberg settled that bill out of taxes.

Hitler was drawn to this city. Outside the walls he built a Roman-style tribune to preside over the annual conventions of the Nazi Party while erecting the world's largest stadium. Here were decreed the infamous Nuremberg Laws (1935), dividing Germans into Aryans and Others. Millions of deaths later, the Nuremberg Trials took place and nine Nazi leaders were hanged for crimes against humanity. Grass grows on the tribune, and the stadium is the world's largest modern ruin.

Nuremberg is Franconian and Protestant. It's a market for hops, a famed producer of toys and *lebkuchen* (ginger cookies, the United States being one of the chief importers), and fond of a two-inch bratwurst eaten off pewter plates.

The tourist area is neatly outlined by the medieval walls and finished on the northwest by the Rock with its fortress. From east to west the Old Town is sliced by the Pegnitz River. From south to north it is bisected by Königstrasse as far as the market; small streets jog on up to the Kaiserburg.

Starting from the south and sauntering north on König, you observe two handsome buildings (the gabled one was a granary, the turreted affair a patrician tower-house), pause to blink at the bronze Virtue Fountain (the Virtues spout water from their breasts), and stop to visit the Church of St. Lawrence.

Thirteenth-century and proud of its rose window, St. Lawrence's is the city's largest and most beautiful church. It's so fully furnished that you'd never guess it to be Protestant. In Nuremberg the Reformation was not destructive. Two of its art works are outstanding. One is a large wood-carved Annunciation by Veit Stoss which hangs from the ceiling: Mary and the Angel stand within a garland of stylized roses. The other is the tabernacle by Adam Krafft, well-described by Sacheverell Sitwell as "a Gothic tower of limestone resting on life-size kneeling figures of the sculptor and his two apprentices, enriched all the way with statues and little carved figures, rising 65 feet, nearly to the roof, and the top of it bent like a crozier."

Beyond St. Lawrence's, at the bridge over the Pegnitz, you enjoy the waterside view of the half-timbered Holy Ghost hospice, now a restaurant. (What interesting houses they built in medieval times!) Then you come to the Hauptmarkt.

On this large square stand two remarkable structures, the Schöner Brunnen and the Frauenkirche.

The fourteenth-century Beautiful Fountain rises like a many-tiered wedding cake adorned with figures and culminating in a fanciful spire.

The Church of Our Lady, belonging to the same century, presents a delightful façade of toy tower below and lacy tower above, ornamental gable and double porch. Daily at noon the automata under its golden clock enact the seven Electors paying homage to Charles IV. Within, the church is over-restored. But look at the Tucher altar (1440), and render the tribute of a nod to a merchant family that has survived every economic catastrophe since the fifteenth century. Tuchers are still in business, mainly in banking and beer.

St. Sebald's is a few steps northwest of the Hauptmarkt, its tall twin towers fronting on the Weinmarkt. Older than St. Lawrence's, it is architecturally more sober. Its prize possession is the huge tomb of St. Sebald, created in 1519 by bronze-founder Peter Vischer. Nobody went to greater lengths with metal. It stands on snails and dolphins, mice run about, there are forests and a population of figures, among whom (try finding them) are the artist and St. Sebald.

More interesting are the three medieval figures on the outer wall, north side, above the entrance. Few persons notice them. First is a knight fully robed in front but naked in back, where dreadful things are crawling under his skin. Facing him from about five yards away is a pretty young woman. Between them an older woman holds up a warning hand. Mama is telling daughter that her brave sweetheart home from the Crusades is being eaten by disease. It could be leprosy or syphilis brought home from the East.

Dürer enjoyed a beautiful house of timber and stone from 1509 until his death in 1528. It is now the Dürer Museum, cared for with devotion. (The half-timbered tavern next door makes a specialty of Rauchbier, smoked beer.)

Above looms the Kaiserburg. This varidated complex of towers and buildings rose as two separate strongholds, Burgrave's Castle and Imperial Castle. The Burgrave was a nobleman who held his part of the Rock in fief. When inherited by the Hohenzollerns this castle became a threat to the townsmen, who called the Hohenzollerns "the lice in the fur," and built defenses against them. A guided tour is indicated.

The National Museum displays Germanic art and *Kultur* in more than a hundred galleries. Look for the Nuremberg section, which fills seven galleries.

Two restaurants have the special Nuremberg touch. Das Goldene Posthorn, in the Weinmarkt, has been a going concern since 1498. Here are atmosphere and good food. There's atmosphere of another kind—crowded, noisy, lively—at the Bratwurst-hausle (Little Bratwurst House) between St. Sebald's and the Rathaus, where fingerlike sausages are grilled to order and rushed by pewter platefuls to clamorous diners. Bratwurst is the whole menu; all you have to decide is whether you want yours with potato salad or horseradish. It's cheap and it's fun. Now and again there's an attempt to set a new record for the number of small doggies eaten at one sitting. When we were there, two good-looking fräuleins did away with 107, which resulted in feature articles in the local press during *Sauregurkenzeit.* "Sourpickletime" is the literal translation—compare the English "dog days."

Nuremberg must be known to millions of American families as the source of *lebkuchen,* especially at Christmas time in those decorated tin boxes a child never forgets.

An easy side trip can be made to the pleasant town of Ansbach—one of many areas in this part of Germany (Hesse) from which Hessian troops were bought by the British and sent to fight against the American rebels.

MUNICH TO BERCHTESGADEN
I

They call Munich Germany's secret capital because it magnetically draws all Germans, be they Franconians, Swabians, or Prussians. This power of attraction is at bottom a tribute to a dynastic family, the Wittelsbachs. They ruled Bavaria from 1180 to 1918, and from 1255 Munich was their capital.

This all-German affection for Munich is odd because the Wittelsbachs stood for Bavarianism and didn't give a damn for German nationalism. But when a city is well regarded and well lived in by its rulers for almost 700 years, it has reason to acquire a happy look and permanent purr. The only Wittelsbach who got scratched was the Ludwig who loved Lola Montez more than his city. He had to abdicate.

In German the city's name is München, which means Monks. It rose on land owned by Benedictines, and is thought to have been laid out by the monks themselves. The city emblem is a tiny monk with outstretched arms. Childlike, he is affectionately nicknamed the *Münchnerkindl*—the Munich Kid.

The most important element in Munich's life is beer. Seven large breweries produce 77 million gallons a year. Every drop of it is subject to a "Pure Food and Drugs Act" of 1516 restricting the ingredients to hops, malt, and water.

Beer ads are fascinating with their coats-of-arms and dates: "Since 1543, Flotzinger-Brau." "Hackerbrau, 1417." "Steiner Biere, 1565." "Since 1397, Spatenbrau." And, awesomely, "Weihenstephaner Bier, since 1040"!

The popular Hofbräuhaus provides the interesting spectacle of waitresses running between beer fountains and thirsty Teutons carrying six foaming steins in each fist.

It was in a Munich beerhall that Hitler in 1920 first came into prominence.

Beery are the tides of life. March is the Strong Beer month and May belongs to Maibock—extra strong. The Oktoberfest, mid-September, sees the world's greatest consumption. In sixteen days Munchners and visitors dispose of some 650,000 gallons. They do this to celebrate the engagement and wedding of Prince Ludwig of Bavaria to Princess Theresa of Saxe-Hildburghausen in—1810!

It was that Oktoberfest-Ludwig who made radical changes in the city. Before settling down to his Bavarian duties he had lived in Italy, where he fell in love with the antique. When he became king in 1825 he proceeded to make Munich neoclassical. But he went too fast for his people. One of the first things they did when they forced him out was to put clothes on the classical statues posing nudely in public.

Later changes were made for the ill-fated Olympic Games of 1972. Streets and squares were widened, miles of underground railway laid, under- and overpasses created along with new boulevard Rings.

To be honest, most of what is worth seeing pre-dates Ludwig I. In Munich, as elsewhere, the nineteenth century didn't create. It copied, producing neo-this and neo-that. Today the copies are not only neo but restored, which makes them neo-neos. However, broad straight avenues lined with those neos, and providing vistas decorated by an arch or fountain, are pleasant when taken on wheels. They make good urban speedways, and their buildings are like stage scenery.

Heart of town is the Marienplatz, where the towered and pinnacled New Town Hall presides in late nineteenth-century neo-Gothic. Daily at 11 A.M. it entertains with a *Glockenspiel.* The dancing, jousting automata are a major attraction. We asked Authority why this endearing show isn't repeated more often. The answer was that while man can fly to the moon, he can't make a *Glockenspiel* any more. This one isn't automatic and has to be set in motion by a man.

Fix your eye on the twin towers with cushionlike caps, and make for them. Munich's landmark, they belong to the big brick

Frauenkirche, the only church that could be called native to Munich in style—a thoroughly German Gothic. It's a fifteenth-century cathedral that looks older. Inside, that tomb as big as a bungalow is a memorial to Louis the Bavarian, a Wittelsbach emperor who died in 1347.

Three small midtown churches are interesting. The Michaels-kirche, begun 1583, was an outpost (architecturally speaking) of the Renaissance, built by Jesuits. Far travelers, they carried not only the Renaissance but the later Baroque and Rococo into some odd places. Palacelike St. Michael's influenced church architecture throughout southern Germany.

The Asamkirche and the Heiliggeistkirche (Holy Ghost) introduce you to the Asam brothers, Rococo fantasists.

In Holy Ghost, they had a commission to make a fifteenth-century church look eighteenth-century fashionable, and redesigned it very prettily. In contrast, their own Asamkirche is Rococo-hysterical. Those metallic gilded garlands looped from an opera-type balcony! Those whorled marble pillars holding up nothing! Those four golden sunbursts with heavy silver clouds! The brothers built this church at their own expense and next door to their house, which they also designed. You'd never know, when in Holy Ghost, they were dreaming up this one as their ideal.

Also in midtown is the Alter Hof, the restored remains of an early ducal residence with pretty, and usually peaceful, courtyard. Hereabouts too is the Hofbräuhaus, where everybody goes to eat or drink at least once.

The Wittelsbachs moved from the Alter Hof to the Residenz, a palace they began in the seventeenth century and kept adding to for more than two hundred years. It spreads around six interior courts and is finished at the north by the formal Hofgarten. Entrance is on Max-Joseph Platz, and at the ticket desk you have to decide what to buy—the Residenz Museum, the Schatzkam-mer, or tickets to both.

Don't hesitate. Choose the Schatzkammer, an exquisite collection of treasures. Outstanding are the crowns, and the St. George in black diamond-banded armor slaying an emerald-tailed dragon which is bleeding rubies.

The Residenz Museum is the palace itself, which goes on forever and is mostly empty, except for restored interior decoration.

You won't want to miss the Cuvilliès Theater, entered from 1 Residenz Strasse through Fountain Court. It has no façade, no exterior. It was a total victim of World War II, but the interior decorations had been saved and the theater was rebuilt to the original design in a corner of the palace.

Elector Max-Emanuel first met François Cuvilliès at a banquet, coming out of a cake. He was a dwarf. Instead of keeping him for court entertainment, the Elector discovered his talent and sent him to Paris to study architecture. Curvilliès returned a master of Rococo. His most famous works are the theater, and the Amalienburg of the Nymphenburg Palace.

On the Odeonsplatz, the Feldherrnhalle is a copy of the Loggia in Florence. The Hitler putsch of 1923 was defeated there.

On the north stretches the lovely English Garden, Munich's Bois de Boulogne. It's the brainchild of American-born Benjamin Thompson, Count Rumford, a British loyalist who left America in 1776. For eleven years he was the Elector's right-hand man.

Among the many museums, we liked best (after the Schatzkammer) the Municipal, showing period rooms, domestic objects, and the famous *Morris Dancers* (1480) by woodcarver Erasmus Grasser. The Neue Staatsgalerie is known for its paintings of the abstractionists and expressionists, including the Blue Knight group with Marc and Kandinsky.

The Nymphenburg, royal summer palace, was well out in the country when begun in 1664. Now it's suburban. Buy the ticket that includes "Schloss, Amalienburg, and Marstallmuseum."

The Schloss is a long building with light Baroque and Rococo rooms concentrating on gilt. The most interesting, of course, is the Gallery of Beauties, with its thirty-six portraits of Ludwig I's court lovelies.

The most famous is Lola Montez, the one-woman bomb who caused a popular revolt. She claimed to be a Spanish dancer, but both her Spanish and her dancing were bad. She was Marie Dolores Eliza Rosanna Gilbert, born in Ireland, daughter of a British army officer. King Ludwig saw her on the stage in 1846 and it was lust at first sight. Only two years later his people made him get rid of her. Lola's varied career after that, unglamorous, included lecturing on fashion in the United States.

The Amalienburg is a hunting pavilion in the palace park, designed by Cuvilliès and considered a gem of Rococo. From its pretty wrought-iron belvedere, Electress Amalie and her court shot pheasants, which had been carefully reared for them in two hundred pruned oak trees all around.

The Marstall is a carriage museum in the old stables, with colossal and tiny, fancy and plain, haughty, sleek, or glittering berlins, phaetons, sleighs, state coaches. Here you meet Ludwig II, Bavaria's Swan King. The fantastic sleighs are his, and that incredible pomposity, his golden wedding coach.

He was Bavaria's golden prince, a handsome young man who came to the throne at eighteen. He went crazy over Wagner and became his patron at no small cost to the treasury until, like his grandfather with Lola, his people demanded Wagner's banishment. He was indifferent to women. A pretty singer flung herself into a fountain before his eyes in the hopes of being noticed. He turned to a servant and said, "Take that lady out and dry her."

Suddenly Ludwig announced his engagement to a cousin, astonishing both her and Bavaria. Her name was Sophie, but he called her Elsa and himself Lohengrin. He had the golden coach created, and it was rehearsed on Munich's streets drawn by six white horses. The preparations dragged on and on, and at last he called off the wedding.

His eccentricities were finally interpreted by his ministers as madness. He had to resign his throne to his uncle and put himself under the care of an alienist. Both he and his doctor were found drowned in Lake Starnberger. It isn't at all certain that this Ludwig was insane, or who drowned whom.

II

Southeast of Munich rears the mountain playland of the Bavarian Alps, where Berchtesgaden is Germany's counter to Austria's Salzburg on the other side.

The geography of this area is on the order of a storm at sea, with resort villages riding the waves. One of the prettiest is Reit im Winkl. We stopped there overnight on the way to Berchtesgaden for the flippant reason that its name beckoned. It seems to mean On Horseback in a Corner.

Reit im Winkl is made to be liked. It lies in a valley pocket on the Austrian border with inviting green hills about, except for one grim mountain, all naked rock, across the border. There's a town hall, a whitewashed church, a post office, a bronze woodman chopping the air on the platz, and little else but hotels, gasthofs, and sweet meadows furnished with *wanderwegs*.

But Berchtesgaden is the focal tourist point of the Bavarian Alps.

No doubt about it, Hitler, ugliest of actors on the world stage, appreciated beauty. Berchtesgaden was his favored hideaway, and Berchtesgaden is one of the world's loveliest *winkeln*. Nature has artfully arranged the contours of its hills and valleys against a backdrop of high mountains which awe but do not intimidate.

The town itself preserves some good houses and streets, its Market Square is comely, and there are nook-and-corner surprises. The one unseemly touch is the railway yards; the eye, from the town above, can't avoid them. But from a score of vantage points on hills within easy stroll—and especially from *Unser* Adolf's "Eagle's Nest" on the Kehlstein, the vistas range from charming to glorious.

Daily tours are run up the Kehlstein. The ride is as spectacular as the setting, for the narrow road, carved out of the mountain, is a major engineering feat on which 3,000 men labored for more than two years, piercing five tunnels.

More labored at Obersalzberg (Hitler's Camp David), forging a complex of underground air-raid shelters and fortified bunkers 120 feet below ground, with all the comforts of home. Here was Gestapo headquarters. Here Hitler entertained Chamberlain, Daladier, and Mussolini at the historic meeting which resulted in "Peace in our time."

The Königssee must be the most spectacular of the Berchtesgadenland's lakes. There's a salt mine to visit for the fun of it, and *wanderwegs* up, down, and sideways.

FREIBURG AND THE BLACK FOREST

I

We checked into the Colombi Hotel, swiftly tidied ourselves and untidied our room, and came down. The clerk looked up as if we had pushed a button and said, "Turn left and go straight on for the spire." We went out. Across the street rose the green slopes of a park tantalizingly just above eye level. An argument happened.

"He said left, didn't he?"

"For the spire. What spire? Let's see the park first."

"The park will stay, we can always see it."

"'Always' means 'never.'"

Husband grasped wife by the elbow. We turned left, down Eisenbahnstrasse, which had overhanging signs and small color-washed houses. Medieval in a sure, quiet way, it was still being well used, well lived in. It was a street we were to walk often and like more each time.

It brought us to a large, complicated building of dark rose stone with green cupolas, curly gables, an angled oriel, a stoneworked balcony, a bas-relief of the Lady with the Unicorn. But no spire. It was the Rathaus.

We crossed the street and made a jog, for surely the clerk hadn't meant us to climb over the Franciscan cloister, and emerged into a broad open space, cobblestoned. And there, unequivocally, was a spire—*the* spire—a soaring tower of lacelike stonework. It belonged to a dusky rose church no less beautiful.

But that was not all.

At the side of the square, among felicitous houses painted blue, green, yellow, brown, stood one that stole the show. It was boldly red, with gilt trimmings. It began with gold-touched arcades. A long balustraded balcony, looking regal, displayed five triple windows with statues between them of four Hapsburg emperors in full armor, each with a canopy, pinnacled, over his head. Side gables, stepped, held a steeply pitched roof from which peered sloping dormer windows, looking like so many hooded eyes. And from the two corners, beside the balcony, jutted corbeled oriels with gold-outlined windows, wearing steep pointed roofs of yellow, green, and red tiles.

This turned out to be the Kaufhaus, or Merchants' Hall, of 1525, now used for civic receptions. A survival of the days of guilds, it sports the architectural fantasies its age delighted in, and that live on here and there to enchant generations which have lost the faculty for putting up happy buildings.

We had not expected much from this capital of the Black Forest. Nothing we had read or been told about it gave us any real idea of what it was like. It is—

You asked about the park? It's Colombi—the hotel is named for it. We've seen pictures of it, but in our four Freiburg days we never did get into it. It was so handy we could see it any time. But we always turned left.

Freiburg is the kind of town for which one feels an immediate affection. It has character and eccentricities. The Dreisam River flows through its streets in curbside rivulets called *Bächle*. Very pleasant, particularly for barefooted children in summer. Underfoot, at many doors the pavement gives way to designs worked in mosaic with pebbles—Rhine-stones, for they are from the Rhine. Street signs are in old Gothic—hard to read but ornamental.

For some sportive reason the 48th parallel of latitude is painted down the middle of Rheinstrasse: *"Parallel-Kreis 48 Grad nördlich."*

Young Freiburgers and guests honor it by ceremoniously leaping it. (As the parallel continues west, it just misses the top of Maine, enters the United States through the topknot of Lake Superior, and leaves by way of Seattle for northern Manchuria and Mongolia. That gives one an idea how twisted are the geographical relations between Old World and New.)

Speaking of Old World and New, it was Freiburg cosmographer Martin Waldseemüller who first put "America" on a map. He did it in 1507 in preparing a guess-map of the New World for an account of Amerigo Vespucci's voyages. This makes Freiburg in some sense responsible for our being Americans and not Columbians or Cabotians.

Freiburgers have a lively sense of humor and wit. They are very like the Baslers just across the border in Switzerland. We were looking at the ruin of a bombed-out structure across from the mayor's offices in the Rathaus and wondering aloud why these tidy people hadn't done something about it after all these post-war years. A man stopped to inform us that it was purposely left so, "to remind our lazy burgomaster, every time he looks out of his windows, that there's work to be done."

It's a fine experience to come upon the Münsterplatz without foreknowledge, as we did, but even when you know what to expect, it should make an impact. It is a two-part open space, the Cathedral or Minster a peninsula thrusting into it and set off by three tall columns holding two saints and a Virgin of 1290. A small fountain has a gilded St. George. Among the tinted houses the Kaufhaus glows. Gaily colorful, the square is at its best during the morning market when fruit, vegetables, and flowers are displayed under striped sunshades, and sausages sizzle on braziers. As closing hour nears, university students swarm to make a quick cheap stand-up *Wurstel* lunch.

The pride of the 150,000 Freiburgers is this Platz, and the pride of the Platz is the Minster, whose 380-foot spire is a masterpiece. The great rose-stone church, begun in the twelfth century, ranks as one of Europe's finest and purest in Gothic. In conception, proportions, and exuberance it announces that the builders were deeply in love with their work, and the burghers with what their money was creating.

It is Gothically busy with buttresses, pinnacles, niched figures, and lusty gargoyles. Some figures prove that local humor is many centuries old. A favorite is the nun on the church's north side. She is feeling for a tooth, having heard that Luther declared any woman with a tooth in her mouth should be able to find a husband. Another is the Rabelaisian gargoyle on the Kaufhaus side, clinging to his high perch by fingers and toes, his naked rear aimed (deliberately, the Freiburger insists) at the Archbishop's Palace. He drips in wet weather and in winter dangles an icicle.

Below, at eye level, are outlined the standard bread measurements so important in market affairs when this church was young. The loaf sizes are four; the date, 1316. The north portal nearest the apse has a wonderful carving of the Creation in primitive style.

The clustered columns of the interior and the stone-framed pointed arches are highly sophisticated. And there are many things to see. The rose window is a St. Catherine's wheel. Peer under the pulpit stairs and you'll see the sculptor, elbows on a carved windowsill, watching you with a bit of a smile; a self-portrait in stone. The figure of the trumpeter under the organ raises trumpet to mouth when the organ plays. Be sure that for hundreds of years children have sat quietly through the services waiting for the magic moment. There's another musician in the vestibule, this one playing his own trumpetlike nose.

The lovely stained-glass windows in the nave were presented by the guilds. Each guild is identifiable by its emblem—architect-masons by square-and-compasses and hammer, bakers by a pretzel, blacksmiths by a horse's hoof, tailors by shears.

Among the painted, stone-carved Apostles on the columns you'll find St. Paul upheld by an Atlas suffering from strain, and St. Peter by a realistic mother monkey with two babies at her breasts.

The Rathaus is two patrician mansions joined. Its courtyard is handsome. The square displays a monument to Berthold Schwarz, a Franciscan monk who invented gunpowder some centuries after the Chinese. The bas-relief on one side shows him playing with retorts; on the other side he's startled by an explosion. Hoist by his own petard. . . . Those Gothic arcades are the remains of a thirteenth-century Franciscan cloister.

Two medieval gateways remain. Martinstor, with its great gilded clock, turrets, and steep roof, spans Kaiser Josefstrasse, the arcaded main street. The Schwabentor, with fresco and clock, is a few streets away, above Oberlinden. The triangular plot of Oberlinden, with the linden tree and the Mary fountain, is a nucleus of very old houses, among them the building with the formidable bear on its sign and the legend proclaiming the Hotel Bären to be Germany's   oldest inn—in business since the early 1300s.

Gerberau, between the two towers, retains a bit of old wall. Parallel to it is Fischerau with a canal and the backs of old houses that still harbor ancient industries, such as the tanner's establishments where we saw a brawny aproned fellow washing a hide at his doorstep.

On Franziskanerstrasse the rose-colored Haus zum Walfisch of 1516 is thought to have been built for Emperor Maximilian I, patron of the university. Front and back are interesting, but the interior has nothing but money—it's a bank.

Freiburg claims to be the warmest and sunniest part of Germany. We were there at tail end of old wives' summer—their Indian summer—and the weather was perfect.

Freiburgers are very wine-wise. The town is built over cellars said to be as deep as the houses are tall.

The Augustinian Museum, in a former monastery, has a good collection of Upper Rhine art and artisanry.

The town has been on the losing side of just about every war that came along. It has been taken and occupied by Swedes, Bavarians, French, and Prussians, and for awhile was Austrian.

A flourishing business is the manufacture of cuckoo clocks. Switzerland is blamed for this gadget, but the Black Forest is the real culprit. A brisk young Freiburger is said to be working on a clock which will cry *oo-kook, oo-kook,* the bird coming out backward, to sell to sophisticated tourists.

II

The town is backed against the tallest mountains of the Black Forest. Like bosomy hills, their highest point is under 5,000 feet.

With our friend Herr Oelke we made a day-long southern sweep beginning with the Schauinsland, Freiburg's 4,000-foot mountain. Herr Oelke was proud of the road up, which makes 170 curves in seven-and-a-half miles, and is the course for an international hill-climbing contest for cars and motorcycles. If carless you can do the trip undizzily by tram to Güntertal, transferring to a waiting bus for the cable car which carries you up in sixteen minutes.

The summit cable station has eat-and-drink facilities, and the nearby Berg Hotel advertises correctly that "Here you can sit and eat either in or out of doors on the very edge of the mountainside looking down on the Rhine valley and across to the Vosges." If you want to relax seriously they bring out a deck chair.

On through pretty Todtnau we went, to stop for lunch at Titisee, a very blue mountain lake with hotels. We chose the Schwarzwald, on a terrace above the water. Like good Freiburgers, after the meal we lay beside the swimming pool inhaling the piney air.

Years ago a boy of fourteen who didn't know he had the seed of greatness in him was hiking, trout fishing, and recording the scenery south of here by Kodak. "We are having a lovely time in the Black Forest," he wrote his grandpapa. He was Franklin D. Roosevelt.

The Black Forest is thick with resorts, some with skiing facilities. Hinterzarten at first glimpse looked tucked away in a fold of nowhere. But from behind the pines emerged a *Kurhaus* and an all-angles modern church, followed by a pair of hotels of the kind that compels a woman to reach for her lipstick and a man for his tie. A *Leckerbissen* (German for *amuse-gueule*) was indicated. The specialty was Black Forest torte, a cake of chocolate, whipped cream, mocha, whipped cream, cherry jelly, and whipped cream. Around us mounds of whipped cream were being ingested by plump people working toward corpulency, while the band played on. Cholesterol would be news in the trimmed wilds of the Black Forest. The Adler, hotel of the torte, had a glassed-in pool, tennis courts, gardens, dance floors, ski jump, restaurants within and without, and a private zoo whose oversexed male deer bellowed at us and charged, but was foiled by the fence. It may be that what he lusted for was a dollop of whipped cream.

Circling home through scenery, we came by way of Höllental and Himmelreich, or Hell Valley and Heavenland. They were named unwittingly by Marie Antoinette. Passing this way to be married to Louis, the future unlucky Sixteenth, she is said to have exclaimed, at the savage mountain gorge, "It looks like hell!" On emerging into the green spread of valley she cried, "Oh, how heavenly!" On this lap of the drive or hike you will see a bronze deer superbly silhouetted against the sky. He's the one who got away from a posse of hunters and hounds by leaping the impossible chasm, and the statue is his Oscar for the feat.

Why "black" forest? It isn't black, nor does it look very foresty, having provided timber since the axe was invented. But you can see how it got its name. On the heights the hills all wear the same suit of clothes—a hundred miles of dark evergreens from Karlsruhe in the north almost to the Swiss border.

With more ambition and less eating than ours, you could make your destination the mountain town of Triberg, where just about all the cuckoo clocks are now being turned out in factories that are making the farmer-woodcarvers superfluous. Triberg has a waterfall in its environs and in its center a Heimat Museum displaying—cuckoo clocks.

ENVOI

We leave you here, claiming nothing more than that we have tried to give you an Introduction to some of what is unique, beautiful, astonishing, eccentric, or miraculous in Europe.

Allegra!

Index

244